Chile in Transition

UNIVERSITY PRESS OF FLORIDA

Florida A&M University, Tallahassee
Florida Atlantic University, Boca Raton
Florida Gulf Coast University, Ft. Myers
Florida International University, Miami
Florida State University, Tallahassee
New College of Florida, Sarasota
University of Central Florida, Orlando
University of Florida, Gainesville
University of North Florida, Jacksonville
University of South Florida, Tampa
University of West Florida, Pensacola

Chile in Transition

The Poetics and Politics of Memory

Michael J. Lazzara

University Press of Florida
Gainesville/Tallahassee/Tampa/Boca Raton
Pensacola/Orlando/Miami/Jacksonville/Ft. Myers/Sarasota

First cloth printing, 2006
First paperback printing, 2011

A record of cataloging-in-publication data is available from the Library of Congress.

ISBN 978-0-8130-3008-1 (cloth)
ISBN 978-0-8130-3568-0 (paperback)

The University Press of Florida is the scholarly publishing agency for the State University System of Florida, comprising Florida A&M University, Florida Atlantic University, Florida Gulf Coast University, Florida International University, Florida State University, New College of Florida, University of Central Florida, University of Florida, University of North Florida, University of South Florida, and University of West Florida.

University Press of Florida
15 Northwest 15th Street
Gainesville, FL 32611-2079
www.upf.com

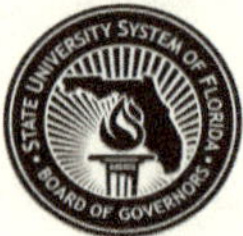

For Julia

Remembering *is* an ethical act, has ethical value in and of itself. Memory is, achingly, the only relation we can have with the dead.

Susan Sontag

Contents

Figures

Acknowledgments

The conceptualization of this project began with my first trip to Santiago in 1995 and has been nourished ever since by the stimulating intellectual exchanges I have shared with friends and colleagues in both Chile and the United States.

As a graduate student at Princeton University, my ongoing dialogue with Arcadio Díaz-Quiñones opened my eyes to the complexities of memory, challenged me to think critically, and helped me to find my voice. Ricardo Piglia, Lucía Melgar, Paul Firbas, James Irby, Ángel Loureiro, and Thomas Trezise were also invaluable interlocutors and sources of inspiration during this project's early phases. Toward the end of my graduate career, I was privileged to participate in Elizabeth Jelin's seminar titled "Memories of Repression and Political Violence." My conversations with Elizabeth at Princeton, and beyond, have caused me to rethink many of my basic assumptions about memory and its narrative rendering.

In Santiago, numerous artists, intellectuals, survivors and colleagues generously helped me understand Chile's memory crisis from the *inside*. I am particularly grateful to Nelson Osorio, Lotty Rosenfeld, Teresa Valdés, Poli Délano, Ana María del Río, Fernando Jerez, Germán Marín, Francisco Simón Rivas, José Luis Rosasco, Antonio Skármeta, Ariel Dorfman, Nancy Guzmán, Pedro Alejandro Matta, Luis Santibáñez, Viviana Díaz, Luz Arce Sandoval, Patricio Aylwin Azócar, Jorge Arrate, María Paz Vergara, Daniela Sánchez, Isabel Donoso, Marisol Vera, and Juan Camilo, to name only a few. Ryan Carlin, both in Santiago and at home, has been a friend and fellow "Chile watcher" over the years. Diamela Eltit and Nelly Richard also deserve special mention for the many exchanges of ideas we have shared and for the abundant richness of their writings. Their work has made mine possible.

Additionally, I would like to express my appreciation to José and Silvia Anadón, María Rosa Olivera-Williams, Timothy R. Scully, C.S.C., Gwen Kirkpatrick, Katie Hite, Victoria Langland, Dan Pastor, Andrea Valenzuela, Alejandro and María Teresa Justiniano, Seth and Kelley Miller, Bill and Rhiana Kehrli, Carlos, Loreto, Loretito, Jorge Andrés, and Carlos Jr., all of whom offered support and insights to enrich my thinking. María Inés Lagos and Patricia Rubio gave invaluable comments that greatly improved my manuscript, as did Amy Gorelick at the University Press of Florida and my Latin Americanist colleagues at the University of California, Davis: Emilio Bejel, Robert McKee Irwin, Linda Egan, and Ana Peluffo.

This book would not have been possible without generous financial assistance from the Princeton Graduate School, the Department of Spanish and Portuguese Languages and Cultures at Princeton University, the Fulbright Foundation, and the Charlotte W. Newcombe Foundation, all of which, in different moments, provided grants for research and writing.

An abridged version of Chapter 1 appeared as "The Poetics of Impossibility: Diamela Eltit's *El padre mío*" in *Chasqui: revista de literatura latinoamericana* 35.1 (May 2006). Part of Chapter 4 appeared in Spanish as "Tres recorridos de Villa Grimaldi" [Three Tours of Villa Grimaldi] in Elizabeth Jelin and Victoria Langland eds., *Monumentos, memoriales y marcas territoriales* [Monuments, Memorials and Territorial Markers](Madrid/ Buenos Aires: Siglo XXI Editores, 2003). I am grateful to the editors for permission to republish these pieces. Selections from Marjorie Agosín's *Las zonas del dolor* [Zones of Pain](New York: White Pine Press, 1988) are also reprinted with the author's permission.

Finally, I would never have had the fortitude or perseverance to see this project through without the constant love and support of family and friends who believed in me every step of the way. My deepest gratitude goes to my parents, Dr. James and Virginia Lazzara, my uncle James M. Doran, my aunt Sue Doran, and my devoted wife Julia, who have, in so many ways, made everything possible.

Author's Note

All translations from the Spanish are my own with the exception of extracts from Marjorie Agosín's poetry, Alosno de Ercilla's *La Araucana,* and Nelly Richard's *Residuos y metáforas*. Two of the works I analyze recently appeared in English: Luz Arce's *El infierno* was translated by Stacey Alba D. Skar as *The Inferno: A Story of Terror and Survival in Chile* (Madison: University of Wisconsin Press, 2004); Carlos Cerda's *Una casa vacía*, translated by Andrea G. Labinger, appeared as *An Empty House* (Lincoln: University of Nebraska Press, 2003).

Prologue

Two Angélicas, Two *Onces*

As General Augusto Pinochet's decrepit political body fades from sight, debates over his seventeen-year dictatorship (1973–1990)—its causes, its legacies—are more salient than ever. This book engages those debates by exploring the many and complex ways in which traumatic memories of political violence have taken textual form during Chile's transition to democracy (1990–present).[1]

In the aftermath of indelible events like torture and disappearance, how much and what kind of memory is most appropriate? Who is authorized to speak about the past, and in what register? What steps are necessary to achieve truth and justice? To what extent is forgetting a logical or necessary response to trauma? These are some of the difficult questions with which Chileans have struggled throughout the post-dictatorship period. While official government discourse has espoused a politics of "looking toward the future" or "turning the page"—a politics based on a wish for national unity and the consolidation of democratic institutions among a deeply divided populace—others seeking truth and justice have been less willing to accept impunity or amnesia and have refused to adhere blindly to the rhetoric of consensus building or reconciliation. For many Chileans, "reconciliation" is little more than a word bandied about by politicians, a synonym for forgetting.

More than thirty years after the military coup of 11 September 1973 that brought Pinochet to power, Chileans are far from unified or reconciled over the meanings of their conflictive past. It is a past that, notwithstanding many important strides toward truth and justice, continues to spark deeply impassioned debates among citizens of different political stripes, especially torture victims, returned exiles, expatriates, and the families of the disappeared. Those who have suffered greatly refuse to bury traumatic memories and struggle daily, despite obstacles, to advance the cause of human rights. For victims engaged in a process of seemingly interminable mourning, politically invoked, symbolic solutions have been perceived as insufficient or incommensurate to their losses.

My research pays special attention to the narrative registers in which Chileans, particularly artists and survivor-witnesses, have attempted to communicate "limit experiences" like torture and disappearance that seem to defy expression. I am interested in investigating some of the multiple lenses through which it has been possible to give form to Chile's traumatic past.

It is true that memories are narrated by individual subjects situated in particular historical and social contexts, but these individual memories are also elaborated and transmitted within inter-subjective social frameworks that tie them together, force them into competition with one another, legitimize them, or silence them. At the same time, narrating memory requires subjects to make decisions, whether conscious or unconscious, regarding *what* aspects of experience will be remembered and *how* those experiences can best be articulated through words or images. It is my belief that despite memory's involuntary machinations, lapses, gaps, and interrupted pathways, subjects (in some regard) exercise *options* at the juncture where remembrance, experience, and narrative intersect.

As my inquiry into Chile's memory problem deepened, I formed a set of working hypotheses that would later guide my analyses of the specific texts studied in this book. I will summarize them briefly here. First, memory stories are dynamic: they respond to the evolution of subjectivity over time as well as to social forces and chance occurrences that allow them to be told and retold toward different ends. Writing memory, consequently, is neither static nor uniform; it is an ongoing, flexible process of composition and recomposition, of casting and recasting the past in its relation to present circumstances and future expectations. Second, memories are selective; rather than confront difficult, painful realities, people often prefer to remember in ways that alleviate cognitive dissonance. Third, because people exist fundamentally in relation to others, memories do not take shape in isolation. Subjects are fragmented; they project themselves across multiple times, spaces, and milieus, crafting their narratives for specific listeners. Consequently, individual memories (as well as the methods for framing them) are inextricably linked to the collective contexts and broader macro-narratives that permit subjects to speak in socially "intelligible" or "acceptable" ways. Last, post-traumatic memories elicit a wide variety of narrative configurations ranging from silence (or the textual rendering of the *impossibility* of speech) to the employment of neat, predictable narrative structures and traditional tropes. This tension between the possibility and impossibility of narrating trauma is one of the fundamental critical questions at stake in this book.

I am constantly struck by the radically divergent narratives about the past I encounter among Chileans. For some, Pinochet is Chile's "savior," a hero who rescued his country from the throes of Marxism, set the stage for its return to democracy, and turned it into an "economic tiger." For others, he is a brutal tyrant, a dictator who gave Chile a neoliberal market economy at the expense and endless suffering of those who dreamed of a different nation: the supporters of Salvador Allende's Popular Unity government (1970–1973). In between those diametrically opposed positions lies a wide spectrum of experiences. For example, there are those who supported the military coup initially, thinking it would provide a quick remedy for a nation left in economic ruin, entrenched in violent rhetoric, and plagued by civil unrest. Many of those same people eventually reneged on their initial support for the General when they realized that his reign of terror would be anything but short-lived. There are also those soldiers within Pinochet's secret police who altruistically aided detainees and suffered grave consequences, or even physical harm, for doing so. Further, there are civilians, once Allende supporters, who either voluntarily, or by force, pledged allegiance to the General or became full-fledged collaborators. Finally, there are those former Pinochet supporters who turned against the General when his criminality became so obvious that it could no longer be denied with any semblance of integrity. It is now clear that facile divisions between the political right (as pro-Pinochet) and the political left (as anti-Pinochet) no longer hold. In the 2000 presidential election, for example, the ultra-right wing candidate Joaquín Lavín, facing indisputable evidence of the dictator's human rights violations, distanced himself from the General to secure his own political credibility. Likewise, the Socialist candidate and eventual winner, Ricardo Lagos, made it clear that he would not be another Allende.

These varied positions, taken together, teach an important lesson: we cannot view Chile's memory conflict in Manichean terms, but must understand Chileans' memory narratives as a series of layered, tempered positions distributed between two diametric poles. If in 1990 (and for several years after the start of the transition) people tended to be either staunchly for or against Pinochet, the ailing dictator's recent fall from grace and obvious criminality have altered the citizenry's attitudes and created important space for the advancement of truth and justice. Memory narratives, to be sure, have become more nuanced since the General's unexpected 1998 detention in the London Clinic. This monumental event, in addition to its wide-ranging effects on international law and the questions it raised about national sovereignty, caused a strong resurgence of memory that made it all but impossible for Chileans to deny that torture and disappearance occurred. More recently, the publication of the *Informe Valech*, a government-sponsored report on torture based on over

30,000 victims' testimonies (2004), the discovery of Pinochet's secret bank accounts exacerbated by suspicions of tax evasion and arms dealing (2005), and the approval of democratic reforms to the 1980 Constitution (2005) have brought disgrace upon the dictator and his family and further weakened the moral and political foothold of Chile's *pinochetista* faction. These recent events have had the added effect of creating a politically necessary, though arguably strategic, distance between Pinochet and many of those who for so long were his closest supporters—particularly, the political right and the military. It remains apparent, nevertheless, that certain *pinochetista* loyalists will continue as apologists for the General even beyond his death.

I would like to note early on that Chile's transition to democracy and its concurrent struggle over memory have been uneven processes. Although it is possible to generalize about the transition's merits and deficiencies, it is also important to keep in mind that the transition is probably best understood not in holistic terms but as a series of "moments," of advances and setbacks in an ongoing struggle occurring on an evolving political scene. I agree with historian Steve Stern's observation that throughout much of the transition, the fight for truth and justice, spearheaded predominantly by human rights organizations, unfolded in tandem with a belief that Pinochet's support base was too large and too strong to make attaining significant degrees of truth and justice viable. The transition governments, for many years after the dictatorship, continued to deal with Pinochet as an imposing body on the political scene. His support base remained firm and his constitutionally ordained authoritarian legacy seemed virtually immovable. The result, Stern claims, was not so much the creation of a "culture of forgetting," but of a culture that oscillated schizophrenically "between prudence and convulsion" (Stern, *Remembering*, xxix). Following Stern's terminology, I am interested in probing these more "convulsive" zones of memory (e.g., collaboration, exile, torture, and disappearance) that not only present tremendous difficulties for narrative telling but also challenge the writing of a smooth and evenly scripted "official story." The individual works I analyze might therefore best be understood as snapshots of different cultural/textual/artistic responses to these convulsive zones in various moments since 1990.

Carrying out this study has taught me that in Chile the political is always personal. A few words based on my own experience might help shed light on the genesis of this book and the inspiration behind its critical questions.

On my first trip to Santiago in 1995, I stayed by chance in the home of a Chilean family who staunchly backed Pinochet and had two boys enrolled in the Military Academy. My immersion among Las Condes *pinochetistas* introduced me firsthand to the extreme opinions of those who supported the dictatorship. Over the past decade, during subsequent research trips to Santiago, I have kept in touch with this family (now close personal friends), and have come to recognize them as a constant reference point for my reflections on Chile. I have always been impressed, though not necessarily for the better, by the way in which, when it came to politics, these friendly, generous people tended to look beyond the dictatorship's human rights violations to focus instead on the here-and-now. They seemed interested only in the end result of Pinochet's "military interregnum"—Chile's so-called "economic miracle"—yet turned a knowing blind eye to the suffering of those who opposed the dictator. Theirs was an "end-justifies-the-means" mentality that I later found to be surprisingly widespread among Chileans of similar social standing and, more surprising still, among those of more modest economic means.[2]

I recall specifically a comment by my host that caught my attention precisely because of its atypical nature: "Since the days of the Conquest, we Chileans have been a subjugated race. And culturally speaking, frankly, you get used to it! ¡*Somos los chilenos gente de rigor*! [We Chileans are a people who respond to strictness!]. We need order and rules to keep us in check. Sometimes it is necessary for a few people to suffer so that a country can move forward and not live in fear." He went on: "Thanks to Pinochet, today I can ride the subway without worrying that some extremist revolutionary is going to plant a bomb and kill me." This attitude, I thought, clearly clashed with a long-standing cultural mythology in which Chileans portray themselves as indomitable warriors who have never been subjugated to any authoritarian power, either internal or external.[3] It occurred to me that my host's comment was a curious inversion of this mythology; its goal was to justify Pinochet's inexplicable violence through a convincing narrative script. Memory, in this case, was transmitted via a tightly reasoned narrative that my host found intellectually satisfying but that I found utterly illogical. Though I could choose to ignore such comments, the fact remained that these types of scripted, rationalized memories were a daily occurrence in my life.

I was constantly reminded that any researcher interested in writing a book about Chilean memories of repression had to "understand *both* sides of the story." My hosts were terribly afraid that my vision of their country's recent history would be tainted or skewed by the left-leaning artists and intellectuals with whom I associated, and this led to hours of after-dinner conversations whose goal was to "deprogram the gringo." I simply listened and took advantage of my strategic position as a cultural outsider trying to absorb and critically question their one-sided memory script. I have since come to discover that although such one-sided narratives remain astonishingly prevalent today, there are definitely more than *two* sides to the story. In fact, the memory debate is not really about being for or against Pinochet but about the different discursive modes through which memories are constructed, as well as the contexts in which those discourses are disseminated and received.

My Chilean hosts' memory narrative included certain emblematic images that have become prominent in the Chilean imaginary of the Popular Unity years.[4] Their story emphasized the "bread lines" and "chaos" under Allende, and they characterized the Pinochet regime's practices of torture and disappearance euphemistically as "excesses" committed in an "irregular war" against communism. I could tell they were reproducing Pinochet's story verbatim. They had internalized the General's master narrative. His language had become theirs. It was as if the dictatorship had socialized them to remember (and speak) in certain ways. Strangely, I sensed that they had begun socializing their own children to remember (and forget) in similar fashion.

At the same time, I found other memories, radically different interpretations of the Allende and Pinochet years, among my colleagues in academia, among the Chilean artists I met, and among many average Chileans who remembered not the bread lines or political instability under Allende but the first real possibility in their lifetimes of a chance for upward mobility for the poor. Although their tones ranged from utopian nostalgia to more critical revisionist history, Allende supporters generally remembered Popular Unity as a vibrant and effervescent revolutionary project, a project forged in true democratic spirit but fated to fail because of government mismanagement, international pressure (largely from the United States) and an insurmountable conservative backlash born from within Chilean society.

I recall especially my experience working with the Chilean poor at Fundación Trabajo para un Hermano [Work for a Brother Foundation] in Peñalolén, a job that prompted my hosts to ask almost daily why I would place myself in "danger" by going to the *poblaciones* [shantytowns]. It was clear that for many of the less fortunate Chileans I met at the Foundation, Allende meant hope. He meant a "half liter of milk for every child." He meant *poder popular*

[popular power] and the dream of a better life. Pinochet meant the end of all that.

On 22 and 23 July 2001, during a research trip to Santiago, I had two temporally juxtaposed experiences that reminded me, on a personal level, of the profound divisions and tensions over the past that continue to estrange Chileans from their compatriots today. These experiences brought into relief the stark truth that two Chiles continue to exist within one nation and that these divisions will likely become less pronounced, less visible, only with the passage of time and the eventual deaths of recent history's protagonists. The following anecdote is just one example of a reality that I perceive in nearly every facet of Chilean life I observe. My hope is that this example, itself a memory, can highlight the general problematic to which this study alludes and frame the debate over memory in tangible, human terms. The example depicts two rather extreme, consciously Manichean, lenses of memory that mark the outer boundaries between which the many-layered, ethically gray and convulsive narratives discussed in this book lie.

22 July 2001: I was invited today to the humble home of a woman named Angélica (mother of a prominent Chilean journalist) to have *onces*, the daily Chilean ritual of teatime, and to look through some old newspaper clippings she had saved pertaining to various landmark human rights cases that interested me for my research. When I got out of the metro at Pila del Ganso, I knew immediately that I was in a different world from the one in which I was living across town in Las Condes. Here the streets were paved with mud and corners were dotted with loitering teenagers. What really struck me, though, was the image of a circus taking place in an open field near the Alameda. This expression of popular culture was clearly at odds with scenes I witnessed in the *barrio alto*. Walking around the Santiago neighborhood of Estación Central, I became acutely aware of my difference, of the way I dressed and the way I walked. I was amazed at how quickly and fluidly (via metro) one can move among distinct cultural and social settings in the city.

When I arrived at Señora Angélica's house, I immediately noticed that it was in less-than-perfect condition. Paint was chipping off the walls and there were old newspapers piled on the floor. The only light emanated from the front room, which I later found to be occupied by two old women sitting at a rickety wooden table. They were Señora Angélica's ailing mother and her sister-in-law.

As I sat with the women and conversed over tea, I looked around at the walls. I saw a poster-sized image of Salvador Allende hanging on one wall, and on the other, the "official" poster from his funeral, as if Allende's funeral were somehow comparable to a rock concert where posters are sold of pop icons. I looked at Señora Angélica's elderly mother, knitting as she watched her soap opera about *la época del salitre* [nitrate era] and began to think about how much history she had witnessed in her lifetime. I wished I could probe her memory and know her story. She sat silently.

The table was set in the customary Chilean fashion: a bit of ham, a bit of *palta*, a bit of sugar and butter, and a few *marraquetas* to accompany our tea, all perfectly arranged on a yellowing tablecloth. As I watched Señora Angélica's mother pick at the insides of her bread and raise the crumbs slowly to her lips, I thought of Gabriela Mistral's poem "Pan" [Bread]: that staple in Chile that gives sustenance and joins families together, that very basic substance that in Proust had the power to open a world of memory. I realized I had been invited that day to break bread with these women, to speak with them about faraway lands and about the ways in which, over the years, I had shared in their culture. They told me about how the violence of dictatorship had affected their family and friends, driving some into exile, leaving others "disappeared." They remembered Popular Unity with flair. How curious, I thought, that Allende's picture hung right there over their dining room table. It was almost as if he were communing with them.

As fate would have it, the next day I found myself in a very different place, this time in Ñuñoa (a somewhat more well-to-do neighborhood than Estación Central), having *onces* with yet another Angélica, a relative of my Chilean hosts with a very different story to tell. I was impressed by the symmetry of the experiences.

The table had been set in exactly the same way as the day before: the same yellowing tablecloth, the same basic foodstuffs. In the course of our conversation, the subject of my research arose. I mentioned to the seventy-three-year-old woman that I had gone that morning to a lecture by well-known Chilean historian Alfredo Jocelyn-Holt Letelier. I could tell she was taken aback. Immediately situating him as a "leftist" and generously sprinkling the term *mijito* [my little child] into our conversation, Señora Angélica subtly asked me if at any point in his lecture Jocelyn-Holt had spoken of "cosas políticas" [political things]. Although I knew the answer to be a resounding "yes," knowing my place, and not wanting a polemic of gargantuan proportions on my hands (words can be incendiary in Chile), I answered her in equally cryptic fashion.

"He spoke," I told her, "more than anything, about 'cosas teóricas'" [theoretical things]. "Ah, qué bien mijito" [Ah, how nice my child], was the answer I received, knowing she would not press the issue further.

While we had our tea and spoke of banalities, Señora Angélica quietly arose from the table and wandered into the bedroom. When she came out, she had something to show me. She was holding a framed certificate that had been given to her "in thanks for her participation in the Chilean fight against Marxism." The date: 1973. She proceeded to tell me (or rather, I should say, *teach* me) that 1973 was, in case I didn't already know, "the best year Chile had ever lived" because it was in that year that the military saved the country from the brink of civil war: a typical discourse, to be sure, but full of fiery passion coming from a woman whose fingers were black with nicotine, whose voice was deep and crackly, and whose eyes seemed to say that she too had experienced much hardship in her lifetime.

Señora Angélica and her husband, Don Lucho, had been the owners of a *latifundio* that was expropriated by the state under Allende's land reform program. As a result of the expropriation, the couple lost everything: their home, their livelihood, and perhaps most important, their dignity. Today they live in an apartment owned by their children, full of antiques that testify to a former life of comfort and social standing, a life that in their memories they are, in some sense, still living.

It was clear that Allende's land reform affected Angélica and Lucho in a very tangible way. Their experience left them enraged and poor. Because of this, Pinochet is Angélica's "savior," and she is proud to take to the streets in his defense at any opportunity. As she told me that day—and I certainly would never have suspected it just by looking at her—"Siempre he sido bien momia, bien política" [I have always been very conservative, a very political person]. In fact, I later found out that she was among the women who picketed publicly for Pinochet's return from London.

Toward the end of our tea, Señora Angélica casually showed me a photograph of a friend. In the background, I noticed a tiny statue of the General staring out at me, strangely dialoguing with the poster of Allende I had seen the day before. I was moved: two Angélicas, two *onces*, two radically different memories, each a testimony to a Chile that remains deeply divided in the public sphere, and even more importantly, behind closed doors.

I realized that day that the rationales shaping each Angélica's memories had everything to do with their individual life experiences. While it was true that under Allende there were cases in which landholders' property was taken under siege without regard for the law, it was also true that under Pinochet individuals were brutally tortured, executed or sent into exile. These were undeniable realities. Logically, such divergent experiences determined powerful differences in outlook. This book is about how those differences are being perpetuated, debated, monumentalized, and written into history.

Though I get the sense that Chilean society is gradually moving away from the polarized positions of these two Angélicas, many Angélicas remain. It is to the education I received from these Chilean women (and many others like them I have met along the way) that I owe the following reflections.

Introduction

The Poetics and Politics of Memory

Human memory is a marvelous but fallacious instrument. . . . The memories which lie within us are not carved in stone; not only do they tend to become erased as the years go by, but often they change, or even grow, by incorporating extraneous features. Judges know this very well: almost never do two eyewitnesses of the same event describe it in the same way and with the same words, even if the event is recent and if neither of them has a personal interest in distorting it. This scant reliability of our memories will be satisfactorily explained only when we know in what language, in what alphabet they are written, on what surface and with what pen. . . .

Primo Levi

Nearly forty years later, 11 September 1973 continues to mark a point of rupture in the life of Chileans. On that day, a coup d'état led by General Augusto Pinochet Ugarte (president, 1973–1990) overthrew Salvador Allende's democratically elected Socialist government, Unidad Popular [Popular Unity] (1970–1973), and ushered in seventeen years of collective fear, torture, disappearances, censorship, and exile. The consequences are still felt deeply and personally in the life of the nation today, sixteen years after Chile's transition to democracy began.

Over the years of transition and despite many significant silences that remain, the history of political violence under Pinochet has gradually, though painstakingly, come to light. Chileans no longer deny the suffering to which many of their compatriots were subjected in the DINA's [Dirección de Inteligencia Nacional/National Intelligence Agency] detention centers and concentration camps. Such denial, which for many years was surprisingly common among *pinochetistas*, now sounds completely implausible following the publication of Chile's *Informe Valech* (2004), a government report mandated by the Ricardo Lagos administration that details the mechanics of torture under Pinochet and records the testimonies of over 30,000 of the regime's victims. Few, moreover, can deny that the bones of the disappeared, where physically locatable and identifiable, have continued to surface from the common graves into which they were abandoned. These bones—a symbol of an unburied past that haunts the present with insistence—testify to the reality of state terror that for so many years the military and the political right brazenly denied.

To be certain, the question today, more than three decades after the coup, no longer has to do with *whether* atrocities did or did not occur, but rather with *how* they are being interpreted, understood, and told. The question has to do with the types of narratives Chileans are writing to make sense of the disaster, with the languages or poetics that either should be or can be deployed to speak a traumatized memory. The issue is at once political and ethical. It implies, on one hand, *naming* torture and disappearance. (Should these realities be characterized as "excesses" or "crimes"?) On the other hand, it implies choosing "appropriate" narrative forms for the telling of "limit experiences" which lead people to the brink between humanity and inhumanity. With what words is it possible to speak the unspeakable? This critical question, so frequently asked throughout the twentieth century, is the challenge artists and survivor-witnesses face in the aftermath of extreme trauma, and it is the key question that informs each of the chapters in this study.

The 1973 coup exacerbated a profound rift within Chilean society that had grown increasingly acute since Allende's 1970 election, a rift that human rights attorney Pamela Pereira once called "una fractura del alma nacional" [a fracture of the national soul] (qtd. in Lira, "Mesa," 206). In the words of Constable and Valenzuela, the coup turned Chile into a "nation of enemies"—a society of "winners" and "losers," "victims" and "victimizers"—embroiled in a bitter war of ideologies that, in the dictatorship's aftermath, has played out as an intense struggle over how to remember the past.[1]

Over the last three decades, we have heard a cacophony of voices attempting to come to terms with Chile's traumatic memory.[2] The coup's supporters offer their version: they remember Pinochet as their "savior," as one who liberated a nation on the brink of "civil war" from a "Marxist cancer." They speak of the regime's human rights violations not as atrocities or crimes, but euphemistically as "excesses" in an "irregular war" whose end result created the conditions of possibility for Chile's return to democracy and its so-called economic miracle. Those who opposed Pinochet—especially people who suffered the direct effects of torture, exile, and disappearance—have a very different story to tell. They remember Pinochet not as their savior but as an evil dictator who destroyed the utopian dream held by thousands of wide-eyed revolutionaries trying to forge a "Chilean road to Socialism." For them, Allende's death meant the death of a political project and the possibility of a more just society for Chile's poor.

Memories of the Pinochet years are therefore multiple and complex. They are narratives written, to adopt Primo Levi's words, in different "alphabets" and with different "pens," (hi)stories crafted with different ends in mind and verbalized through diverse discursive lenses. This study attempts to address this complexity by exploring some of the *poetics of memory* that have surfaced in Chile's transition. My intention is to lay bare the political aims of these poetics, as well as to question their ethical consequences. I would like to ask: When a nation has suffered a traumatic and scarring episode, in what "languages" is it possible to convey the experience?

Each chapter highlights one of these languages—one of the *lenses of memory* through which Chilean artists and survivor- witnesses have attempted to give voice to the nation's traumatic memory. Each chapter, furthermore, understands the construction of memory narratives not only as a subjective process (inextricably linked to individual identity) but also, following Elizabeth Jelin's insight, as a discursive battleground on which different versions of the past lay claim to the truth (*Los Trabajos,* 26–27). Testimonial narratives have the particularity that they want to be taken as fact, to be believed on their own terms. I argue, to the contrary, that we cannot approach memory discourses as transparent narrative acts but rather must evaluate them critically in order to reveal their motivations, benefits, and drawbacks. What do memory narratives cover up in their telling? What do they reveal, and why?

In his often-cited essay "What Is a Nation?" Ernest Renan observed that "forgetting... is a crucial factor in the creation of a nation" and that "historical enquiry brings to light deeds of violence which took place at the origin of all political formations" (45).[3] Indeed, history teaches that after traumatic episodes, nations often find it easier to forget the past and look toward the future, to cover up what is most painful and focus instead on moments of glory and heroism that bolster the national self-image. When societies, like individuals, gaze upon their wounds, they feel shame they would rather not face. But forgetting, as all of the artists whose works I analyze would argue, bears important consequences. It means ignoring traumas that, if left unacknowledged, will linger unresolved into future generations. Forgetting means letting the voices of the drowned remain lost forever; it means giving in to the victors' history.[4]

The artists and survivor-witnesses whose works I examine—Diamela Eltit, Luz Arce, Silvio Caiozzi, Marjorie Agosín, Claudio Pérez and Rodrigo Gómez, Carlos Cerda, Pedro Alejandro Matta, and Germán Marín—all, in different ways, tell the "story of the conquered" [*la historia de los vencidos*] and probe the limits of understanding traumatic experience. Their novels, poems, testimonies, documentaries, and photographs offer varied approaches to writing the past, engage some of memory's most convulsive zones, and call into question narrative's very possibilities for telling. Their contributions share an ethical exigency to rescue from oblivion the voices of the "expressionless" (Benjamin) set adrift on history's tides.[5] From outside the state's institutional apparatus, they contest and challenge the writing of an "official story."

The Official Story

What is the official story against which these Chilean artists and survivors have risen up in defiance? To understand how Pinochet's master narrative has been challenged, it is first necessary to say something about the nature of that narrative, for only in so doing will it be possible to understand the lenses through which dissenting narratives have been constructed.

Perhaps no one document better encapsulates the traditional *pinochetista* version of history than the "Carta a los chilenos" [Letter to the Chilean People], written in December 1998 during Pinochet's detention in the London Clinic. The letter, which at the time of its publication was widely disseminated in the Chilean press and on the internet, rehashes the well-known image of Pinochet as the "good soldier" who saved Chile from the clutches of communism—"esa verdadera antirreligión" [that true anti-religion]—and made Chile into a modern democratic state. Imprisoned in London and hoping to be sent back to Chile, Pinochet portrays himself as the victim of a terrible injustice:

> He sido objeto de una maquinación político-judicial, artera y cobarde, que no tiene ningún valor moral. Mientras en este continente, y específicamente en los países que me condenan mediante juicios espurios, el comunismo ha asesinado a muchos millones de seres humanos durante este siglo, a mí se me persigue por haberlo derrotado en Chile, salvando al país de una virtual guerra civil. Ello significó tres mil muertos, de los cuales casi un tercio son uniformados y civiles que cayeron víctimas del terrorismo extremista.
>
> [I have been the object of a cunning, cowardly, judicial and political machination that is devoid of moral value. While on this continent, and specifically in the countries that condemn me through spurious judgments, communism has killed many millions of people in this century, I am persecuted for having conquered it in Chile, for having saved my country from a virtual civil war. That meant three thousand dead, almost a third of whom were military and civilians who fell victim to extremist terrorism.] (7)

Pinochet's letter is steeped in Christian rhetoric and even goes so far as to portray him as a martyr who will "accept the cross" he has been given to bear if his suffering can ultimately contribute to the unity, pacification, and reconciliation of the Chilean people. His story plays out as a classic manifestation of the struggle between civilization and barbarism:

> El dilema era: o vencía la concepción cristiana occidental de la existencia para que primara el respeto a la dignidad humana y la vigencia de los valores fundamentales de nuestra civilización; o se imponía la visión materialista y atea del hombre y la sociedad, con un sistema implacablemente opresor de sus libertades y de sus derechos.
>
> [The dilemma was: either the Western, Christian concept of existence—which respects human dignity and the fundamental values of our civilization—would win; or the atheistic and materialistic vision of man and society, with its implacable oppression against freedoms and rights, would impose itself upon us.] (3)

According to Pinochet's "salvationist" version of the events of 11 September 1973, the grave human rights violations perpetrated by the dictatorial state must be understood as a price that had to be paid to save the nation from Marxist terrorists.[6] Even today, Pinochet's supporters rarely use the word "dictatorship" and prefer instead a more sterile and benign lexicon: "military regime," "authoritarian government," "state of exception," and other such euphemisms.

Two details about Pinochet's letter are striking. First, Pinochet did not pen the document himself; it was actually written by former commander in chief of the army (2001–2006), General Juan Emilio Cheyre. This detail is important because it subtly signals a point of continuity between the military under Pinochet and the military today. Though Cheyre, primarily as a reaction to the *Informe Valech* and Pinochet's financial crimes, has attempted to distance himself from the dictator's legacy, details of this nature indicate a nefarious institutional cohesion that still exists.[7]

Paradoxes abound. On one hand, it is true that Cheyre has publicly assumed responsibility for the military's human rights violations, but on the other, he has stressed repeatedly the need to view those violations in their proper historical context. Cheyre, too, has vociferously advocated speeding the judicial process and reducing the sentences of human rights violators willing to collaborate with the courts. Though Cheyre takes distance from Pinochet in his public discourse, he continues to support the ailing dictator symbolically by visiting him regularly at his home. Consequently, Cheyre's gestures toward achieving truth and justice often appear politically motivated or aimed at achieving a forgetful reconciliation, while at the same time, it is clear that his actions are also linked to an (understandable) institutional imperative to "modernize" the army and move forward, unfettered by a sordid past. In addition, it is noteworthy that many of those affiliated with the Pinochet regime still refuse to offer information that could help reconstruct the history of political violence or determine the whereabouts of more than 1,000 Allende supporters who remain "disappeared." Several politicians from the Pinochet era remain active in politics, knowing they are best served politically when public opinion connects them only peripherally to the former dictator.

A second, more personal observation is also quite telling. While conducting research in Santiago in 2000, I wandered into one of Chile's most prominent commercial bookstores, Feria Chilena del Libro, and was surprised to find on display a hardcover "Collector's Edition" of Pinochet's letter. Since almost every book printed in Chile is a paperback, it struck me that Pinochet's letter was published as a handsome hardcover volume. The letter was printed on high-quality linen stock, in a cloth cover, and shrink-wrapped in plastic. The book, as an aesthetic object, spoke to me of the value that many still place on the version of history therein. In this commemorative Collector's Edition, Pinochet's official story was indelibly preserved for all time. It would forever adorn the nightstands and coffee tables of those who believed (and continue to believe) in his "civilizing" mission.

Obstinate Memory

To understand the sociopolitical context of the works discussed in this study, it is necessary to say something, however brief, about the major achievements and challenges of Chile's first three transition governments in the area of human rights. It is a story that reveals the obstinacy of Chile's traumatic memory despite a future-oriented politics and a general institutional inertia toward amnesia.

The Concertación [center-left coalition] governments of Patricio Aylwin Azócar (1990–1994), Eduardo Frei Ruiz-Tagle (1994–2000), and Ricardo Lagos Escobar (2000–2006) have called repeatedly in their public discourses for "reconciliation" and "consensus" among Chileans, two key words that through their exhaustive repetition in the mass media have become the hallmarks of Chile's official politics of memory.[8] Nevertheless, each of these governments has faced unique and difficult challenges in its tenure that have made it all but impossible to achieve what might be called national unity, consensus, or reconciliation.[9] All three governments have had to contend with a traumatic past that continues to divide the Chilean citizenry; all three, with varying degrees of dedication and success, have made attempts to resolve what in political discourse is often referred to as the "problem" of human rights; and all three have tried to forge a democratic future for a country cloaked in the shadow of its authoritarian past. The legacies of these three governments, taken together, indicate that there is no easy resolution to Chile's traumas. Ghosts, despite all attempts to hold them at bay, insistently return to haunt the nation.

Alexander Wilde has used the term "irruptions of memory" to describe those "public events that break in upon Chile's national consciousness, unbidden and often suddenly, to evoke associations with symbols, figures, causes, and ways of life which, to an unusual degree, are associated with a political past that is still present in the lived experience of a major part of the population" (475).[10] Whether it be the unearthing of disappeared bodies, the unanticipated arrest of Pinochet in London (1998), the declassification of secret CIA files, the testimony of a public figure who for years remained silent, the annual commemoration of the military coup, or the discovery of Pinochet's secret accounts in New York's Riggs Bank, Chile's past has refused to stay buried. And with each irruption of memory, the country has become, as Wilde correctly observes, "an arena of deeply divided public discourse, shot through with contending and mutually exclusive collective representations of the past" (475). Reconciliation and consensus have, in those moments of traumatic resurgence, proven more a utopian dream than a reality.[11] The name given to Chile's so-called *democracia de los acuerdos* [consensus-based democracy]—a phrase often used by political scientists and cultural critics—is a far from accurate description of the ongoing contentious and fractious debate over human rights.

Behind the Concertación's consensus-based politics lurked a desire to eclipse the traumas that divided Chileans. This desire was based on a fear that too much memory might disturb the consolidation of a still fragile democracy, while exacerbating long-standing political animosities. Tomás Moulián, in his influential and widely cited analysis *Chile actual: anatomía de un mito* [Chile Today: Anatomy of a Myth], reminds us that "El consenso es la etapa superior del olvido" [Consensus is the most advanced stage of forgetting] (37). The victory of the Concertación meant, in Moulián's opinion, the annulment of politics as it was practiced in Chile before 1973, that is, politics as a struggle among competing visions of society, and its replacement by a neoliberal regime put into place by Pinochet, a regime that preserved in its very makeup many characteristics of the authoritarian government that preceded it. Moulián notes how the transition governments, interested primarily in representing Chile as an "economic tiger" and a model for other nations to envy, have found it easier to espouse a politics of "turning the page" and "looking toward the future" than to confront the past directly.[12]

Patricio Aylwin Azócar, the transition's first president, knew how difficult it would be to propose a satisfactory resolution to the human rights issue as long as the military's authoritarian enclaves continued to permeate Chile's fledgling democracy. Aylwin's now famous promise to achieve truth and justice "en la medida de lo posible" [insofar as it was possible] speaks to the difficulties faced by a democracy founded in the shadow of dictatorship. When Aylwin assumed the presidency in 1990, addressing Chile's traumatic memory appeared to be his first priority. On more than one occasion, he told the media that he wanted to be remembered as the "Reconciliation President" and that he would take any steps necessary to effectuate a "reencuentro entre los chilenos" [coming together of the Chilean people]. Especially in his first year as president, Aylwin made admirable strides in the area of human rights policy: he erected a monument to the disappeared in Santiago's General Cemetery, staged his inauguration in the symbolically charged National Stadium, asked forgiveness on national television, brought Allende's body to Santiago for a proper burial, and convened a National Commission for Truth and Reconciliation, headed by Senator Raúl Rettig, whose job would be to investigate and report on the nature of human rights violations under Pinochet.[13] The Commission's work produced the two-volume *Informe Rettig* [Rettig Report], a lengthy document that listed by name more than 3,000 Allende supporters who died or disappeared, detailed the types of human rights violations committed, and enumerated the historical causes that led to the breakdown of democracy.[14] Presented in 1991, the report constituted the first official state recognition that crimes against humanity had occurred, and it seemed a promising sign despite the profound discontent it evoked among *pinochetistas.* Yet from the time of its publication and for many years after, the *Informe Rettig* was acerbically criticized for not adequately addressing the needs of thousands of torture survivors. Since the report allowed reparations only for the families of those who died (i.e., *ejecutados* and *desaparecidos*), it left the question of torture pending and made survivors feel as if the state had abandoned them. More than a decade later, the unaddressed issue of torture forced President Ricardo Lagos to finish the work Aylwin began. Realizing that human rights were a grave and inescapable public concern, Lagos convened a second truth commission

(2003–2004) whose aim was to acknowledge, address, and "repair" torture. The more than 600-page *Informe Valech*, a milestone document based on over 30,000 individual testimonies, brought into public consciousness for the first time the use of torture as a widespread institutional policy under Pinochet.

The transition governments' impetus toward reconciliation and their limitations in the area of human rights were undoubtedly related to the difficult conditions under which the transition was organized. When Aylwin came to power, the courts and many public service positions were packed with Pinochet supporters. Provisions included in the 1980 constitution allowed the ex-dictator to remain in place as Commander in Chief of the Armed Forces until 1998 and then to assume a seat in congress as a "senator-for-life." Moreover, the so-called *amarras* [ties to the past] that shackled the new Chile to the old would not allow Chilean democracy to be consolidated easily. The destruction of important archives detailing the whereabouts of the disappeared, the 1978 Amnesty Law that made it virtually impossible to bring perpetrators to justice, the extremely conservative nature of the press, a new liberal business class loyal to Pinochet, and a citizenry used to living in fear were all factors that made it difficult for Aylwin to forge the reconciliation he so desired. Although he tried many times to overturn the 1978 Amnesty Law, he was always unsuccessful. Consequently, by late 1991, a frustrated Aylwin began to turn his attention away from human rights.[15]

As time wore on, the first transition government's interest in memory seemed to wane. This was particularly apparent in September 1991 when 135 "disappeared" bodies were disinterred from the infamous Patio 29 in Santiago's General Cemetery and no government official attended the ceremony. The discovery of the bodies came only shortly after Aylwin's decision to declare publicly that the transition was complete (7 August 1991): "La transición ahora se ha cumplido. En Chile vivimos en democracia" [The transition is now over. In Chile we live in democracy]. From that moment forward, human rights all but disappeared from the administration's public agenda, and the struggle to remember came to be associated almost exclusively with human rights organizations or with the victims themselves. Memory took a back seat to other concerns; it ceased to be a moral politics actively fostered by the government or a guiding framework within which to grow Chile's new democracy (Wilde, 494). It became an issue that, at least in official circles, would best be left shrouded by a tacit pact of silence.

Eduardo Frei Ruiz-Tagle took power in 1994 assuming that Chilean democracy had been "consolidated" and that Aylwin had handled the human rights issue adequately. But Pinochet's 1998 detention proved that was not true. The General's arrest represented a critical turning point in Chile's memory saga. Not only did it cause old passions to resurface vengefully but it also triggered an important redefinition of public opinion, especially among younger generations now more aware of Pinochet's criminality because of the international attention drawn to his crimes. Following the London arrest, a flood of testimonial books and other studies about the dictatorship poured into Santiago's bookstores, and people on both sides of the political spectrum took to the streets either for or against the ex-dictator. General Ricardo Izurieta, Pinochet's successor as commander in chief who had been trying to distance himself from the General's incendiary legacy, was forced to put his project of military modernization on hold and declare his support, vociferously and publicly, for Pinochet's return to Chile. Pinochet's detention in London, independent of one's feelings about the dictatorship, was viewed in Chile as an issue of national autonomy.

By August 1999, Pinochet's fate still pending, Frei's minister of defense, Edmundo Pérez Yoma, convened the Mesa de Diálogo—an unprecedented attempt to bring together a wide range of voices to discuss (and hopefully settle once and for all) the "problem" of the disappeared.[16] Representatives of the Catholic Church, members of the Jewish community, Freemasons, human rights attorneys, intellectuals, representatives of the armed forces and police, as well as politicians of different ideological stripes all sat down with the intention of drafting a document that would contribute to national reconciliation and affirm the participants' (and, by extension, the nation's) commitment to the core values of truth, justice, and reparations. Despite its drawbacks, the Mesa's most useful outcome was that it served as a forum for staging a pluralistic and public debate about the past. Though the military continually emphasized the importance of "contextualizing" the violations historically, for the first time since 1973 there was at least an implicit assumption of responsibility by the military. However, the Mesa de Diálogo's temporal coincidence with Pinochet's detention caused tensions about the past to run high and made it exceedingly difficult for the Mesa's participants to reach a lasting agreement.[17] After ten drafts and many hours of discussion, they ultimately produced a document that expressed in no uncertain terms the nation's commitment to finding the *desaparecidos*. The document demanded that the armed forces inform the president in writing of the victims' whereabouts within a period not to exceed six months. Sources would be protected by privilege so that those who came forward would not have to worry about prosecution. This last detail sparked many critiques from the human rights community that justice was being traded for truth.

The military's final report was disappointing. Only 200 of the more than 1,000 Chileans still disappeared were even mentioned, and much of the information volunteered was later proven inaccurate. Bodies were not where the military claimed they were or, in the cases of at least two *desaparecidos* who had purportedly been thrown into the sea, their bodies had already been documented and identified by the Servicio Médico Legal [National Medical Service]. With more than 300 court cases pending against perpetrators, the military, despite outwardly good intentions, was not entirely forthcoming. The armed forces feared that if they revealed key information, either their officials could suffer damaging judicial reprisals or their public image would become tarnished.

As the thirtieth anniversary of the coup approached (11 September 2003), what to do about the past again irrupted in Chilean life and was forced to the top of President Ricardo Lagos's political agenda.[18] Three detonating factors can help explain this latest resurgence of memory.

The first factor was a shocking political maneuver by Pablo Longueira, one of Pinochet's staunchest political supporters and president of the UDI [Unión Democrática Independiente, Chile's party of the extreme right], who in June 2003 announced publicly that he had been engaged since the late 1990s in a dialogue with eight families of the disappeared.[19] According to Longueira, the dialogue sought to "resolve" the human rights issue by the thirtieth anniversary of the coup and to demonstrate the UDI's genuine Christian compassion for their compatriots' suffering. The move was quickly criticized by the Concertación as a political stunt whose goal was simple: to bolster the public image of right-wing candidate Joaquín Lavín in the 1999 presidential campaign. In reality, Longueira's proposal amounted to little more than a Chilean "Punto Final" [Final Stop]. He recommended, in the interest of national reconciliation, that all pending court cases against military officials be closed, that the 1978 Amnesty Law be applied, and that the government make reasonable financial reparations to the families to help heal their wounds. Money was Longueira's proposed way of dealing with the family members' pain. His "La Paz Ahora" [Peace Now] proposal not only hoped to establish a definitive political solution to the human rights problem, thus freeing his party from the *pinochetista* stigma that historically had been attached to it, but also to renovate the UDI's image and place the political right in better electoral position for the 2006 presidential race.

The second detonating factor was General Juan Emilio Cheyre's "Nunca Más" speech of 13 July 2003 (Cheyre, "Declaraciones"). Attempting, like his predecessor Ricardo Izurieta, to foster an image of the military as a modern organization in the service of Chilean democracy, Cheyre made a speech in which he called for national reconciliation and for an end to the "desfile de militares en tribunales" [parade of military officials through the courts]. In his discourse, he expressed hope that the army would not remain a "prisoner of the past," and, in a bold move, announced publicly that "los atropellos a los derechos humanos no tienen justificación" [human rights abuses have no justification]. These statements were echoed in a later, even more important document entitled "Ejército de Chile: el fin de una visión" [Chilean Army: The End of a Vison] (*La Tercera*, 4 November 2004), in which Cheyre directly admits the army's responsibility for human rights violations under Pinochet, though always with the caveat of historical contextualization. Cheyre's statements, nevertheless, were widely interpreted by the Chilean media as important steps in the struggle for human rights and understood as an expression of the military's genuine desire to distance itself from Pinochet. A close reading of Cheyre's speeches, however, reveals that his call for "Nunca Más" was couched in ambiguous rhetoric that, between the lines, jabbed at Popular Unity, diffused the blame for the coup, and implicitly reaffirmed the military's role in bringing "Order" to Chilean society. His words were neither the apology nor the acceptance of responsibility that many of the dictatorship's opponents wanted to hear.

The third detonating factor was a brief statement denouncing human rights violations signed by eight generals who had occupied prominent positions in Pinochet's government (7 July 2003).[20] The statement, a response to a flurry of news reports about the illegal exhumation of bodies, publicly condemned the brutal disinterment of many *desaparecidos*. The document represented a major coup within the military's ranks, drawing a clear line in the sand between those officers who decidedly remained silent about the past and a small "renovated" faction who wanted to demonstrate their commitment to the civilian authority's reconciliatory project. Yet the generals' statement, like Cheyre's "Nunca Más," was carefully worded and deliberately vague. Although the officers affirmed their commitment to "Nunca Más," they never renounced the Pinochet regime outright nor did they condemn *all* human rights violations specifically. Moreover, the statement did not mention torture or disappearance at all; it referred only to the illegal exhumation of bodies as a kind of special, particularly reprehensible violation of human rights.

These three detonating factors, which might be read as strategic moves by certain *pinochetista* political actors to mitigate the consequences of an obstinate memory, caused President Lagos to convene his advisory committee and draft a formal proposal on human rights. The proposal, entitled "No hay mañana sin ayer" [There Is no Tomorrow without Yesterday], was presented live on Chilean television and radio on 12 August 2003 and was carefully drafted only after consultations with every political party, the Catholic Church, and the family members of the disappeared. It reiterated the government's commitment to the ideals of truth, justice, and reparations.

Lagos's plan contained a few particularly salient features, both positive and negative. First, it made a clear distinction between the "intellectual authors" of human rights crimes and those who were "just following orders." Following the South African model, Lagos suggested that judicial immunity be granted to those "less severe" offenders who contributed substantially to reconstructing the truth or to finding the bodies of the disappeared. Second, Lagos's proposal did not suggest legislation to overturn the 1978 Amnesty Law and advocated instead the expeditious closure of pending court cases.[21] The president signaled a need to "avanzar más aceleradamente en el cierre de nuestras heridas" [advance more rapidly in the closure of our wounds] and "facilitar y agilizar las investigaciones judiciales" [facilitate and streamline the judicial investigations]. This would be done in the interest of finalizing prosecutions of military officials by the end of General Cheyre's tenure as commander in chief. Third, the document proposed a modest increase in reparations already being paid to families of the disappeared as well as an expanded definition of those eligible for compensation. Most notably, torture victims would receive "una indemnización austera y simbólica que determinará el ejecutivo" [a modest and symbolic sum to be determined by the chief executive]. If, until 2003, torture victims felt abandoned by the state, Lagos's proposal sought to rectify that situation by including them among those whom the state now officially recognized as victims. Finally, Lagos' proposal acknowledged for the first time a reality that Chile's transition governments had never fully accepted: the nation's deeply entrenched wounds could not be healed easily. If Chile were to achieve real reconciliation, a fuller acknowledgment of the past would be required by every sector of Chilean society. To that end, Lagos spoke the following words to the nation:

> Una fractura social, política y moral de la magnitud que los chilenos vivimos, no se cierra en un acto y en un momento determinado. No es po-

sible extirpar el dolor que vive en la memoria por medio de un conjunto de medidas, por muchas, bien intencionadas y audaces que éstas sean.

[A social, political, and moral fracture of the magnitude we Chileans lived cannot be closed with an act or in one particular moment. It is not possible to take away the pain that lives on in memory through a series of measures, plentiful, well-intentioned, and bold as they may be.] (Lagos, "No hay mañana")

The government's proposal on human rights was greeted with both acceptance and criticism. Some saw it as a significant step forward in Chile's journey toward reconciliation, others as a chance for permanent closure to the country's traumatic past.[22] Some saw it as politically strategic and excessively conciliatory to the military and the political right, while others, particularly families of the disappeared, openly criticized it for failing to include a provision to overturn the Amnesty Law. For victims unwilling to sacrifice justice for truth, Lagos's proposal only promised further impunity.

No matter what its long-term outcomes, Lagos's proposal demonstrates that Chile's memory struggle is far from finished. Even as Pinochet falls deeper into disgrace, Chileans remain divided over the past.[23] Many perpetrators go unprosecuted, and memory comes in and out of vogue with changing political circumstances. At the same time, increased economic, social, and symbolic reparations for victims in Chile, coupled with the Argentine legislature's recent decision to repeal that country's "Final Stop" and "Due Obedience" laws, are positive signs that a new chapter is opening in the Southern Cone's fight for truth and justice. After years of intense struggle, it is heartening that the victims' voices are being heard more loudly than ever. Perhaps this is a sign that their traumatized memories will ultimately have greater historical resonance than the voices of the "victors" who wanted to silence them.

Dissenting Voices

If, until now, I have spoken only of the "official story" as it was told by the military government and of the ways in which Chilean institutions have scripted and negotiated the past from *inside* centers of power, it is important to recognize that there is also an *outside*: voices in Chilean society that have offered important critiques and combated the politics of forgetting from more marginal, less powerful, social positions.

The Chilean artists and survivor-witnesses whose works I analyze in this book are some of the most important among these voices. So, too, are the families of the disappeared and other survivors of repression who have borne witness publicly to the regime's injustices and crimes. Through their works and actions, they have questioned the writing of historical master narratives and offered ethical challenges to those who would forget or allow impunity to reign.

Writers like Diamela Eltit, for example, have cultivated an aesthetic that focuses on what Nelly Richard calls "residual" zones of culture: those marginalized loci of cultural production from which it becomes possible to speak in an-other voice, to question power structures and interrogate the "logic" of the transition. As Nelly Richard defines it, the "residual," as a critical hypothesis, "connota el modo en que lo secundario y lo no-integrado son capaces de desplazar la fuerza de la significación hacia los bordes más desfavorecidos de la escala de valores sociales y culturales, para cuestionar sus jerarquías discursivas desde posiciones laterales y descentramientos híbridos" [connotes the way in which the secondary and the nonintegrated are capable of displacing the force of signification toward borders less favored by the scale of social and cultural values, in order to question their discursive hierarchies from lateral positions and hybrid decenterings] (*Residuos,* 11). Richard's work has played a pivotal role in debates about memory in Chile's transition and has influenced my own, particularly for the way it moves freely across modes of discourse (e.g., artistic, political) to unveil with critical fervor "ideological plots, representational folds, semantic cuts and ruptures" as well as "fragments of social discourse . . . and aesthetic symbolizations" that fall beyond our normal frame of reference, but that, when seen, reveal much about a given cultural milieu and its problems (*Residuos,* 14). Her essays offer a critical vocabulary with which to deconstruct and critique the "design of the present, its logic and rhetoric," and an alphabet in which to write about the complex ties among memory, language and representation (*Residuos,* 13). Like Richard, I am interested in exploring these connections as they play out in some of the transition's most challenging textualities of memory. Politically, I agree with Richard that focusing on the local, the minoritarian, the fragmentary, the other, can be productive ways to undermine the construction of facile or exclusionary macro-historical accounts. Yet I am also interested in deconstructing the macro-narratives themselves and in showing how such narratives can influence the ways certain minoritarian subjects craft their own memory stories. Luz Arce, for example, rationalizes her collaboration with Pinochet's secret police—arguably one of the most residual and gray zones of post-dictatorial experience—by appealing to one of the transition's most dominant political macro-narratives: the discourse of reconciliation (see Chapter 2). In this sense, the "macro" and the "micro," the dominant and the residual, always exist in a complex and inseparable dialectic.

This book also owes an important intellectual debt to the scholars who have reflected intelligently on Chile's memory crisis in the pages of the *Revista de crítica cultural* (*RCC*): Eltit, Avelar, Thayer, Galende, Moreiras, Moulián, Pérez, Santa Cruz, Olea, Brito, and others. Founded by Nelly Richard in 1990 and published twice annually, the *RCC* has been one of the most significant forums for debate on Chilean post-dictatorial culture and has established an important dialogue, from Chile, with other prominent post-dictatorship journals like Argentina's *Punto de vista*, under the direction of Beatriz Sarlo.[24] From an interdisciplinary perspective, the contributors to the *RCC* have attempted to name and interrogate the margins and identify what official narratives exclude. The *RCC* has espoused a notion of culture as a force field linked to power structures whose elements either mirror or challenge hegemonic authority, establishing a necessary dialogue between politics and aesthetics and showing artistic production to be a site from which to question the political and, in some instances, to found an alternative politics.

Nelly Richard's critical project, however, despite its importance for memory debates in Chile, has not gone uncritiqued. I recall specifically an occasion during my research when I discovered the intensity of the debates that occur within what I have called the *outside* (extra-institutional life). I feel it is important to acknowledge the reality and salience of these debates insofar as they point to an undeniable fact: critical discourses on memory are themselves memory narratives and cannot be taken at face value. It is clear that critical discourses like Richard's, similar to the objects of their gaze, exercise political and aesthetic *options* and pass judgment on the materials they examine. For that reason, such discourses have been an important source of tension among Chilean intellectuals and activists interested in remembering a traumatic past. (How should that past be remembered? Whose voices should be privileged?) Though it is true that all fields of intellectual inquiry are battlegrounds upon which different visions and theories vie for legitimacy, I cannot help feeling that when historical memory is at stake the risks are somehow higher. This is so because the debate over memory is not a debate that occurs only in theory, only in the abstract. Rather, it is a high-stakes debate whose outcomes have a profound political, social, and moral impact in the present.

I appeal to an anecdote based in personal experience to emphasize the tensions among intellectuals and activists to which I am referring:

On 26 July 2001 I conducted an interview with Chilean journalist Nancy Guzmán, well known for her hard-hitting interview with the torturer Osvaldo Romo Mena. The interview appeared in part on Univisión in 1995 and later, in book form, as *Romo: confesiones de un torturador* [Romo: Confessions of a Torturer] (Santiago: Planeta, 2000). In *Residuos y metáforas* [Cultural Residues], Richard dedicates two pages to describing what she calls an "obscenity": namely, how the airing in Chile of Guzmán's Romo interview produced virtually no reaction among Chileans (72–73). Guzmán, however, told a very different story. Contrary to Richard's claim, she admitted having received numerous death threats from the military after a portion of her interview aired on Chilean television. The military sent representatives to speak to Guzmán in order to confiscate her original interview tapes. Fearing that his testimony might incriminate certain military officials, they wanted to know exactly what Romo had said. Guzmán was forced to lie to her interrogators. She told them the tapes had been left in the United States and subsequently erased. Supposedly, the only part of the interview that remained was the brief segment shown on Univisión.

Beyond its direct personal effects on Guzmán, the airing of the Romo interview also caused a stir within Chile's human rights community. Many families of the disappeared spoke out against it, arguing that Romo's televised image lent validity to a torturer's voice and tainted their loved ones' memory. They feared that the explosion onto the national scene of such an insidious figure would hinder the construction of "heroic" narratives about their disappeared relatives (i.e., that the disappeared resisted torture and died as "martyrs" for Popular Unity). Guzmán defended her project; she spoke of how Chile "needed" to hear Romo's voice. Brutal and terrible as it sounded, she thought that understanding the torturer's logic was important, too, for reconstructing history. Because she believed so passionately in revealing the perversity of Romo's words, she subjected herself to the psychological stress of visiting him daily in Santiago's Penitentiary. The "second-hand trauma" that resulted from her contact with the torturer frequently manifested as physical illness. As Guzmán told me, she would often return home from her interviews, curl up in an armchair and break down crying. She felt she had sacrificed greatly to bring the torturer's evil voice to light.

On the same day I met with Guzmán, I also spoke with Nelly Richard, who had recently published an acerbically critical article on Guzmán's book

("Las confesiones," 2001). Richard characterized Guzmán's work as an "abusive journalistic montage" that "betrayed" the memory of the victims by narrating their dramas and traumas in "crude and simple" terms. She questioned whether Guzmán's book contributed anything to the memory debate, or if instead it should be seen as just one more artifact in the flood of "memory merchandise" to fill Santiago's bookstores following Pinochet's 1998 arrest. Richard was wary of the ramifications of privileging a torturer's voice within the pages of a book.

I bring this anecdote to light because it reflects the complex and often tense interactions among actors on the *outside*. In this case, a prominent public intellectual (Richard) and a journalist (Guzmán), both interested in saying something about Chile's memory crisis, offer radically different interpretations of how best to tell the victims' story, of whose voice to privilege. Guzmán claims that if we are to understand what happened to the victims it is vitally important to deconstruct the thinking of their victimizers. Richard, in contrast, argues that although this may be necessary, privileging a torturer's voice carries important ethical risks. Both, however, firmly believe in the validity and ethical bases of their respective projects.

The discrepancy between Richard and Guzmán proves the construction of memory to be a complex battleground on which differing voices and interests vie for legitimacy. The anecdote ultimately teaches an important lesson: there is, indeed, no one way to write the victims' history, even for those on the *outside* who agree it should, in fact, be written.

Writing (at) the Limits

How, then, to write about limit experiences like torture and disappearance that seem to defy expression?

Many scholars (Elaine Scarry, Giorgio Agamben, Sarah Kofman, Shoshana Felman, and Cathy Caruth, to name only a few) have theorized that there is something about traumatic experience that is not reducible to discursive representation. Agamben, for example, in his seminal book *Remnants of Auschwitz: The Witness and the Archive* (1999), offered a theoretical starting point for this study by proposing the figure of the *Muselmann*—the one who "touched bottom" and "saw the gorgon" in the camps—as a "lacuna" inscribed within all testimonies after Auschwitz. Agamben posits the *Muselmänner* as the "complete witnesses" to the horrors of the Nazi extermination who, paradoxically, because they died in the camps, cannot bear witness today to Hitler's reign of terror. Their absent voices mark a gap, an archival void in the history of the Holocaust, and it is to this gap that every living survivor testifies. The *Muselmann* signals the very limit of human knowledge in genocide's aftermath.

Elaine Scarry's important work *The Body in Pain: The Making and Unmaking of the World* (1985) also raises important questions about the torture victim's possibilities for verbalizing trauma. For Scarry, the torture victim's world is "unmade" in the torture chamber, and her pain somehow defies words. The act of torture, Scarry tells us, culminates in the destruction of the prisoner's *voice* and the simultaneous magnification of her *body*: "Physical pain does not simply resist language but actively destroys it, bringing about an immediate reversion to a state anterior to language, to the sounds and cries a human being makes before language is learned" (4). In torture, the victimizer assumes a powerful, godlike posture, imposing himself upon his victim as a menacing voice devoid of a body. The torturer's goal is to destroy his victim physically in order to turn her into a traitor, a collaborator, separated from her own voice, subjectivity, and autonomous agency.

Cathy Caruth has also spoken of the impossibility of bearing witness after trauma. For Caruth, the traumatic event "is not assimilated or experienced fully" at the time of its occurrence, but rather "belatedly, in its repeated possession of the one who experiences it" (*Unclaimed Experience,* 4–5). The trauma victim therefore struggles, after the fact, to incorporate the traumatic moment and find a language in which to articulate an event that cannot be fully known or apprehended because it was "not fully perceived as it occurred" (8). In Caruth's theory, the traumatic moment marks a "collapse of witnessing," an inability fully to know the empirical event itself, and thus "challenges us to a new kind of listening, the witnessing, precisely, of impossibility" (10).

Caruth's theory of trauma as "missed experience" has been the source of much critical debate and begs asking both how traumatic events are actually experienced by individuals and about what constitutes "experience" itself. Is experience solely constituted through discourse? That is, are events "experienced" only when they can be narrated? Or is trauma experienced or inscribed upon victims independently of their ability to verbalize or translate it into a system of symbolic representation? When we refer to trauma's "unspeakability" or "unsayability," what is it exactly about trauma that is *impossible* to narrate? Is this impossibility related, on one hand, to the nature of the event itself or to an essential deficiency in the symbolic systems available to us for representing (i.e., representation's "always already" mediated character)? Does this impossibility reside in the difficulty victims face when trying to construct a place from which to speak? Or does it have to do, as Dori Laub has suggested, with the reception of testimony—with the outside listener's inability ever to understand fully the victim's plight because of its absolute otherness? (Felman and Laub, 1992)

I would like to advance the idea that "experience," particularly when it is conveyed as memory, is never pure, never unmediated. Post-traumatic memory narratives, instead, are attempts to "materialize" the meanings of the past in the form of "actions and expressions" (Jelin, *Los trabajos*, 37). Instead of representing an event literally, exactly as it occurred, memory narratives incorporate the past *performatively* via modes of transmission that render the experience (or some aspect thereof) intelligible to a specific audience, and for a specific reason (37). In writing memory, subjects generally appeal to narrative modes with which they are familiar or which are available to them, and which create the conditions of possibility for telling. Narrating individual memories, in this sense, cannot be disconnected from the broader collective archive of discursive practices and symbols that facilitates their transmission, circulation and reception.

The impossibility of saying to which Agamben, Scarry, and Caruth refer, moreover, does not allay the survivor's impulse to speak his or her trauma. Although it is true that some survivors, like Jorge Semprún, have opted for silence in trauma's immediate aftermath, many others have been compelled to assume the challenge of bearing witness, even if it meant confronting failure. The Freudian notion of "working through" trauma points to the fundamental need victims feel to integrate the traumatic moment into a broader life narrative: a biography that "makes sense" chronologically as a *before*, *during*, and *after* trauma. The traumatic moment seemingly defies expression yet, paradoxically, never ceases to recur in the victim's nightmares. It is a moment from which the victim cannot break free.

The *imperative to tell* pitted against the *impossibility of saying* leaves survivors in a bind. Unable to remain silent, the witness nevertheless feels she lacks words with which to convey the extent and weight of her experience. To narrate therefore implies risk. Yet if one is to bear witness at all, it is necessary to engage in an act of narrative reconstruction and choose a strategy of representation. Only by risking language's failure to express trauma can the survivor come any closer to understanding or incorporating the traumatic moment.

The question thus becomes, *How* should one speak the disaster? This study aims to show, through specific textual examples, that there are indeed multiple ways of narrating limit experiences, and that each strategy of representation necessarily implies political, aesthetic, and ethical decisions. Although testimonial discourse (understood in its broadest sense) often posits itself as a transparent or exhaustive representation of truth, I maintain the necessity of challenging these truth claims and questioning the political and ethical motivations that give rise to testimonial works. What narrative techniques does the witness employ? What is his or her speaking position (social, ideological, gender, etc.)? Acts of witnessing, to be certain, are always motivated; they are never innocent. It therefore becomes acutely necessary to ask *how*, *why* and *to what end* a witness remembers (Young, *Writing and Rewriting*, 1988).

I propose the term *lenses of memory* as way of referring to the witness's (or the artist's) subjective speaking position. The lens, as a metaphor, evokes the prismatic refractions (ideological, generic, or otherwise) to which memories are subjected in their telling. Lenses shade: they distort and alter what filters through them. To the one who writes or tells, of course, the memories projected are entirely "seeable." They exist in a coherent and convincing narrative context that the testimonial subject has created—a symbolic world that makes "sense" to her. When one experiences an identity crisis, for example, memories are often made to conform to a vision of the self that fosters a sense of coherence and unity (Jelin, *Los trabajos*, 26). Frequently, memories are rendered through complex narrative frameworks that help the speaker project a self-satisfying image that relieves post-traumatic cognitive dissonance or instability in subjectivity. Considering these points, we must understand memory narration to be a highly subjective, highly personal undertaking.

Moreover, to narrate in the aftermath of the twentieth century's traumas and genocides is, as Walter Benjamin intuited, to confront the ruins of history. Benjamin's well-known reading of Klee's "Angelus Novus" in his "Theses on the Philosophy of History," a reflection offered in the midst of Nazi fascism, captures the dilemma that Chile and other nations struggling to make sense of the disaster continue to confront.[25] When writers gaze upon the wreckage of the past, they stand in awe like Klee's angel: wings spread, mouth wide open, frozen between a past that can never be fully recovered (or rendered comprehensible) and an unknown future that cannot be adequately embraced. Though the angel (the witness) would like to "awaken the dead and make whole what has been smashed," the storm of progress violently blows him toward tomorrow as the ruins of history pile skyward, strata upon strata, leaving him powerless in its wake (Benjamin, *Illuminations*, 257).

Thinking about Benjamin's reflection in the context of Chile's transition, it seems almost impossible not to associate the word "progress" with the country's current neoliberal landscape: a landscape where the new constantly replaces the old and where forgetting the past often seems much easier than doing the painful work of memory. Blown toward the future by winds of amnesia and change, how is one to deal with the wreckage of history and attempt to restore what has been irrevocably destroyed? Benjamin once suggested that memories are uncovered through a process of "digging" through the strata and layers of memory, of returning over and over again to the same strata to form new associations that lead to new understandings (*Selected Writings*, 576). This archaeological metaphor, a way of dealing with ruins, alludes to re-membering as a process of piecing together the fragments and shards of experience in ways that permit innovative and unforeseen narrative constellations. Memory, for Benjamin, is never complete, nor is it static; it is a dynamic process that requires resisting the winds of change and the inertia toward forgetting. He insists that we *do* something with the ruins of history: return to them, analyze them, assemble them. But how these ruins are assembled depends entirely upon the lenses through which they are projected. Identifying or collecting memory traces (either voluntarily or involuntarily) is one thing; deciding how to deploy them is yet another.

The chapters that follow emphasize some different *lenses of memory* through which Chile's traumatic experience has been narrated: the lens of madness (Eltit), the lens of conversion and reconciliation (Arce), the lens of the *desaparecido* (Caiozzi, Pérez and Gómez, Agosín, and Cerda), the lens of the torture survivor (Matta), and the lens of the returned exile (Marín). Each analysis draws attention to the political, ethical, and aesthetic concerns born out of the speaking positions and narrative techniques the witnesses employ. Each of the lenses examined, moreover, projects a different degree of *narrative resolution* to the past. Some narrative forms are decidedly open and ambiguous; others tend toward closure or wish to establish a set of indisputable "facts." Is it best, for example, to write about the past in linear terms and with identifiable narrative tropes (Arce), or to employ an aesthetic based on the fragment (Eltit, Caiozzi), an aesthetic that alludes in its very composition to the impossibilities of witnessing? Is it better to tell a story about the impossibility of telling (Cerda, Marín, Pérez and Gómez) or to offer an "intelligible" narrative that renders the limit experience more comprehensible, more transparent to the listener (Matta)? What problems arise when writers attempt to speak for the dead (Agosín)? The texts I analyze reveal a perennial tension between *open* and *closed* narrative forms, between works that try to make "sense" of the past—to tell a story of the catastrophe or provide resolution to the traumatic moment—

and works that, in their very composition, seek to reveal the limits of narrative representation after trauma.[26]

Primo Levi, in his essay "On Obscure Writing," opines that "one should not write in an obscure manner, because a piece of writing has all the more value and all the more hope of diffusion and permanence, the better it is understood and the less it lends itself to equivocal interpretations" (170). Levi lashes out against writers like Paul Celan who attempt to communicate limit experiences through an obscure "non-language" (175). "It is not true," he writes, "that the chaos of the written page is the best symbol of the ultimate chaos to which we are fated: to believe this is a typical vice of our century" (174). Levi would most certainly question writers like Eltit whose aesthetic option challenges the notion of clarity when writing about trauma. This project, to the contrary, wishes to propose the possibility that certain aesthetic options bordering on what Levi calls "obscurity" can, in fact, offer another kind of truth—the truth of literature—which tells of the past through its own unique cadences, metaphors, tropes, and symbols. Might it be true that those artistic responses that resist putting hasty or undue narrative resolution ("closure") to the past are the ones that can best stand up to the ethical and epistemological challenges facing post-dictatorial societies?

My desire is to show how literature remembers in other ways.

The Sites of Memory

The corpus of works I have chosen reflects a small but representative selection of the cultural artifacts that have circulated in Chile's transition. The works are consciously heterogeneous and have been selected because they make possible a fruitful debate about trauma's representability. I would like to clarify from the beginning that I am not proposing a radically new theory for reading the literature of trauma, nor is it my intention to survey all of the many cultural artifacts the Chilean post-dictatorship has offered. Neither is it my intention to focus on one genre or author in particular. My analyses simply hope to raise key questions about the rhetoric(s) and operations of memory at both the level of the individual and the social level.

Pierre Nora proposed the term "sites of memory" [*les lieux de mémoire*] as a way of referring to those material, symbolic and functional spaces in which societies anchor and relate their memories of the past: books, monuments, archives, anniversaries, depositions, films, festivals. Nora rejects the notion that the past can be resurrected in its totality by the historian and claims instead that we experience the past as fractured, fragmented, distant, remote, and complex (17). The cultural artifacts and practices into which memory is condensed are further characterized by their lack of fixed meaning. Unlike the "monumental" writing of history that Nietzsche decried in *The Use and Abuse of History*, Nora's sites of memory are open to critical interrogation precisely because of their dynamic quality, their "capacity for metamorphosis," the "endless recycling of their meaning," and the "unpredictable proliferation of their ramifications" (19). Inspired by Nora's conception of site, I move freely among a wide array of cultural materials (novels, documentaries, poems, testimonial works, and photographic projects), all of which share a desire to bear witness. Though my central focus is on literature and the arts, I have been compelled to move beyond the boundaries of one particular academic discipline or genre and draw on different kinds of cultural artifacts and scholarly materials. My hope is that the diversity of the corpus I have chosen will reveal that memory is all around us and that its textualities continually challenge formal delineations of genre and discipline.

The theoretical perspectives that inform my writing are equally varied. As I thought through issues of memory, trauma, and narrative, I found myself led in many directions and into many different sections of the library. Readings in literary and cultural studies, psychology, sociology, political science, history, philosophy, and theology all influence the pages of this study, as do readings about other cases of political violence and genocide in the twentieth century (e.g., Argentina, South Africa, and the Holocaust). Though each chapter is inspired by my personal contact with Chilean culture, I would be pleased if the broader insights I offer could open lines of inquiry for thinking beyond Chile. My focus on one cultural context, nevertheless, stems from a firm belief that although we can (and should) consider the topic of traumatic memory in comparative perspective, it is nonetheless necessary to recognize that each democratic transition, each instance of trauma, each cultural milieu, refers us to a particular history, a particular set of dilemmas and cultural idiosyncrasies that cannot necessarily be extrapolated or transferred. Andreas Huyssen, in that vein, has warned against the projection of the Holocaust as a "universal trope" onto other instances of trauma and genocide. "The global and the local of Holocaust memory," Huyssen notes, "have entered into new constellations that beg to be analyzed case by case; while Holocaust comparisons may rhetorically energize some discourses of traumatic memory, they may also work as screen memories or simply block insight into specific local histories" (24). I would like to avoid the trap to which Huyssen refers. My goal is to maintain a consistent focus on the local, drawing on other scenarios (e.g., Holocaust studies) only where they can usefully illuminate my thinking about Chilean texts.

At the same time, reading and learning about other cases of genocide has helped me to understand that what happened in Chile between 1973 and 1990 is not at all a new phenomenon but a sad commentary on the pervasiveness of political repression and human rights atrocities in modern history. A visit to the National Holocaust Museum in Washington, D.C., for example, deepened in many ways my thinking about Chile's traumatic memory and its representation. So, too, has observing daily events in the U.S. War on Terror.

Allow me to offer a brief schematic of the book's organizational rationale:

Chapter 1, "The Poetics of Impossibility" proposes a reading of Chilean writer Diamela Eltit's *El padre mío* [My Father] (1989) as a text which, through an aesthetic of the fragment, foregrounds the impossibility of bearing witness in trauma's aftermath. The chapter also discusses the possible role for literature in a post-dictatorial politics of memory. Between 1983 and 1985, Eltit recorded the testimony of a schizophrenic homeless man who was jailed and tortured by the Pinochet regime. She published the vagabond's discourse in the transition's early days as a *counter-memory* that could disrupt the scripting of an "official story." The text, with its fragmentary and illogical prose, stood as a challenge to the possibility of writing a clean, linear narrative of trauma and served as a reminder of how history tends to leave behind certain voices with important stories to tell. Furthermore, the text called into question how traumatic memories could (or should) be written. My interpretation suggests that *El padre mío* be read as a political, aesthetic, and ethical response to the way in which official versions of history are elaborated and negotiated. My discussion of impossibility is informed by the critical perspectives of Primo Levi, Philippe Lacoue-Labarthe, Sarah Kofman, and Jean Améry, and particularly by Giorgio Agamben's book *Remnants of Auschwitz: The Witness and the Archive* (1999).

If Chapter 1 studies an aesthetic of memory based on the fragment, Chapter 2, "The Poetics of Reconciliation," looks at how one individual survivor narrated her terrible and traumatic story in the "official" language of reconciliation. Luz Arce's *El Infierno* [The Inferno] (1993) is the testimony of a "traitor" to the Chilean left who, after the 1973 coup, became an informant and later a functionary of Pinochet's secret police. Arce's confessionary text is a *mise en scène* of a subject grappling publicly and privately with shame: the shame of having been tortured, the shame of having collaborated with the regime, and the shame of having been labeled a "puta y traidora" [whore and a traitor]. Writing is the vehicle by which she works through her trauma and seeks atonement with God, self, and nation. How does a subject who speaks from the "gray zone" (Levi, *The Drowned*) deal not only with "survivor guilt" but also with the shame of her own de-subjectification through torture? Critical reflections by Agamben, Derrida, Scarry, and Foucault help frame my reading of Arce's testimony as a text which, through a curious double movement, offers a glimpse at the objectification and reconstitution of a subject whose testimony—radically different from the broken, fragmented poetics of *El padre mío*—strangely mirrors Chile's official discourse of reconciliation. In the end, the languages of reconciliation and conversion give Arce narrative ground upon which to stand, a place from which to say "I."

Chapter 3, "Presence and Absence," stems from a conviction that the story of the Pinochet years cannot be told without considering the figure of the *desaparecido*. My analysis seeks to understand two different (and often simultaneous) strategies that Chilean artists have used to represent the disappearance of former left-wing militants by the dictatorship: *marking the absence* and *marking the presence*. If the general political tendency has been to forget the disappeared in the interest of looking toward a more promising, less divisive future, Chilean artists have used their artworks to call attention to absent voices and bodies and to decry the politics of forgetting. Art has been a space in which the dead have been made to speak. Through the examination of four works, Chapter 3 posits the dialectic between presence and absence as a guiding principle for a post-dictatorial poetics of memory.

First, Silvio Caiozzi's documentary film *Fernando ha vuelto* [Fernando Returns] (1998) narrates the process of exhumation and identification by forensic scientists of the remains of one of Pinochet's victims. The film foregrounds images of a disappeared man's fragmented bones—a body whose presence, through forensic identification, now makes possible a process of personal and collective mourning. Caiozzi's documentary communicates an ethical imperative to remember and suggests the need to provide a decent burial for the regime's unidentified victims. Second, Claudio Pérez and Rodrigo Gómez's *Muro de la memoria* [*Memory Wall*] (2002), a monument to the disappeared located at Puente Bulnes (Santiago de Chile), uses the photograph as a medium through which to make present the disappeared. By displaying the faces of the forgotten dead in a prominent urban thoroughfare, Pérez and Gómez seek to remind Chileans that the *desaparecidos*, years after the dictatorship, continue to haunt the nation, to cry out for truth and justice. Third, Marjorie Agosín's poetic cycle "La desaparecida" [The Disappeared Woman] in *Las zonas del dolor* [Zones of Pain] (1988) uses prosopopoeia to give voice to those who cannot bear witness for themselves. The poet acts as a vessel through which the "impossible" voices of disappeared women assert their ghostly presence. And finally, Carlos Cerda's novel *Una casa vacía* [An Empty House] (1996) evokes the memory of the disappeared by marking their absence, by calling attention to Chile's denial of their voices. The novel implores us to heed the mute cries of those ghostly beings within the "house"—a metaphor for the nation—who want so desperately to be heard.

Chapter 4, "Lenses of Memory (On Narrating Villa Grimaldi)," re-emphasizes the diverse lenses through which a single object of inquiry can be represented by exploring the complex interplay among memory, site, and subjectivity. To that end, the chapter takes Villa Grimaldi, one of the Pinochet regime's most notorious torture centers, as its principal object of inquiry. Although a former army general destroyed the site before the end of the dictatorship with the hope of erecting a modern condominium complex, thanks to the work of human rights activists, a "Park for Peace" (1997) has been built there. In the park, the former torture center's ruins remain partially intact. My reading desires to understand the relationship between narrative and ruins, and to unveil the political, ethical, and aesthetic struggles involved in preserving (and narrating) a physical site of memory.

The chapter begins with an analysis of the aesthetic design of the park. I then proceed to explore two very different and, in many ways, opposing narratives of the site. The first is that of Mr. Pedro Alejandro Matta, a survivor of Villa Grimaldi who offers a well-polished memory script to the tourists he guides through the park's ruins. Matta's narrative, I feel, reveals very specific personal and political motivations, as well as a desire to legitimate his version of the past as uncontestable. I then proceed to compare Matta's discourse to that of German Marín's narrator in his novel *El Palacio de la Risa* [The Palace of Laughter] (1995). Marín's narrator is a returned exile who, having living abroad for seventeen years, returns to Villa Grimaldi's ruins and struggles to construct his version of what happened there. The novel is a profound literary reflection that upsets the possibility of establishing polished, uncontestable narratives about the past; it privileges instead memory's precarious and fragmented nature, while referring to the multiplicity of truths that have circulated in the post-dictatorship.

1

The Poetics of Impossibility (Diamela Eltit's *El padre mío*)

At a certain point, it became clear that testimony contained at its core an essential lacuna: in other words, the survivor bore witness to something it is impossible to bear witness to.

Giorgio Agamben

[Schizophrenics] destroy imposed speech, which is violating in its claims to proper, exclusive, totalitarian meaning. . . . They explode that meaning which for them had always been meaningless—in order to get back down to, and play around with, its categorical and lexical components, its underlying articulations.

Luce Irigaray

As Chile's transition to democracy began, President Patricio Aylwin (1990–1994) established the National Commission for Truth and Reconciliation, whose goal was to create a public record of the Pinochet regime's human rights violations, explain the context in which the violations took place, and list the names of those executed or disappeared.[1] Hoping to ascertain the truth about the dictatorship's nefarious crimes, the government invited victims and their families to set aside fears, come forward, and speak publicly to the commission's officials about their suffering and loss. At its conclusion, the truth commission issued the *Informe Rettig* [Rettig Report](4 March 1991), a lengthy document that constituted the first official recognition by the Chilean state of the military regime's human rights violations.

When the commission finished, the main critique of its work had to do with how it defined victimhood. The Rettig Report clearly stated that the commission's mandate was to catalogue only "the most serious violations of human rights *resulting in death and disappearances*" [emphasis mine] (Rettig, *Summary*, 11). What would become, then, of countless other victims who passed through the regime's detention centers and concentration camps and survived the experience? How would their testimonies be preserved for the historical record?

In 1989 Diamela Eltit (b. 1949) entered into the debate by publishing the fragmented, seemingly nonsensical testimony of a schizophrenic homeless man whom she called "El Padre Mío."[2] The publication, whose date marked the temporal passage from dictatorship to transition, implicitly reflected on the extent to which the legacies of authoritarianism would continue to haunt the nation's psyche post-Pinochet. Eltit's book sought to grant legitimacy to the discourse of an indigent and anonymous victim whose voice and truth, without her intervention, would otherwise be forgotten forever. El Padre Mío's testimony, with its elliptical, illogical prose, stood as a challenge to the dictatorship's clean, linear vision of history and proposed, from the margins of society (poverty, madness, indigence), a counter-memory that could disrupt the process of scripting an official story. For Eltit, the discourse of madness became a narrative lens through which to found a poetics of traumatic memory, a discourse that would incite her readers to question language's very possibilities for narrating the disaster.

As she reveals in her prologue, Eltit encountered the vagabond whose tape-recorded testimony she transcribes as part of an improvised research effort aimed loosely at understanding the "city and its margins" (*El padre mío*, 11). Beginning in 1980, she and visual artist Lotty Rosenfeld set out on foot to explore what they considered to be the most marginal areas of Santiago. They wandered through "multiple hostels, brothel towns and diverse instances of vagabond life" with the hope of capturing "an aesthetic that could generate cultural meanings"—a voice that could serve as a "photographic negative" of Chilean society and reveal something about the general atmosphere of social fragmentation, violence and political corruption they read as having existed in the dictatorship (*El padre mío*, 11). The results of the artists' search are documented in a number of film reels shot by Rosenfeld between 1981 and 1985.[3] The films show Eltit interviewing a homosexual man, a woman bedecked in gaudy jewelry selling trinkets in the street, and a woman who had undergone a sex change operation. In every case, Eltit appears interested in understanding how the marginalized city dwellers perceive themselves in relation to Chilean society and larger power structures.

When she met El Padre Mío in 1983, Eltit was struck not only by his physical marginality (he lived on a vacant lot surrounded by cut-up fragments of newspaper that he read diligently) but also by the poetics of his voice. He spoke to her without prompting, and his words poured forth in a monotonous, circular, and fragmentary way, yet always with an insistence that he had a truth to tell: "Pero debería servir de testimonio yo" (*El padre mío*, 57). The intuition that the vagabond had something important to say prompted the artists to return to the vacant lot where he resided and record his testimony again in two subsequent years (1984 and 1985). On these visits, the homeless madman spoke in the same frenzied, illogical fashion. But despite the "illogic" of his words, Eltit sensed in his discourse three overarching concerns that, to her mind, summed up the dictatorship's legacy: politics, economics, and violence. These preoccupations led her to posit the vagabond's fragmented voice as a metaphor for Chile's own infected psyche:

> Es Chile, pensé. Chile entero y a pedazos en la enfermedad de este hombre; jirones de diarios, fragmentos de exterminio, sílabas de muerte, pausas de mentira, frases comerciales, nombres de difuntos. Es una honda crisis del lenguaje, una infección en la memoria, una desarticulación de todas las ideologías. Es una pena, pensé.
>
> [It's Chile, I thought. All of Chile fragmented in this man's illness; torn-up newspapers, fragments of extermination, death syllables, the pauses of lies, business jargon, names of the deceased. It's a profound crisis of language, an infection in memory, the de-articulation of every ideology. It's a pity, I thought.] (Eltit, *El padre mío*, 17)

Eltit found her inspiration for *El padre mío* in a little-known journalistic project by André Gide entitled *La Séquestrée de Poitiers* [*The Sequestered Girl of Poitiers*] (1930), which, like her own book, raises important questions about marginality, torture, testimony, truth, and justice. Gide's text tells the true story of a young French girl named Mélanie Bastion who, in the late nineteenth century, was locked away by her blue-blooded mother for having become pregnant out of wedlock. Gide narrates in graphic detail the physical tortures to which the girl is subjected during her twenty-five-year captivity. Forced to live in isolation and left to fester among rats and insects at the back corner of her family's mansion, Mélanie is so severely mistreated that she eventually loses her mind. Her madness makes it difficult, if not impossible, for her to bear witness to her ordeal intelligibly.

Gide's book is a pastiche of different texts—oral testimonies, journalistic articles, interviews, and legal depositions—the most interesting of which are two interviews in which Mélanie attempts to talk about her harrowing experience in her own voice. Prior to the girl's discursive intervention, we are told that the doctors who assessed her in the asylum all agreed she would "never regain her ability to reason," thus setting the stage for a voice that will make little rational sense (*La secuestrada,* 72). Gide, however, frustrates the reader's expectation of unintelligibility by salvaging only those snippets of Mélanie's testimony that can be deemed "intelligible." On more than one occasion, the girl's first-person account is interrupted by sentences like "Ms. Mélanie Bastion makes some incomprehensible statements" or "Ms. Bastion appears perturbed and pronounces some words we cannot understand." In those moments, Gide (as author/*autoritas*) suppresses and censors the madwoman's discourse, forcing it to conform to the logic of textual intelligibility. Mélanie's words are subjected to reason's judging eye.

Though Eltit is fascinated by Gide's incursion into the relationship between madness and truth, she does not follow his modus operandi. If, as I have said, Gide textually suppresses madness, testing his subject's words against the benchmark of logic, it is precisely El Padre Mío's *illogic* that Eltit foregrounds, celebrates and allows to speak on its own terms. Sensing that the *loco*'s incoherent ramblings can open up new possibilities for the creation of metaphorical meanings, she invites her reader to consider the *alternative logic* at work in the madman's speech.

Luce Irigaray, in a fascinating essay entitled "Schizophrenics, or the Refusal of Schiz," posits the schizophrenic as a figure in search of a true form of expression, a subject free from language's imposed constraints. Irigaray reads schizophrenic discourse as a challenge to the rigid, codified nature of linguistic systems and to the one-to-one correspondences between signifiers and signifieds. Schizophrenics, Irigaray tells us, break with totalization of sense, dissociating themselves from the imposed restrictions of the mother tongue. Their discourse is inherently transgressive.

El padre mío, following Irigaray, forces readers to ask if it is possible to speak of a schizophrenic "logic." Should the discourse of madness be discounted as insane or nonsensical (as in Gide), or conversely, be taken as a reservoir of hidden meaning (as in Eltit)? Although she leaves the question unresolved, Irigaray offers a compelling image of the schizophrenic as a subject who "unspeaks," as one who breaks through "the closure of constraining discourse in an attempt to find the laws of its engendering" (*To Speak,* 183–184). Schizophrenic discourse appears as a torrent of signifiers in flux (in a state of free play) around an unnamable signified: a signified that "occults, bars, blocks, occupies the space of a gap or a hole," or even "of the unspeakable" (*To Speak,* 186). It is precisely this tension between discursive freedom and psychological subjugation that attracts Eltit to the vagabond's voice.

Recent debates on bearing witness after traumatic experience—particularly reflections by Giorgio Agamben, Primo Levi, Jean Améry and Philippe

Lacoue-Labarthe—focus on the lacunae or silences bound up in the testimonial act. In *Remnants of Auschwitz: The Witness and the Archive* (1999), for example, Agamben suggests that all testimony paradoxically bears witness to an impossibility of bearing witness. This is because those who could have described the Nazis' crimes most fully (those whom Agamben, following Levi, calls the *Muselmänner* or "complete witnesses") all died in the camps. Consequently, the survivor-witness's speaking position is that of one on the brink between the inside and outside of experience, of one who speaks "by proxy" in the name of the dead. Agamben offers a compelling model of testimony as a force field in which tensions among humanity and inhumanity, subjectification and desubjectification, speech and silence play out. Testimony takes place on the subtle ridge that divides these categories from one another, and the testimonial subject's discourse bears witness to the complex relationalities among these terms.

Taking as my point of departure Agamben's theory on testimony's impossibility and Irigaray's understanding of schizophrenia as a liberation of discourse from totalitarian control, I would like to propose a reading of *El padre mío* as a text which, through an aesthetic of the fragment, challenges the possibility of bearing witness after extreme trauma, while simultaneously opening up the possibility of reading testimony literarily. In what senses are we to understand testimony's impossibility in *El padre mío*? And what can we discover by reading the *loco*'s discourse (his "truth") from the vantage point of literature?[4]

In addition to Eltit's book, I will also consider a video montage of El Padre Mío's testimony that Eltit and Rosenfeld compiled in 1985. Some of the images that appear in the video were to be used in the book but for reasons of cost were never included. The video images permit additional insight into how Eltit wants to portray the vagabond and open a space to reflect on her own role as secondary witness.

In short, I will offer a reading of *El padre mío* as a textual project in which the boundaries that separate delirium from sanity, imagination from reality, and testimony from literature become blurred. My wager is that by reading the text from the vantage point of literature, we can attend to the vagabond's "truth" as lying somehow *beyond* empirical facts, and admit the possibility that testimony, understood through a literary lens, "means" on other levels.

The Fragment

El padre mío can best be understood within the context of what Nelly Richard once designated as Chile's *Escena de Avanzada* [neo-avant-garde cultural scene]: a group of artists who responded to the Pinochet regime's grammar of power and censorship by exploring the relationships between art and politics and questioning the ways in which discourses are configured. The works of the *Avanzada* (which included artists like Eltit, Raúl Zurita, Lotty Rosenfeld, Carlos Leppe and Eugenio Dittborn) sought to develop a "poetics of ambiguity" that "resisted any totalization of sense" (Richard, *Margins*, 19). These artists frequently employed techniques such as fragmentation, montage, and collage as ways of contravening the dictatorial state's rigid surveillance of language. Contrary to Pinochet's discourse of "order," coherence, and intelligibility, the *Avanzada* rebelled against hegemonic discursive configurations and focused instead on those marginalized subjects and fragments of experience that fell outside the scope of the regime's official line.

According to Richard, the *Avanzada* emerged at a particular historical moment (post-1973) in which the Chilean social fabric had been torn asunder by political repression, violence, torture, the failure of the Left's revolutionary mission, and the destruction of a long-standing democratic framework for governance. She notes that with the coup "all sense floundered, not only because of the failure of an historical project (that of Popular Unity), but also because of the breakdown of a whole system of social and cultural references which, for Chileans up to 1973, provided the clues to all reality and thought" (Richard, *Margins*, 17). In Richard's opinion, the coup ushered in a "crisis of intelligibility" that left people struggling to make sense of contradictions between the regime's seemingly transparent discourse and the violence they witnessed on a daily basis.

In that context, some members of the Left and many who went into exile were afraid to abandon an aesthetic based on the intelligibility and rationality of historical narratives. Because they perceived that the social fabric had been radically fractured, their approach to writing history was to piece it back together hoping to forge a lost sense of solidarity among Chileans. *Solidaridad* [Solidarity] and *compañerismo* [brotherhood] were prevalent and emotionally charged terms in the imaginary of Popular Unity; to restore solidarity in post-coup Chile meant to stress the importance of a collective "we," of national traditions and customs that unified all Chileans. Estranged from the *patria* and left with vivid memories of the "romantically" charged Allende years, writers in exile wrote about how exile communities scattered around the world latched onto certain national symbols (e.g., the Chile of "vino tinto y empanadas" [red wine and empanadas]) as a way of convincing themselves that all was not lost, that history had not been irrevocably shattered and that Pinochet would one day fall, thus permitting their return to Chile.

The *Avanzada*, on the other hand, operated separately from the traditional Chilean left and, in fact, was accused by many of its members, particularly those in exile, of wanting to erase the past. As Nelly Richard writes:

> Contrary to the exiles' desire for [the] *continuity* [of history], for a complete and transcendental meaning, for an origin and a destiny, the *Avanzada* worked with a particular historical time which was not only deprived of heroism but also impossible to express: a time disrupted and scattered by different voices and stories, by contradictory symbols and interpretations, by a clash of memories and counter-memories threatened with oblivion and struggling to piece together the meaning of a shattered nation. (*Margins*, 112)

There thus emerged two opposed conceptions of history: that of the exile community, which insisted on the possibility of writing a "linear" history that emphasized the continuity of national traditions, and that of the *Avanzada*, which rejected historical macro-narratives, monuments, and museums, and opted instead for privileging the fragmentary and the marginal as the most appropriate lenses for imagining a shattered nation.[5] As Nelly Richard reminds us in *Residuos y metáforas* [Cultural Residues], through their artistic projects and political commitments the members of the *Avanzada* brought into relief the difference between "un saber controlado" [the control of knowledge]—a phrase she uses to refer to how the dictatorial state tried to control both public discourse and the minds of its subjects—and "el descontrol del pensar" [the unwieldiness of thought]: those gestures, cultural symbols, subjectivities and discourses that floated diffusely upon Chile's cultural scene (Richard, *Residuos*, 139).

During the dictatorship, the Pinochet regime attempted to control language by appealing to rational arguments to cover up its brutal crimes. Grave human rights violations and disappearances were explained away as "excesses" of a wartime scenario, and the coup was scripted as the moment in which the armed forces saved Chile from the verge of communism and chaos. Leftist militants were cast as enemies and criminals to be tamed and defeated, and it quickly became the regime's primary mission to extirpate an ever-growing "Marxist cancer" from the body politic.[6]

Once the regime took power, strict censorship laws were imposed and freedom of expression was severely curtailed. Writers and journalists like Máximo Gedda (National Television Network), Jaime Vargas (*La Tercera* newspaper), and Aristóteles España (poet) were detained, tortured, or killed. Even more went into exile (e.g., Poli Délano, Ariel Dorfman, Antonio Skármeta). As of 1973, any writer hoping to publish in Chile had to submit his or her work to an office of "Censura Previa" [Previous Censorship] that would edit "subversive" elements and accept or deny publication. Works denied publication were those that, in the regime's language, "atentaron contra la moral, el orden público, la seguridad nacional o la vida privada de las personas" [endangered morality, public order, national security or the private life of the citizenry] (Baltra Montaner, *Atentados*, 17).[7]

Through censorship, the regime tried to silence voices that would challenge its authority. Linguistic ambiguity was suppressed and supplanted by the regime's monologic discourses. As Diamela Eltit notes in an essay entitled "Las dos caras de la moneda" [The Two Faces of La Moneda or The Two Sides of the Coin], from its first moments in power the junta began to elaborate a "new national lexicon" whereby terms like "patriotism," "order," and "justice" were redefined according to the regime's logic. At one point in her essay, Eltit emphasizes the theatricality of the junta's television appearance on the afternoon of the coup:

> Los cuerpos de los militares que encabezaban el golpe comparecían, en las últimas horas de la tarde, como el último elemento que faltaba para completar la escenografía, esa puesta en escena de una obra política que se iba a representar por los próximos 17 años. Allí estaban, sentados tras una mesa oficial, los cuatro uniformados *elaborando discursos entrecortados y no exentos de confusión*, señalando el fin de los partidos políticos, el fin de prácticamente todo para dar inicio a una nueva era—la era del orden—en las postrimerías de uno de los días chilenos más álgidos y caóticos del siglo . . . .
>
> [The bodies of the soldiers in charge of the coup seemed, in the waning hours of that afternoon, like the final element needed to complete the scene, that mise en scène of a political show that would play on for the next seventeen years. There they were, seated behind an official table,

four uniformed men *elaborating their choppy and confusing discourses*, calling for an end to political parties, an end to practically everything, in order to pave the way for a new era: the era of Order. All this in the waning moments of one of the most algid and chaotic Chilean days of the century. . . .] (Emphasis mine) (Eltit, *Emergencias*, 21)

Eltit sees through the junta's theatrical masks to the confusion and choppiness of its discourse. Although the military spoke of restoring "order" to the nation, the chaos and violence of the coup, coupled with the initial wave of state terror, undermined the military's would-be transparent rhetoric. Eltit correctly perceives something illogical, out-of-sync, or even mad about the way in which life was suddenly turned upside-down. People were expected to obey a curfew; many citizens were labeled political subversives, detained, and tortured; friends and neighbors became informants. Who could one believe? Who could one trust? In effect, Eltit senses that the junta, because of the lack of synchronicity between its public discourse and the lived reality of violence and chaos, began to undo Chileans' fundamental faith in the link between "words" and "truth."

Within the confines of censorship and state control, Eltit cultivated an aesthetic of the fragment as a way of questioning ordered systems (social, political, linguistic, artistic). Particularly in early works like *Lumpérica* [E. Luminata] (1983) and *Por la patria* [For the Fatherland] (1986), both novels written under dictatorship, the space of writing functions not as a locus of control (in the Foucauldian sense) but as a space in which to foreground language's silences and discontinuities. These books are full of violent images and violated bodies, of subjects who want to bear witness but who can do so only in a language bordering on non-sense. Likewise, in *Los vigilantes* [Custody of the Eyes] (1994), both literature (i.e., the act of writing) and life are constantly threatened by powerful men and watchful "neighbors" keen on legitimizing the neoliberal order left in place by Pinochet (those who want to "guard the West's fate") (65). Eltit's characters' minds are subjected to a terribly violent manipulation by authoritarian powers—a manipulation whose essence can perhaps best be captured in a single sentence uttered by Coya/Coa in *Por la patria*: "Tengo el cerebro trizado" [My mind has been cut up] (157).

Factual Truth versus Truth Effect

Sarah Kofman once observed that "about Auschwitz and after Auschwitz no story is possible, if by a story one means: to tell a story of events which makes sense" (*Smothered Words,* 14). *El padre mío* challenges the idea of "story" as chronologically ordered narrative and places readers in a precarious and disoriented position with respect to the *loco*'s broken monologue.[8] Allow me to focus for a moment on two specific textual operations that offer insight into the mechanics of the vagabond's discourse and the difficulties it presents for interpretive reception: the presence of silence (ellipsis) and the disconnection between signifiers and signifieds.

Silence is a key motive, both thematic and formal, in the vagabond's testimony. In the course of his "Primera Habla" [First Speech Act]—the first of the book's three sections—he explains how powerful men who exercised control over him put him in a mental institution for two years in order to silence him:

> . . . en el Hospital Siquiátrico estuve dos años para silenciarme, por lo que le estoy conversando. Allí fui llevado a la fuerza. Yo fui planeado por asesinato y enfermo mental con las personas que le estoy conversando, el señor Colvin que es el señor Luengo y el Padre Mío, para quedarse con las garantías ilegales de los derechos que le estoy conversando.
>
> [. . . I was put in the Psychiatric Hospital for two years to shut me up, because of what I'm telling you. I was taken there by force. I was pegged to be murdered and as a mental case by the people I'm telling you about, Mister Colvin who is Mr. Luengo and El Padre Mío, to keep the illegal guarantees of those rights that I'm telling you about.] (Eltit, *El padre mío,* 29–30)

Various fragments indicate that he has been persecuted unjustly and that he now seeks redress for being tortured. Consider the following series of fragments, noting especially the use of the word "electricity" and the vagabond's reference to the current, weakened state of his body:

1. A mí me quería tener en un recinto recluido para silenciarme.
   [He wanted to have me locked away to silence me.] (28)
2. Yo estoy planeado más de veinte años.
   [I have been on the hit list for more than twenty years.](33)
3. Antes de perder la firmeza de mi cuerpo, de una sola cachetada podía

tumbar a un hombre yo, pero ya no soy el mismo, porque yo no le convenía, por lo que le estoy conversando.

[Before I lost the firmness of my body, I could knock a guy out with a single blow. But I'm not the same anymore, because I was worthless to him, because of what I'm telling you.] (34)

4. . . . el procedimiento del medicamento y la electricidad . . .
[. . . the procedure of medication and electricity . . .] (40)

5. . . . Ya que yo soy comunista y socialista . . .
[. . . Because I'm a communist and a socialist . . .] (68)

6. Ya que yo persigo lo mismo, para que se les haga justicia, si es que ustedes quieren.

[Because I'm after the same thing, that justice be done, if that's what you want.] (67)

From our reading, we surmise that at some undetermined point in the past the vagabond collaborated with the powerful men who are now trying to silence him. Consequently, he possesses knowledge about the corruption of certain high-ranking individuals. Yet despite several allusions to his own complicity, he repeatedly affirms his own innocence: "Yo no soy cómplice de ellos, con el exterminio general" [I am not their accomplice, nor with the general extermination](47). His schizophrenic vacillation between complicity and self-exoneration situates his voice in an ethically liminal position reminiscent of Primo Levi's "gray zone."

Wanting to denounce a situation of injustice, El Padre Mío seeks interlocutors (Eltit and Rosenfeld) as the "others" toward whom he will project his words. His discourse pours forth such that we keenly sense the urgency in his speech; his incessant repetitions and insistence on his own truth contribute to this sense of desperation. Nevertheless, as readers we have tremendous difficulty understanding what he is saying. Meaning breaks down as words are produced, and we are left wading among lost antecedents and vague references.[9] It is also worth noting that each of the book's three sections ends with an ellipsis—a syntactical detail that signals both the endless nature of the vagabond's discourse and the silences bound up within it. The reader gets the feeling that the madman will speak *ad infinitum*, and wonders as much about what he has *not* said as about what he has.

Beyond silence, the disjuncture between signifiers and signifieds also points metaphorically to the impossibility of communicating trauma. For example, in the *loco*'s monologue we find chains of textual references to men whose names are grammatically equated with one another such that they lose their individuality and come to represent a general structure of power and corruption he wants to denounce (e.g., el señor Colvin, el señor Luengo, el Padre Mío, el señor Allende, el señor Pinochet, el rey Jorge, etc.). These signifiers are emptied of their individual meaning and become practically substitutable for one another. As a result, meaning is displaced from particular one-to-one correspondences to a broader semantic network of signifiers in flux. The repetition of these masculine names signals a state of generalized patriarchal surveillance and discipline to which the vagabond is beholden. These names, moreover, are discursively juxtaposed with a series of institutional and political structures, equally undifferentiated, whose mere existence instills fear in the speaker: "la Administración" [The Administration]; "la Organización Gamal Abdel Nassar" [The Gamal Abdel Nassar Organization]; "los compromisos con el Perú, con Argentina y con Centroamérica" [commitments to Peru, Argentina, and Central America] and "las Embajadas y los Consulados" [The Embassies and Consulates]. Given these disparate references, what seems to be at issue is not so much the sorting out of specific factual details, but rather the reception of a broader message—the madman's denunciation of an overwhelming and seemingly omnipresent structure of repressive power. The incessant repetition of the phrase ". . . por lo que les estoy conversando . . ." [. . . because of what I'm telling you . . .] points to the speaker's innate desire to have the "facts" of his case understood. However, as readers we cannot understand the details of his story. His dizzying flurry of references leaves us wondering what sense, if any, we are to make of his disjointed speech.

In her chapter on *El padre mío*, Gisela Norat proposes one possible solution. Following Reader-Response Criticism, she argues that the reader should work to "fill in the gaps" of the madman's narrative and impose "order" upon his testimony (*Diamela Eltit,* 70–84). She reads the *loco*'s discourse with an eye toward subjecting it to what she terms an "ordering principle," announcing that her main goal is to figure out "who does what and why" (83). The result of Norat's analysis is a sophisticated story in which the critic takes the vagabond's fragments and rewrites them in linear terms. She guesses at whatever meaning she can glean based on the clues the *loco* provides.

I would question Norat's approach. Certainly, I would agree that there is a story embedded somewhere in El Padre Mío's discourse—a story which, as I have said, he urgently wants to communicate and to which only he is privy. However, I would disagree with Norat's assumption that order—if by order we mean a linear or chronological sequence of causes and effects—should be imposed upon the text. *El padre mío*, though it does permit certain moments of illumination, essentially frustrates attempts to impose order at every turn. This, of course, does not quell the reader's desire to do so (indeed we are trained to read in linear terms and respond favorably to texts we can grasp easily). Yet I cannot help feeling that Eltit's text, at least from her authorial perspective, desires to be read in a different way.

I would argue that the schizophrenic's Babelian speech invites us to consider not its factual truth but its "truth effect": what the *loco*'s testimony—in its very linguistic errantry—can tell us in more general, metaphorical terms about Chile under dictatorship, as well as about the nature and limits of bearing witness. Regarding the problem of "truth," it is useful to recall Derrida's comments on the relationship between truth and discourse in his response to Lacan's seminar on Poe's "The Purloined Letter." Derrida states, "Even if communication communicates nothing, it communicates to itself" (Derrida in Muller and Richardson, 40). With this observation, he allows us to consider all speech acts—even those that intend to deceive—as an "unveiling of truth." The issue, for Derrida, is not so much the difference between truth and lies, or their admixture in a given instance of speech, but the very "birth of truth in speech."

In the case of *El padre mío*, or of any subjective testimonial utterance for that matter, truth is born through an act of witnessing that the speaker professes to be factual (i.e., via the production of signifiers that from the witness's unique perspective make sense to him and that he finds intellectually convincing and emotionally satisfying). Given the speaker's conviction that what he says is true, the reader is asked to place blind faith in the veridicality of his utterance and accept it at face value. This leap of faith, without discounting the importance of testimony's "facts," allows us to shift the terms of the debate momentarily away from the truth/falsehood distinction toward other levels of reading. If we accept the vagabond's speech act as "true" (in the sense that it is faithful to his convictions), we can begin to search for higher-order meanings within his discourse. In other words, we open ourselves to the possibility that it is precisely the nonsensical nature of the madman's speech that refers us, metaphorically, to the general state of social paranoia that has invaded his psyche and to the overarching "crisis of intelligibility" (Richard) originated by the dictatorship.[10]

In her Holocaust memoir *None of Us Will Return*, Charlotte Delbo includes a telling epigraph that I find relevant for reading *El padre mío*: "Today I am not sure that what I wrote is true [*vrai*]; I am certain that it is truthful [*veridique*]"

(1). Perhaps it is for its "truth effect"—its veridicality or correspondence to the real rather than for its brute factuality—that we are to read the *loco*'s testimony. If we opt to read his broken speech in this way, we sense immediately amid his baroque babble a series of keywords that recall the general atmosphere of Chile under Pinochet, words that have to do with violence, power, and the economy. A glossary of his keywords might consist of terms like *colaboración* [collaboration], *usurpación* [usurpation], *Administración* [Administration], *complicidad* [complicity], *bancario* [fiduciary], *exterminio* [extermination], *asesinato* [assassination], *legal* [legal], *ilegal* [illegal], *compromiso* [commitment], *matar* [kill], *garantías* [guarantees], *diputado* [deputy], *senador* [senator], *Presidente de la República* [President of the Republic], *órdenes* [orders], *silenciar* [silence], *reclusión* [reclusion], *dinero* [money], *Rey* [King], *progreso* [progress], *socialista* [socialist], *comunista* [communist], *razón* [reason] and *fuerza* [force].

Thinking about how dictatorships attempt to control their subjects' minds—how they drive subjects to the edge—invites us to consider the extent to which El Padre Mío's fragmented psyche is a by-product of the regime itself. It is worth asking: What is the source of the subject's *locura*? Is it social rejection? Is it economic ruin? Is it the torture he has suffered personally? Is it because he lives within a culture of violence (Chile in the 1980s)? Or is he just mentally unbalanced? The text does not permit us to resolve these issues satisfactorily.

Impossibility

This enigmatic word comes up time and again in the pages of testimonial writing. What is it, precisely, that is impossible to bear witness to after trauma? In what sense does testimony confront us with the limits of memory or the limits of language? And what can the testimony of a madman reveal about this impossibility?

It is necessary to understand that the impossibility of *bearing witness* is not the same as the impossibility of *giving testimony*. Indeed, many survivors of trauma have testified to their experiences of abjection. In the Chilean case alone, there are countless books and documents written in the first person that attempt to describe the horrors of Pinochet's torture chambers. This sheer quantity of oral and written testimony reveals an undeniable urgency among victims to speak their experiences so that such suffering will "Never Again" occur.

The urgency to communicate, however, leads to a paradox: the victim's *desire to speak* pitted against her *inability to say*. Although some victims opt to remain silent after trauma, others feel an urgent need to make sense of the experience and incorporate it into an overall life narrative with a before, during, and after.[11] Torture survivors frequently write about how in captivity the impulse "to live" becomes inextricably linked to an impulse "to tell" of the injustices suffered. Political prisoners will themselves to endure terrible odds hoping they will one day be free to denounce publicly the crimes committed against them. Yet once in the outside world, they often discover that living to tell is not enough. As both Dori Laub and Susan Brison confirm, survivors must also "tell to live" (Brison, 66; Felman and Laub, 78–79). Narrating trauma thus becomes essential to the reintegration of self and the reestablishment of ties to the broader community; it is an important step in "remaking" and reclaiming subjectivity (Scarry, *The Body*).

Despite survivors' compulsion to tell, no amount of telling is ever sufficient. Dori Laub notes that "[t]here are never enough words, or the right words; there is never enough time or the right time; and never enough listening or the right listening to articulate the story that cannot be fully captured in thought, memory and speech" (Felman and Laub, 78). Laub intuits that to bear witness after trauma is in some sense impossible, yet his main explanation for this impossibility pivots on a lack of reception for the victim's discourse: "Some hardly even spoke of [their traumas], but even those who have talked incessantly feel that they managed to say very little that was heard" (79). The lack of reception for testimony is, of course, one sense in which we can understand impossibility and reinforces Laub's thesis that the testimonial act requires the reestablishment of a community between "I" and "You"—between self and Other—that was broken by Nazism. But impossibility has other senses as well.

Perhaps it is impossible to bear witness to trauma because it is simply too painful for the victim to talk about the violence perpetrated against her. Many times victims opt for silence, feeling it is safer to repress memory than risk vulnerability. In another sense, impossibility may be linked to the shame victims feel when they gaze upon their wounds.[12] To admit victimization can be humiliating for those who do not want to be viewed as "abnormal" or different from their peers. And in yet a third sense, the impossibility of witnessing may reside in the insufficiency of language (or other symbolic systems) to convey trauma exactly as it occurred, in all of its painful immediacy. I am referring, of course, to narrative's "always already" mediated-ness.

To explore the idea of impossibility further, it is useful to recall a text by

Primo Levi that may shed additional light on *El padre mío*. In his opening chapter to *Remnants of Auschwitz*, Agamben analyzes Levi's reference in *The Reawakening* (1963) to a child named Hurbineck: a "nobody," a "child of death," "a child of Auschwitz," who was held along with Levi in the infirmary of the big camp. I cite extensively from Levi:

> [Hurbineck] looked about three years old, no one knew anything of him, he could not speak and had no name; that curious name, Hurbineck, had been given to him by us, perhaps by one of the women who had interpreted with those syllables one of the inarticulate sounds that the baby let out now and again. He was paralyzed from the waist down, with atrophied legs, as thin as sticks; but his eyes, lost in his triangular and wasted face, flashed terribly alive, full of demand, assertion, of the will to break loose, to shatter the tomb of his dumbness. The speech he lacked, which no one had bothered to teach him, the need of speech charged his stare with explosive urgency: it was a stare both savage and human, even mature, a judgment, which none of us could support, so heavy was it with force and anguish. . . .
>
> After a week, Henek [a Hungarian boy of fifteen who tended to Hurbineck] announced . . . that Hurbineck "could say a word." What word? He did not know, a difficult word, not Hungarian: something like "mass-klo," "matisklo." During the night we listened carefully: it was true, from Hurbineck's corner there occasionally came a sound, a word. It was not, admittedly, always exactly the same word, but it was certainly an articulated word; or better, several slightly different articulated words, experimental variations on a theme, on a root, perhaps on a name.
>
> Hurbineck continued in his stubborn experiments for as long as he lived. In the following days, everybody listened to him in silence, anxious to understand, and among us there were speakers of all the languages of Europe; but Hurbineck's word remained secret. . . .
>
> Hurbineck died in the first days of March 1945, free but not redeemed. Nothing remains of him: he bears witness through these words of mine. (Levi qtd. in Agamben, *Remnants,* 21–23)

What is bound up in this secret word that the dying Hurbineck utters repeatedly with sustained force? To what is the dying child trying to bear witness with his inarticulate babble? Agamben describes Hurbineck's obstinately secret word as a kind of non-language akin to the rumbling or "background noise" in Celan's poetry—a "dark and maimed language" that pours forth from the mouth of a dying man. Hurbineck's indecipherable utterance seems to bear witness (and with extreme urgency) to what is unsayable about Auschwitz. His situation dramatizes perfectly the victim's paradoxical need to speak pitted against the impossibility of saying. Hurbineck has a truth to tell, but that truth transmits as a series of broken syllables, an obstinate sign that remains wholly unintelligible to the other prisoners. Levi intuits that the dying boy's truth can only be conveyed "through these words of mine," by proxy, for Hurbineck is the "drowned," while Levi, by some unexplainable twist of fate, has been "saved." Hurbineck, in effect, is the lacuna bound up in all testimony. His voice marks the moment in which the possibility and impossibility of bearing witness enter into a profound tension (Agamben, *Remnants,* 36–39).

Is Hurbineck's nonsensical babble the real "truth" of Auschwitz? Is the truth something that is impossible to state, that can only be sensed? Is the fragmented, broken word (*mass-klo, matisklo*) something akin to a *poetics of the impossibility of bearing witness*? Does the truth of testimony somehow exceed language's ability to convey?

The question of finding a language with which to bear witness responsibly informs all post-traumatic testimonial literature and must be taken into account when considering a text like *El padre mío*, which not only stands as a challenge to the possibility of converting the horrors of dictatorship into a readily communicable "story," but which also reads as the discourse of a subject whose desire to tell outweighs his ability to capture in words the magnitude of the offense committed against him.

The madman's monologue is riddled with references to violence perpetrated against him and others. At one point, he even warns his interlocutors (Eltit and Rosenfeld) that if they are not careful they, too, will suffer violence at the hands of the powerful: "Si ustedes no se ponen de acuerdo, la mayoría, están todos planeados para el exterminio" [If you all don't stick together, you'll be on the hit list too] (28). Allusions to threats against the vagabond and his family are scattered throughout his monologue, yet are never described in much detail. His testimony records only the superficial marks (the exteriority) of his suffering without ever voicing its particulars. Words like *atropellado* [run over], *chocado* [hit], and *triturado* [cut up] allude to a terrible reality that remains hidden from view, whose exact causes and effects can be sensed but never concretized. It is impossible to say why the vagabond does not speak in greater detail about the physical harm he has suffered. What is clear is that the lack of detail regarding violence, coupled with the presence of innumerable signifiers that point cryptically to that violence, demands that we reflect on language's very ability to render "visible" the vagabond's trauma.[13]

Wondering about the possibility of describing life in the Nazi concentration camps, Sarah Kofman asks:

> How . . . can one tell that which cannot, without *delusion*, be "communicated"? . . . How is it possible to speak, when you feel a "*frenzied desire*" to perform an *impossible* task—to convey the experience just as it was, to explain everything to the other, when you are seized by a veritable *delirium of words*—and yet, at the same time, it is impossible for you to speak. Impossible, without *choking*. (emphasis mine)(*Smothered Words,* 14, 38)

For Kofman, Auschwitz represents an experience so beyond description, so beyond rational explanation, that it cannot be borne witness to in words other than those of delusion, delirium or frenzy. To read *El padre mío* is to get a sense of what Kofman might mean when she suggests that the traumatized subject bears witness through the language of madness, that he "chokes" on the words as they try to escape from his mouth.

At the Mind's Limits

How does life in the camps defy logic? In what sense does authoritarianism's extreme violence resist explanation in rational terms?

Jean Améry's essay "At the Mind's Limits" brilliantly details his personal discovery of the intellect's failure to ascribe "logic" to the camp. Unlike in "normal life" (Améry's term), where intellectual acumen is generally rewarded and valued, the intellect was of no worth in Auschwitz. The physically strong, not the intellectually savvy, were the ones most likely to survive because they could be exploited for manual labor. Binary divisions like human-inhuman, rational-irrational, life-death, dignity-indignity ceased to be applicable, and power was wielded over detainees in a wholly arbitrary way: "In Auschwitz the intellect was nothing more than itself and there was no chance to apply it to a social structure. . . . Thus the intellectual was alone with his intellect, which was nothing other than pure content of consciousness, and there was no social reality that could support and confirm it" (Améry, *At the Mind's Limits,* 6).

In the course of his essay, Améry recalls an occasion in the camp on which he tried to strike up a debate with a French philosopher from the Sorbonne.

Longing for an intellectual conversation, Améry believes that the learned man will reply to his queries. Yet to Améry's surprise, the philosopher gives only "monosyllabic, mechanical answers and finally [grows] silent entirely" (7). This unusual occurrence causes Améry to ask how it is possible that a man of such brilliance could be reduced to stammering and silence. His ultimate explanation is that the intellectual does not stammer because his senses have been blunted by violence, but rather because "he simply no longer believed in the reality of the world of the mind" (7–8).

Améry's anecdote refers not only to a breakdown of logic in the camp and to language's inability to explain or represent the violence suffered there (e.g., the professor's stammering) but also to the receptor's difficulty in understanding the traumatized subject's speech (e.g., Améry's failure to make sense of what he hears). What purpose could reason serve in a space of madness where modes of comportment and codes of ethics that applied to life on the outside no longer held? Every category once useful for situating or explaining "normal life," according to Améry, was nullified in Auschwitz:

> In the camp the intellect in its totality declared itself to be incompetent. As a tool for solving the tasks put to us, it admitted defeat. However, and this is a very essential point, it could be used for its own abolishment, and that in itself was something. For it was not the case that the intellectual—if he had not already been destroyed physically—had now become unintellectual or incapable of thinking. On the contrary, only rarely did thinking grant itself a respite. But it nullified itself when at almost every step it ran into uncrossable borders. The axes of its traditional frames of reference then shattered. Beauty: that was an illusion. Knowledge: that turned out to be a game with ideas. Death veiled itself in all its inscrutability. (Améry, *At the Mind's Limits*, 19)

Like Améry, Primo Levi also articulates a vision of the camp as an illogical space—a "gray zone" of moral indeterminacy where ethical lines blur and people are made to act irrationally (*The Drowned*). Levi's famous example of the soccer game between the SS officers and the *Sonderkommando* (deportees forced to lead their fellow prisoners to death and then shovel their ashes from the incinerators) evokes metaphorically how the camps compelled prisoners into nefarious complicity with their captors, making them breach ethical boundaries to prolong their own lives, even if only for brief periods of time. Like the game Levi describes, the camp operated using a skewed, predetermined set of rules that contaminated everyone within its scope, victims and victimizers alike.

It is precisely this contamination that we read in *El padre mío*. The vagabond's erratic discourse defies rational criteria and testifies to a context—dictatorship—in which "logic" no longer functions as a tool for explaining the "normal" occurrences of everyday life (e.g., slanted discourse, political violence, lies, disappearances, curfews, censorship, and betrayal). His words are tainted by the regime's totalitarian language, and his biography is marked by both collaboration and de-subjectification. It is not insignificant that the madman's discourse is a repository for linguistic fragments gleaned from newspapers found on the vacant lot where he lives. His voice, clearly, is not "pure" but rather a filter for multiple discourses, official and otherwise—a polyphonic, heteroglot register of memories and counter-memories.

Who Bears Witness?

El padre mío confronts the reader with a double act of witnessing. The vagabond, of course, is the text's *primary witness*, but at the same time Eltit, as author, acts as *secondary witness*. She frames the vagabond's voice in her prologue and, in so doing, uses it to her own political and aesthetic ends. By publishing her book, she not only presents her subject's speech act as a metaphor for Chile's fragmented psyche, but also remains faithful to her broader political concern (present from her very first publications), incorporating marginalized voices into her literary project. Here, the "low class" urban speech of a vagabond (orality) is afforded the authoritative status of the written word (literacy), thereby allowing the vagabond's oral ramblings to permeate the sacrosanct space of the written Law. Eltit's transgressiveness lies in using her clout as an established writer to carve out a public niche, albeit a small one, for the voice of a madman, thus allowing him access to the public (the Other) he so desires: ". . . pero me tienen que conseguir un locutor y un periodista para que el hecho se dé a conocer . . ." [. . . but you have to get me an announcer and a journalist so that the matter can be made known] (*El padre mío*, 58).

Yet Eltit is conscious of her position as secondary witness and of the ways in which she is using her subject. Her prologue indicates that she is fully aware that the vagabond's voice will never reach an audience other than through her. Consequently, the primary and secondary witnesses (the vagabond and Eltit) enter into a pact of solidarity borne out of mutual desire.[14] On one hand, Eltit went searching in marginal areas of urban Santiago for a poetics that would metaphorically emblematize the dictatorship's effects on ordinary citizens; on the other, El Padre Mío needed someone to listen to his delirious monologue and connect him to an audience.

Eltit, as reader, recognized in the vagabond a Chilean everyman (recall that his proper name is unknown to her): a subject, terrorized and terrified, beholden to power structures of the dictatorial state. Yet more important, she read in his repetitions, silences, rhythms, and rhymes the broken poetics of a citizen "at the mind's limits." As she indicates in a passing reference in her prologue, the vagabond's voice reminded her of Samuel Beckett. Certainly El Padre Mío's disjunctive speech recalls a work like Beckett's *Not I* (1963), a short play in which the audience sees only the mouth of a traumatized madwoman as she produces an incoherent discourse. Beckett's madwoman tells no "story," offering only a shattered language that alludes to, yet does not render comprehensible, the nature of her plight. Like Eltit, Beckett invites us to focus on the materiality of the vagabond's speech, to listen to it as if it were a secret voice whose story, whose trauma, evades reconstruction but necessitates the attempt. In that sense, both Eltit (as reader) and the reader of *El padre mío* are seemingly cast in the role of psychoanalyst.

Ricardo Piglia points out that the psychoanalyst and the writer share a common bond: they are both attentive to secret, hermetic narratives. The pairing of disparate elements, of fragmentary words and phrases is, for the psychoanalyst, a way to narrate experience. Piglia notes that a writer like Joyce recognized in psychoanalysis a *narrative model*: "Joyce percibió que había ahí (en el psicoanálisis) modos de narrar y que, en la construcción de una narración, el sistema de relaciones que definen la trama no debe obedecer a una lógica lineal, y que datos y escenas lejanas resuenan en la superficie del relato y se entrelazan secretamente" [Joyce perceived in psychoanalysis modes of narrating and that, in narrative construction, the system of relations that defines the plot should not obey linear logic, that remote details and scenes sound upon the surface and become secretly intertwined] (Piglia, *Formas*, 61). As in Piglia's reading of Joyce, Eltit seems to recognize in the vagabond's discourse a narrative model. By foregrounding his testimony, she acknowledges the secret aspects of his trauma that remain silenced or which, perhaps, cannot be said.

Eltit's project also capitalizes on the father-daughter duality. In the vagabond's discourse, the phrase "El Padre Mío"—whose syntactic configuration recalls the religious overtones of "El Padre Nuestro" [Our Father]—comes to designate the maximum representative of an authoritarian power structure (the Pinochet regime) to which the homeless man is subject: "Porque hasta mi nombre ha elegido él" [He has even chosen my very name] (Eltit, *El padre mío*, 27). The vagabond posits himself as a kind of spectral inversion of an almighty father figure who wields absolute power over him. If the dictatorial father (Pinochet) is all-powerful, the son (the vagabond) appears alienated, marginal, and powerless. Yet Eltit, by calling the schizophrenic man "My Father," resituates the marginalized subject and allies herself with him politically and aesthetically. She rejects her dictatorial father (Pinochet) and chooses for herself a different father (the vagabond). As the vagabond's "daughter," she rescues and empowers his voice, incorporating it into her own aesthetic project, thus affording it a public editorial platform. She foregrounds the extreme pain of his discourse and places herself in the position of a second-generation daughter trying to access her father's unknowable traumatic past.

Moreover, in the father-daughter duality the feminine becomes a locus for subversion—a conceptual space through which to disrupt established masculine hierarchies and question power structures. If a masculine power has stripped the vagabond of his subjectivity, the feminine, through the figure of the daughter, will act as a site of liberation and reaffirmation of the marginal subject's worth. The Pinochet regime wanted its subjects to accept the dictator's *patria potestas*, and consequently, to legitimize his discourse as Logos. Eltit's text wholeheartedly rejects this claim, offering one of society's most downtrodden subjects as an alternative father figure and source of truth.

At the end of her prologue, Eltit adds that after visiting the vagabond in 1983, 1984, and 1985, respectively, she returned again in 1986 to the vacant lot where he lived. To her surprise, she was told by other shantytown dwellers that he was gone: "—Se fue, me contestaron" [—He left, they answered me] (18). She concludes with the following lines: "La publicación de este libro permite compartir su peso, dejar abiertas otras identificaciones. Me permite, especialmente, diluir su ausencia" [The publication of this book permits me to share his importance, to leave open other identifications. It permits me, especially, to dilute his absence] (Eltit, *El padre mío*, 18). The vagabond has disappeared. But where has he gone? Has he moved away? Have the powerful men he speaks out against finally caught up with him? Whatever the case, it is significant that Eltit emphasizes his absence. He is no longer there to speak for himself. The responsibility, therefore, falls to her to rescue his voice from oblivion.

Voice and Image

The question of *framing* El Padre Mío's testimony is an important aspect not only of Eltit's book but also of a video entitled *El padre mío* (1985) produced by Eltit and Rosenfeld as part of the work of C.A.D.A. (Colectivo de Acciones de Arte/Art Actions Group). I would like to focus briefly on the ways in which Eltit and Rosenfeld, in their video, employ visual images to guide our reading of the vagabond's voice. Through techniques like superimposition, juxtaposition, and montage (all frequently employed by the artists of the *Avanzada*), the artists establish a clear linkage between the vagabond's voice and the broader sociopolitical context of the dictatorship, thus inviting us to consider possible relationships among the vagabond, other marginalized urban subjects who appear on screen, and the overarching power structures of the dictatorial state.

As the nine-minute video begins, the viewer sees Santiago's shantytown dwellers engaging in street protests against the dictatorship in 1983, a year that marked a critical moment of political aperture in Chile.[15] From there, General Pinochet, dressed in his starched white military regalia, imposes himself upon the scene. The red, white, and blue sash he is wearing symbolically evokes the idea of nationhood. Though we cannot hear what the General is saying, we notice he is standing behind a podium giving a public discourse.

These juxtaposed images of the dictator (emblematic of the regime) and the protests of 1983 (emblematic of the opposition) are soon eclipsed by yet another image: that of an eight-year-old girl named Marisol Díaz. Marisol is pictured in her school uniform reading an essay in front of the camera. In her speech, she focuses on the domestic violence that occurs in her home. We learn that her brother and father are both abusive and that her mother has tried to abandon her: "Mi papá le pega a mi mamá, y no sé por qué" [My father hits my mother, and I don't know why]. Her childlike innocence situates her as the victim of patriarchal abuse—a kind of domestic abuse that echoes in the private realm the abuse of patriarchal (dictatorial) authority in the public sphere.

After this, the video spins into a cacophony of competing voices and images. Pinochet reappears, his mouth again moving as if giving a speech. Yet the voice we hear is not Pinochet's; it is the vagabond's. This superimposition of visual images and audio clips seems to suggest two things: (1) that the violence of the Pinochet regime is responsible for creating a psychic rupture in the speaking subject whose voice we hear; (2) that the public discourse of the dictator himself, when compared to lived reality, might very well be construed as *locura*.

As El Padre Mío's voice plays on, more images are superimposed on the dictator to reveal the "other side" of Chilean reality (poverty, killings, drug use, etc.), and these images undermine his discourse of order and reason. Two images are especially striking: the image of a meeting by a group of *pobladoras* [shantytown women] who are conversing about how the dictatorship has not helped them escape poverty and the image of a shantytown dweller holding up to the camera what looks like a bag of cocaine.

The video ends with a sustained image of the vagabond giving his testimony. The camera lens zooms in on his face and lingers there, forcing us to take note of his extremely wrinkled, sun-dried skin, his broken teeth, the deep circles under his eyes, and the gnats that occasionally fly around his head. His face is cracked, broken, fractured, fissured, such that its image echoes the fragmentation we hear in his voice. Even his physical body bears the marks of *rotura* [brokenness, indigence].

The video version of *El padre mío*, like the book, thus causes us to reflect on how both bodies and minds were affected by the Pinochet regime's violent actions and contradictory gestures. Simultaneously, it serves as an example of how artists of the *Avanzada* used fragmentation, montage, and juxtaposition as well as the superimposition of voices, bodies, memories and counter-memories as a response to the dictatorship's monolithic language. By combining and recombining cultural signifiers in innovative and provocative ways, Eltit and Rosenfeld challenge our desire to accept what we see and hear at face value.

El padre mío as Literature

> *Hube de ubicarme, otra vez, en un lugar diverso, un espacio de suplantación que no apela a revertir nada, a curar nada, como no sea instalar el efecto conmovedor de esta habla y la relación estética con sus palabras vaciadas de sentido, de cualquier lógica, salvo la angustia de la persecución silábica, el eco encadenatorio de las rimas, la situación vital del sujeto que habla, la existencia rigurosamente real de los márgenes de la ciudad y de esta escena marginal.*
>
> *En suma, actuar desde la narrativa. Desde la literatura.*
>
> *[I had to situate myself, again, in a different place, a space of subversion that didn't seek to change anything, or cure anything, only to inscribe the moving effect of this discourse and the aesthetic relation to its words, empty of meaning, of any logic other than the anguish of syllabic persecution, the incessant echo of its rhymes, the life circumstance of the subject who speaks, the very real existence of the city's margins and of this marginal scene.*
>
> *In short, I wanted to act from narrative, from literature.]*
>
> Diamela Eltit, "Prologue" to *El padre mío*

At first glance, it would seem that El Padre Mío's discourse can be read from any number of disciplinary angles (e.g., psychology, anthropology, history, sociology), and each of these lenses would likely offer valuable insight into the reality to which the speaking subject bears witness. Why, then, does Eltit suggest we read the madman's testimony *as literature*?

The question forces us to consider the different levels on which testimony "means." Eltit clearly understands that the madman's testimony, as I have insisted, does not tell a story that can be read chronologically or according to parameters of cause and effect. Instead, she attunes her ear to the poetics of the vagabond's testimony, reading there a metaphor for the fracture of memory, language, and sense during the Pinochet years. Based on her intuition, Eltit's "Prologue" becomes a space in which to challenge her readers to consider the figurative value in testimonial discourse and to read it in a way that goes beyond the level of literal facts—in short, to read it as literature.

Philippe Lacoue-Labarthe maintains that "the singularity of experience cannot be rendered in language" (15). This statement, as I have attempted to show by referring to testimony's impossibilities, may be particularly applicable when it comes to post-traumatic memories following authoritarian regimes. The extreme violence perpetrated on the metaphorical body politic and on the real bodies of political prisoners leaves victims at an impasse, unable to convey through language the weight or depth of their physical and mental pain. All attempts to bear witness only *allude* to the singularity of the offense without capturing its dimensions fully. Capitalizing on this idea, Lacoue-Labarthe suggests that poetry, especially poetry after Auschwitz (and here I understand the term "poetry" metonymically as a stand-in for literature) is "en route" to a destination—*experience*—that it never fully reaches or captures.

In his impressive analysis of Paul Celan, Lacoue-Labarthe reads Celan's poetry as an attempt to make sense of a reality (Auschwitz) so terrible and so complex that it evades words. Reminiscent in his tone of Agamben's reading of Levi, Lacoue-Labarthe points out that it is precisely Celan's poetic stammering and stuttering that permits us to feel, to sense, to acknowledge what is unsayable about Auschwitz. Celan, in effect, bears witness to an impossibility of making sense of the camps. His texts communicate the "dizziness" of memory, the vertiginous character of a discourse that wants to say everything, but that cannot do so coherently.

Despite this impossibility of telling the "story" of Auschwitz, Lacoue-Labarthe reassures us that "all is not lost"; in a broken poetics like Celan's "a possibility of articulating something still remains, if only in an incomprehensible and incommunicable language . . ." (*Poetry*, 23). The dark, often obscure murmurs of Celan's verse, for Lacoue-Labarthe, signify something quite powerful: they allude to the singularity, the un-representability, the profound pain, the catastrophe of Auschwitz. Here, the notion of *allusion* is key insofar as it signals an often overlooked part of testimony's "value": meaning is bound up not only in what the testimonial utterance says, but also in what it keeps silent or cannot say. To read literature after Auschwitz, consequently, means to learn to listen attentively to these silences and search within them for meanings of a different order.

I have argued in this chapter that *El padre mío* highlights metaphorically the difficulties of bearing witness to trauma in rational terms while challenging the writing of clean, polished or deceptively transparent narratives of the Pinochet years. Eltit's book privileges the fragment, the "residual" and the impossible as hallmarks of a post-dictatorial poetics of memory, rejecting the linear and the rational as viable modalities for writing the disaster.[16] Not only does Eltit's book serve as a space for exploring totalitarian power's mind-altering effects, it functions as a site of political subversion where a marginalized voice is upheld as an important source of truth. Through the lens of *locura*, Eltit offers a compelling reading of a nation torn asunder by extreme violence and rampant fear. Her urban artistic intervention invites us to consider alternative methods of reading testimonial discourse and challenges us to search for meaning in unexpected places.

2

The Poetics of Reconciliation (Luz Arce's *El infierno*)

La Flaca Alejandra, Luz y Carola traicionaron, pero Gladys Díaz y Miriam Ortega lograron callar. A pesar de los sufrimientos atroces, las cinco sobrevivieron. No hay lógica en estos lugares. Uno puede hablar sin traicionar. Uno puede empezar a traicionar sin entregar nada importante. Pero pasó de otro lado, les pertenece.
[Skinny Alejandra, Luz, and Carola became traitors, while Gladys Díaz and Miriam Ortega managed to keep silent. Despite their atrocious suffering, all five women survived. There is no logic in these places. One can speak without betraying. One can start to betray without giving up anything important. But, in either case, she has crossed over to the other side; she belongs to them.]

Carmen Castillo

La literatura es una forma privada de la utopía.
[Literature is a private form of utopia.]

Ricardo Piglia

How is it possible to convey in words the weight and depth of traumatic experience or articulate a coherent vision of the self after the fibers of identity have been torn asunder in the torture chamber? How can one gain *narrative control* over intrusive memories and integrate the traumatic episode into a rational "life story"? To narrate trauma—or more precisely, to integrate trauma into the narrative of a life—survivors must speak *from* somewhere: that is, they must construct a locus of enunciation and opt for a narrative mode that can offer the possibility of communicating adequately a profoundly painful experience. (Of course, when I say "adequately" I realize that any mode of representation will almost always seem inadequate or insufficient to survivors of limit experiences.) In the previous chapter, I highlighted Diamela Eltit's *poetics of impossibility* as one possible narrative response to trauma whose aim was to question the "sayability" of extreme violence perpetrated by the dictatorial state. Here, in a radical turn, I would like to explore the consequences of a very different type of poetics: the suturing of traumatic experience into integral narratives that alleviate cognitive dissonance in survivors precisely because they allow trauma to be explained through coherent or rational frameworks. I will focus on one such framework that, as I see it, has penetrated deeply in both the public and private discourses of Chile's transition: the *poetics of reconciliation*.

Perhaps more than any other book published during Chile's transition, Luz Arce's *El infierno* [*The Inferno*] (1993) brings into relief the political and ethical dilemmas that arise in representing traumatic memory, as well as the artifice with which a subject who has survived a hellish and morally disturbing personal journey manages to say "I" in its aftermath. Arce's book guides the reader through the darkest confines of life inside DINA [Dirección Nacional de Inteligencia] and CNI [Central Nacional de Informaciones] (Pinochet's secret police organizations) and describes in graphic detail the brutal violence, fear, and human frailty that were part of that world. The text is unique among Chilean post-dictatorial testimonies because it emanates from an unstable ground of moral indeterminacy: Arce is neither entirely victim nor perpetrator, but one of many former left-wing militants who were "broken" in Pinochet's torture chambers and later compelled into complicity with the regime. In fact, aside from Marcia Alejandra Merino Vega (known in Chile as "La Flaca Alejandra" [Skinny Alejandra]), whose similar testimony *Mi verdad: más allá del horror, yo acuso . . .* [*My Truth: Beyond Horror, I accuse . . .*] was also published in 1993, Arce is the only Chilean collaborator to publish a book about her experience.[1]

Rejected by the left as a collaborator and by the right for betraying her loyalties to DINA, Arce's status in Chile at the time of writing is precarious, to say the least. Following years spent in silence, confusion, and self-loathing, her textual project is to come forward and publicly confess her "sin" of collaboration. More than a decade after resigning her post as a functionary of Pinochet's secret police (1980), she emerges from hiding and stands before the nation as a repentant convert to Christianity who, having discovered God, asks forgiveness of her fellow countrymen.

In *El infierno*, the discourse of reconciliation takes on a profoundly personal dimension. It ceases to be an official state-sponsored rhetoric aimed at establishing social peace and the necessary conditions for governance; instead, it is taken by Arce in its Judeo-Christian sense: as the radical re-orientation of her life, a turning toward God and away from sin, and an embracing of the "other." Moreover, Arce's public assumption of shame has had an important though somewhat unexpected consequence in Chile: it has allowed other collaborators to use her as a scapegoat while portraying themselves as valiant, as having resisted giving up names or party-related information under torture. However, the commonly acknowledged reality among Chilean human rights activists is that more political prisoners than not were broken by Pinochet's henchman. Yet, to avoid public stigma, these other Chilean collaborators have, in almost every case, remained silent, hidden behind masks of martyrdom, while Luz Arce and La Flaca Alejandra have been made to shoulder (metonymically) the collective shame of collaboration. As Arce writes, she and La Flaca are the "putas y traidoras" [whores and traitors] who have been symbolically saddled with the guilt of every militant who "talked." Consequently, Arce is an emblematic figure whose voice and public image are of great relevance for understanding the political and ethical problematic of Chile's traumatic memory. It is precisely because of the unique position from which Arce's voice emanates—the *in-between* of collaboration—that her book deserves to be read rigorously, both for the moral dilemmas it raises and for its political complexity as a cultural artifact. *El infierno* reminds us that post-dictatorial memory is not just about the disappeared, the executed, or Pinochet's neoliberal legacy, but about thousands upon thousands of traitorous bodies driven to absolute abjection and forced to live with the consequences (e.g., rejection, ignorance). These broken subjectivities in desperate need of reconstitution (and recognition) are one of the dictatorship's most obstinate legacies. They, too, must be taken into account, however painful or difficult that may be.

Luz Arce's discourse emerges not only from a desire to reconcile with her traumatic past but also from a profound sense of responsibility toward fellow victims and the Chilean citizenry in general. She wants to bear witness for those who cannot speak for themselves, and often, as a means to that end, "names names": those of the victims who died as well as the perpetrators who killed them. Yet she remains careful to guard any information that may be too sensitive or damaging to third parties. Acutely aware of Chile's fragile political climate, she makes clear that she will not interfere with any legal proceedings either impending or already in progress.[2] As a result, her act of truth telling is not unconditional, not anarchical: she will not tell the whole truth at any cost, but is limited by the social, political, and judicial constraints of the day.

Furthermore, *El infierno* is temporally and ideologically enmeshed in the broader institutional framework of the transition. The book appeared just three years after Arce testified formally before the Truth Commission (1990) and served as a vehicle for expanding both the factual and emotional aspects of her deposition. In her deposition, as in her book, Arce affirms that she speaks out of a desire for truth, justice, and reconciliation, noting that her courage to acknowledge her shame publicly is a direct result of her conversion to the

Roman Catholic faith.[3] And it is this conversion experience, coupled with the institutional legitimacy afforded her testimony by the Catholic Church and Chilean government, that compels Arce to come forward. At the same time, the context of the transition is crucial, as the "appropriateness" of the historical and political moment is such that Arce *can*, in fact, break her silence.[4] The truth commission creates a political space in which Arce can testify "safely" and view herself not as a criminal (as for years she had been labeled by her compatriots, particularly by a significant sector of the human rights community), but as a victim who can offer invaluable testimony to the workings of DINA/CNI from the *inside*.

In the opening paragraph of her "Palabras preliminares" [Preliminary Words], Arce admits that a "black legend" has stained her name in Chile: "Existe sobre mí una suerte de 'leyenda negra,' una historia imprecisa, elaborada al tenor de una realidad de horror, humillación y violencia" [There is a kind of "black legend" about me, an imprecise story, elaborated in a context of horror, humiliation, and violence] (*El infierno*, 19). Her book is an attempt to debunk that story and correct her public image. Through writing, she hopes to vindicate her tarnished name and dispel certain myths that others have propagated about her (e.g., that she was the one who gave up the names of the vast majority of the detained and disappeared). Her text is at once a plea for forgiveness ("pido perdón, pero no lo espero" [I ask forgiveness, though I do not expect it]) and a struggle to reconstitute her fractured identity ("¡Qué complicado resulta a veces dar coherencia a la propia vida!" [How complicated it sometimes is to give coherence to one's life!])(19, 20).

The question of identity is central to *El infierno*. Arce appears as a subject whose identity is in constant flux. The narrative traces her journey from her early days as a militant in Chile's Socialist Party, and later goes on to describe her detention and torture, the nature of her collaboration, her integration into the ranks of DINA/CNI, her subsequent conversion to Christianity, and the ultimate reconstitution of her "self." Along the way, she assumes innumerable false names and repeatedly expresses doubts regarding the nature of her true identity. For nearly four hundred pages, she appears embroiled in a constant struggle, from youth onward, to answer the question *Who am I*: "Me di cuenta que yo nada sabía de mí" [I understood that I didn't know anything about myself] (24). In the midst of this existential dilemma, her conversion experience functions as a stabilizing mechanism to mitigate her identity crisis. Christianity (with its focus on forgiveness and reconciliation) permits Arce a framework within which to subsume her disparate identities: the militant, the torture victim, the collaborator; it gives her a place from which to say "I." Arce's story, therefore, reads as the narrative of a broken woman, estranged from herself, who discovers an uncanny capacity for healing, rooted in Christian doctrine, and a space for rearticulating her identity in the newly democratized Chile. She concludes her book with the following exhortation:

> El país tiene que rescatarse a sí mismo y enfrentar su verdad para poder dejar en el pasado lo que pertenece a éste, y pensar y construir un futuro libre del olvido o la mentira. Me doy cuenta que yo necesité hacerlo. Fue importante, fue indispensable para decirme otra vez: mi nombre es Luz, Luz Arce.
>
> [The country has to save itself and confront its truth in order to leave in the past what belongs to the past, and to conceive of and build a future free of forgetfulness and lies. I understand that I had to do so. It was important; it was indispensable so I might once again say to myself: My name is Luz, Luz Arce.] (387)

In the opening lines of "The Gray Zone," Primo Levi notes that survivors of limit situations have often tried to understand (or make others understand) the complexities of their experiences. But, Levi is quick to point out, "what we commonly mean by 'understand' coincides with 'simplify': without a profound simplification the world around us would be an infinite, undefined tangle that would defy our ability to orient ourselves and decide upon our actions" (*Drowned*, 36). In Levi's estimation, human beings seek to render complex experiences knowable by reducing them to schematics, by explaining them in terms of narratives (or fictions) the mind can grasp or perhaps justify. In a similar vein, Sylvia Molloy suggests that particularly in the case of autobiographical narrative, it is necessary to choose from an "archive" of available forms for narrating the self (*At Face Value*, 5). In other words, the "I" exercises an *option* in autobiography that is at once political, ethical, and aesthetic.

Ángel Loureiro adds another dimension to the debate by stressing that autobiography is, first and foremost, a performative act: an art of self-representation that emerges as an ethically motivated address directed toward an other, an address that seeks a response (in Arce's case, forgiveness by the reader). Contrary to previous scholarship on autobiography, Loureiro notes that rather than finding its genesis in "cognitive pretensions" or in the idea of truth as an "adequation to past experience," autobiographical writing affirms the writer's "belief in his own truth" (*The Ethics*,14). As critics frequently note, autobiographical and testimonial texts, Arce's notwithstanding, emanate from the authority of a witness whose truth, because it is based in her own lived experience, is put forth as incontrovertible. Arce's authority stems from the fact that she "was there," that she witnessed firsthand the horrors of Chilean repression and knows from personal experience what collaboration means. Her testimony, in that sense, is self-legitimizing insofar as those who did not experience the gray zone themselves are left with little basis upon which to contest her discourse. This self-proposed incontrovertibility is, in general terms, the testimonial text's pretension of veridicality: the reader is asked to defer to the authority of the witness's discourse because of his or her privileged relationship to the truth.

Considering that Arce testified before the Truth Commission before publishing *El infierno*, it seems necessary to distinguish between testimonial writing in book form and testimony given in a legal forum. Something particular must have compelled Arce to expand her original legal deposition into a book-length narrative. What might the gesture of writing provide that witnessing in a legal forum cannot?

Two hypotheses come to mind. First, the space of writing provides Arce greater discursive freedom than does the genre of a legal deposition. Whereas the structure of legal testimony is fundamentally oral and dialogic (based on a rigid structure of questions and answers and consequently subject to manipulation), testimonial writing (especially when, as in Arce's case, it is not mediated by an interviewer), though equally subject to manipulation, leaves the speaker at liberty to express her experience as she sees fit, unconstrained by the formulas of legality.

Second, we might also consider the objective of bearing witness. Agamben notes that the law's ultimate goal is to produce judgment, a sentence (*Remnants*, 18). A legal proceeding must generate a concrete result: someone will always be convicted or exonerated regardless of whether the truth has been uncovered in the process. Testimonial writing is different. Its objective is not to bring about legal resolution (though admittedly testimonial writing almost always seeks to influence or produce an impact in the real world), but rather to establish a truth that stands somehow *beyond* the law. Thus, testimonial writing is inscribed, first and foremost, not in the realm of legality, but in the realm of ethics. Therefore, when Luz Arce writes *El infierno*, independent of the "facts" of the case, her utterance emerges out of an ethical obligation toward the truth.

Yet, I would add, the construction of truth takes place only in the production of discourse. In autobiography, identity is constructed through a narrative act. And this narrative act, following Foucault's postulation of a historicized subject, cannot occur outside the range of discourses available to the testimonial subject in the given cultural or historical moment of writing. Consciously or unconsciously, autobiographical (or testimonial) subjects become "attached" to the discourses that constitute them: "Autobiographers necessarily write through the mediation of scientific, philosophical, psychological, historical, political, sexual, moral, religious, linguistic, and literary discourses, to name just a few, in which they believe or which have currency in their time, as well as in the context of practices and institutions that allow them to speak" (Loureiro, *The Ethics*, 13). It is worth remembering Foucault's comment in "Truth and Juridical Forms" that "the political and economic conditions of existence are not a veil or an obstacle for the subject of knowledge but the means by which subjects of knowledge are formed" (15). When one says "I" in testimony (as Arce does), she says it rooted in a particular position in historical time. She speaks, that is, via the lenses and discursive modes available to her as an historically situated subject.

The theoretical insights I have outlined here are central to my analysis of *El infierno* insofar as they support my claim that Arce exercises a political and aesthetic option through her choice of narrative form. Specifically, Arce employs the generic model of a confession (in the tradition of Rousseau and Augustine) as the privileged mode through which to tell her experience. Such a choice, I think, is not an innocent one but may very well reveal something deeper about the cultural (as well as the purely circumstantial) forces that operate *on* and *through* Arce as a testimonial subject and that shape the way in which she writes her life in a particular historical and political moment: the Chilean transition of the early 1990s. My contention is that *El infierno* can be read as a text implicitly, yet intricately intertwined with the Concertación's politics in the early moments of the transition. Arce's book is a mise en scène of a subject who, having embraced the dominant discourse of reconciliation, uses it to bring narrative resolution to the shame of collaboration. Confession, religious conversion, and forgiveness are the narrative tropes—though, at the same time, we must not forget that they are also real, lived convictions—that Arce adopts to write herself a place in the nation and clear her tainted name. (Here I feel compelled to note that the line dividing trope from belief in Arce is undoubtedly a blurred one. She certainly does not think of her text in terms of the narrative devices she employs but simply lives her life in accordance with the Christian values that guide her autobiographical act. It is only *a posteriori*, in the eyes of the literary critic, that belief becomes trope.)

What might be the possible consequences of a political and aesthetic choice that would posit collaboration and trauma as "resolvable" or subject to a harmonious ending? I do not wish to imply that the reader ever feels that Arce's trauma is resolved (or even remotely so). The text's overall effect is, in fact, quite the opposite. What I wish to stress is that both the narrative form and content of *El infierno* communicate a profound *desire* to gain closure and assuage the shame of a morally ambiguous experience. Mindful that such a narrative gesture may, in fact, belie the very complexities of the gray zone, I will explore how Arce's personal (and textual) process of reconciliation occurs on three successive levels: reconciliation with self, God, and nation. In tandem, I will show that there are admittedly certain moments of tension and rupture in *El infierno* that contradict Arce's overall project of achieving narrative harmony and challenge the very limits of the "sayable"—moments in which torture and collaboration appear to defy verbalization and resist a "happy ending."

In short, I will explore the consequences of Arce's narrative strategy to suggest that *El infierno*, in its textual desire and narrative impulse, emblematizes and echoes the utopian discourse of reconciliation that has been the hallmark of Chile's transition.

Stage 1. Reconciling with Self: Overcoming the Shame of Torture and Collaboration

I would like to begin by thinking about what reconciliation with self might mean, about how it might be possible to come to terms with victimization and culpability after torture and collaboration. Without a doubt, to say "I" after trauma is a daunting task that requires that a victim scrutinize her life in order to determine how she arrived at her present condition. For the sake of clarity in my discussion, I will examine torture and collaboration (and its subsequent bureaucratization) as separate "moments" that Arce must integrate into a logical narrative progression. I examine them each in turn, beginning with torture, understanding that these experiences are organically connected to one another in Arce's text.

Recent theoretical reflections on trauma's effects stress that torture's goal is to annihilate subjectivity, to turn victims into "bodies in pain" deprived of autonomous voices and coerced to speak the language of betrayal. As Levi points out, prisoners taken to the Nazi concentration camps were brutally objectified: registration numbers were branded on their bodies to remind them that they would no longer be viewed as human beings with names and individual identities, but as numbers, as dehumanized objects within Hitler's machinery of death (Levi, *Drowned*, 118). If we understand torture to be a process whose goal is the destruction of subjectivity, then the arduous process of recovery (insofar as it is possible) should logically imply a reconstruction of the self that somehow accounts for and attempts to integrate the traumatic moment into a rational life plan. One thing is abundantly clear: the victim who speaks after trauma is not the same subjectivity who spoke prior to the traumatic moment. Put more concretely: Luz Arce, driven to the point of complete and utter abjection in DINA's torture chambers, is not the same subjective consciousness who writes *El infierno* ten years later. When she takes up the pen, Arce is a "broken" and confused subject who uses writing as a means by which to regain control of intrusive memories from which she cannot escape, to construct a voice that will permit her to project herself into the future.

The self is an unstable category, a dynamic and constantly evolving narrative construct. As philosopher Susan Brison points out, subjectivity is not unitary, nor is the traumatic moment entirely recoverable because of the lapses and fissures it leaves in memory. Consequently, post-traumatic subjects find themselves in a bind: they struggle to articulate a coherent sense of identity that can satisfactorily integrate diverse "selves" in different temporal moments (e.g., the self before torture, the tortured self, the post-traumatic self, the self of textual enunciation, the projected future self)(*Aftermath*, 56). Narrative acts offer victims a chance at self-reparation, a chance to insert disorderly experiences into a chronological frame and thus exercise control (autonomy) over intrusive memories. After trauma, victims want to be made anew (one often hears the term "to be made whole") and this implies not only understanding who they are in the present in relation to who they were in the past, but also the projection of their narratives toward real or imagined interlocutors capable of empathetic listening. Working through or "mastering" trauma involves confronting shame honestly and directly; it implies integrating the shards of a fragmented identity so as to gain the necessary confidence to reestablish ties to both self and community.[5] This, however, is easier said than done. For the victim, forced to live with her scars, integrating trauma can be an exceedingly difficult if not insurmountable task.

In an ongoing interview conducted between 2002 and 2005, Luz Arce told me that torture survivors are not the same people they were before the offense, but instead "meras reconstrucciones de las personas que fueron antes" [mere reconstructions of the people they once were]. In light of this comment, it seems clear that she writes *El infierno* not to recover a lost identity but rather, following the logic outlined above, to narrate a *new* version of self that can integrate her many faces: the militant, the torture victim, the collaborator. Significantly, her narrative begins with a metaphorical moment of rupture that establishes a temporal and existential rift in Arce's being (11 September 1973):

> El 11 de septiembre lo viví como una irrupción en lo que era mi mundo, como un poder destructivo que aniquiló lo importante de mi vida. La catástrofe que tornó todo en algo incoherente, incomprensible. Que llenó mi vida de pena, ¡Dios! si sólo fuera eso, era un vacío anestesiado, no ver, no saber, no nada.
>
> [I lived 11 September 1973 like an irruption in my world, like a destructive power that annihilated everything that was important in my life, a catastrophe that made everything incoherent, incomprehensible, that filled my life with pain. God, if it were only that! It was an anesthetized void: no sight, no knowledge, nothing.] (*El infierno,* 34)

Plagued by recurring trauma and years of repressed memories, Arce writes that on 4 December 1989, as she was walking home through downtown Santiago, she noticed a copy of the left-wing magazine *Punto Final* hanging on a newsstand. Realizing that this was the first issue of *Punto Final* to be published since the coup and that the numbering picked up where the last issue left off seventeen years earlier, the experience was a revelation to her: it made her realize that life, after Pinochet, must somehow, in some form, continue. When she finally arrives home, Arce goes to her window, gazes upon the San Cristóbal Virgin atop the Santiago cityscape and prays to her heavenly mother for strength to probe memory's minefields. Once again calling attention to her ruptured subjectivity, she wonders:

> ¿Podré retomar mi vida? Sentí pavor. Me pareció que por más de una década y media estuve ausente de mi propio ser y que se acercaba la hora de la verdad. Me detuve, cerré los ojos, abarcando con el pensamiento ese oscuro paréntesis donde lo vivo y lo llameante me estaba consumiendo en una hoguera, y volví a percibir el miedo que me paralizó durante años.
>
> [Can I regain control of my life? I felt scared. It seemed that for more than a decade and a half I had been estranged from my being and that the moment of truth was near. I stopped. I closed my eyes, thinking about that dark parenthesis in which life and the flames consumed me, as in a bonfire. And I felt once again the fear that had paralyzed me for years.] (*El infierno*, 34)

The estrangement from herself of which Arce speaks is the product not only of fear but of the shame that stems from knowing she has been violated and has suffered extreme dehumanization. For years, Arce admits, she tried constantly to repress the memory of her time in the camps, to forget consciously and actively the horrors she experienced and witnessed. Forgetting seemed necessary if she were to build any sort of viable future for herself and her family.[6] But her desire to forget was trumped by the sting of shame—a shame which, in the course of her narrative, takes on many faces: the shame of being violated and objectified under torture, the shame of collaboration, and the shame of having survived while many of her *compañeros* perished.[7]

In his enlightening discussion of shame, Agamben highlights Levinas's study *De L'évasion* [On Evasion], in which shame is understood as an "intolerable presence of the self to itself," an extreme situation in which one cannot hide from herself what she would very much like to conceal (Levinas qtd. in Agamben, *Remnants*, 105). "In shame," Agamben writes, "the subject . . . has no other content than its own desubjectification; it becomes witness to its own internal disorder, its own oblivion as a subject. This double movement, which is both subjectification and desubjectification, is shame" (106). Very much in line with Levinas' observation, Arce presents herself as a wayward woman racked with shame, unable to evade the intolerable memory of her past. The "traitorous" self she for so long kept at bay eventually emerges as a force with which she must reckon: "Nunca me había enfrentado tan desnuda ante mí misma" [I had never been so naked before myself] (*El infierno*, 339).

Arce uses the first half of her text to lay the groundwork for the construction of her newly imagined subjectivity: that of the Christian penitent. Yet there can be no remaking of the self (or attempted justification of her collaboration) without first narrating the "un-making" of subjectivity and the conditions under which collaboration took place. Consequently, Part I of *El infierno* focuses on Arce's desubjectification through torture, seeking to establish a clear, unambiguous picture of her as a *victim* of the Pinochet regime. Indeed, if she writes herself in this way, her discourse has a better chance of gaining moral credence with her readers, who she hopes will see her as fallibly human, swept up by the nefarious current of the totalitarian state. In our personal interviews, Arce summarized her position quite succinctly: "Nunca sentí que yo fuera parte de la DINA en ningún momento, ni como prisionera colaborando, ni como funcionaria" [I never felt like I was part of DINA at any moment, neither as a prisoner collaborating nor as a functionary]. Certainly, she accepts her collaboration, yet she feels that ultimate blame lies with the highest ranking leaders of DINA and with Pinochet himself.[8] She holds that she was a mere cog in the wheel of state terror.[9]

Arce's choice of language and imagery throughout Part I speaks metaphorically to the destruction of voice and subjectivity and further emphasizes her position as victim. For example, she describes her brutal torture at Londres 38 in March 1974 using phrases like "soy una muñeca desarticulada" [I am a doll torn apart] and "tengo la boca enmudecida" [my mouth has been muted]. In other moments, she speaks of her desire to "not exist," to be a "nobody" (*El infierno*, 56, 77–78). This dehumanized status is further brought into relief when she is divested of her name (her individuality) and assigned a number: Prisoner 54.

Other scenes, too, refer to Arce's loss of voice. While under the care of military doctors at Tejas Verdes for wounds incurred during torture, Arce feels a strange compulsion to thank a soldier who takes pity on her (he is just one of many characters in the book who demonstrate some degree of compassion in a morally degraded world). Interestingly, she lacks the linguistic ability to do so: "Traté de hablar, quería agradecerle, pero me salió un quejido raro. . . .—¡Tiene la boca y la lengua rota!—dijo otra enfermera . . . [I tried to speak. I wanted to thank him, but a strange shriek came out. . . .—Her mouth and tongue are broken!—said another nurse . . .] (61). Later, when she is transferred to the Military Hospital (HOSMIL) for further treatment, she again calls attention to her inability to speak:

> Una enfermera se acercó y me dijo:
> —¿Cómo se llama?, dígame. . . . ¿Cómo se llama?
> Sin responder, abrí la boca y ella vio mi lengua.
> —Tiene la lengua hinchada, doctor.
> La enfermera seguía hablando:
> —Creo que no puede hablar, doctor.
> El médico se acercó a mí y comenzó a explicarme lo que ocurría con mi pie.
> [A nurse drew near and asked me:
> —What's your name? Tell me. . . . What's your name?
> Without responding, I opened my mouth and she saw my tongue.
> —Her tongue is swollen, doctor.
> The nurse kept talking:
> —I think she can't speak, doctor.

The doctor came over and started explaining to me what the problem was with my foot.] (*El infierno*, 67)

As a final example of the destruction of subjectivity, the scene in which Arce narrates her repeated rape by a sergeant in charge of hydrotherapy treatments at the Military Hospital is telling. During her treatments, the evil sergeant drowns Arce in a bathtub, pushing her to the brink of death while violating her brutally and sadistically. Here again, Arce describes herself as a non-entity (una "no-persona"):

> Recuerdo la cara desfigurada del sargento a través del agua, y la sensación de asfixia. Pero sobre todo impotencia, dolor, deseos de desaparecer. De no existir. De ser nadie. . . . Era como si la propia voz no sonara; como si uno no existiera. No era una persona.
>
> [I remember seeing the sergeant's disfigured face through the water, and the feeling of asphyxia. But, above all, impotence, pain, the desire to disappear, not to exist, to cease being. . . . It was as if my own voice couldn't sound; as if I didn't exist. I wasn't a person.] (*El infierno*, 77–78)

This scene, however, is not just interesting for the way in which it alludes to Arce's "un-making," but also for how Arce textually "resolves" this horrifying experience. At a certain point, she is temporarily set free under surveillance, and during this period she has a chance encounter with the same sergeant who raped her in the Military Hospital. The following dialogue occurs toward the end of their conversation:

> —Sí sargento. Estoy libre.
>
> —Que le vaya bien—dijo despacio, y se fue.
>
> Yo sé que mi mirada fue dura y creí ver tristeza en sus ojos. Pero me llamé la atención diciendo: "Luz, eres bien huevona, ¿qué te importa este maricón sádico?"
>
> [—Yes, sergeant. I'm free.
>
> —Be well—he said slowly, and he left.
>
> I know that my look was hardened and I thought I saw sadness in his eyes. But I got it together and said to myself: "Luz, you're such an idiot. Why does that sadistic faggot matter to you anyway?"] (88)

This interchange constitutes a foundational moment in *El infierno* insofar as it confronts the reader with the dilemma of how Arce will ultimately deal with her shame and foreshadows the project of reconciliation that will be developed more fully later in her book. Despite the fact that she chastises herself for bothering at all with such an evil man, Arce's reference to the sergeant's look of sadness (*tristeza*) opens the possibility that on some deep, unmanifested level he feels remorse for his actions. This possible glimpse of remorse in her torturer is critical to the book's narrative progression insofar as it allows the reader, early on, to consider the feasibility of mutual forgiveness between victim and victimizer. Arce's reading of shame in the sergeant's gaze, in effect, makes the second half of her narrative possible.

Having looked at Arce's "desubjectification" (her unmaking) through torture, and having noted how the early part of her testimony paves the way for her reconciliatory project, I would now like to turn to a second "moment" in Arce's life trajectory: collaboration and its subsequent bureaucratization.

Arce's testimony, it is clear, becomes even more problematic when having established her speaking position as a victim she begins to tell the story of her collaboration with DINA, all the while employing attenuating statements that read as justifications for her actions. To be fair, Arce does at one point specifically write the words "no pretendo justificarme" [I don't pretend to justify myself], but in order to confront her shame in a productive and therapeutic way she nevertheless feels compelled to offer reasons for why she acted as she did (*El infierno*, 171). Why did she not choose death? Why did she "allow" herself to be broken in the torture chamber? What cannot be justified, one might argue, cannot be integrated into her story. Self-justification, independent of its merit, is therefore a fundamental and perhaps inevitable element in Arce's project of subjective reconstitution.

Arce's collaboration is complex and multifaceted. It consists of (1) giving up names of her comrades under torture (at least two of whom eventually became *desaparecidos*); (2) participating in the so called *poroteos* (raids by DINA/CNI whose aim was the entrapment and capture of left-wing militants); (3) using her knowledge of the power structures of groups like MIR [Movimiento de Izquierda Revolucionario/Leftist Revolutionary Movement] to sketch organizational diagrams for Pinochet's secret police; (4) teaching classes on Marxism to military officials; (5) assuming false identities and carrying out clandestine operations in Uruguay as part of Operation Celeste; and (6) engaging in amorous relationships with a number of military officers, particularly Rolf Wenderoth Pozo. Her narrative describes her seven-year-long process of transformation (1973–1980) from detainee to full-fledged "functionary" of DINA/CNI. Throughout this process, Arce is constantly plagued by pangs of conscience. "Aún en los peores tiempos existió algo que podríamos llamar conciencia, pero el vivir tan reducida como persona de alguna manera hace que la conciencia se va achicando" [Even in the worst times, there existed something we might call a conscience, but living in such a reduced state of humanity somehow makes the conscience shrink], she confessed in our private interviews. Arce thus offers one of her most salient defenses for her collaboration by proposing the limit situation as a scenario in which the category of conscience becomes altered. On numerous occasions, she points out that she only gave up the most "peripheral" information and the most "peripheral" names. Such behavior, she notes, was in accordance with the revolutionary training manuals she studied as a militant, which claimed that a "good revolutionary," when pressured, should give up only information that would not damage the integrity of the movement as a whole. To this day, Arce maintains that she did not give up everything she knew—just enough to survive—and consequently, the information she kept silent became like a salve for her shame: "el bálsamo era lo no entregado" [the balm was what I didn't give up].

She further attenuates her shame by drawing a distinction between the terms *culpabilidad* [culpability] and *responsabilidad* [responsibility], where the former term carries the connotation of legal guilt and the latter term remains inscribed solely within the realm of ethics.[10] Her contention is that she is not fully to blame for her collaboration because she was not able to act with complete autonomy in the camps, as one theoretically could in the outside world. She makes a point of noting that her collaboration occurred under duress as a "hostage" of DINA/CNI and that therefore she cannot be held accountable for her actions as a functionary in a juridical sense. In short, Arce is willing to claim moral responsibility for her collaboration, but not legal responsibility (culpability).[11]

There has been much debate in the post-dictatorship period about whether collaborators should be held responsible for actions they carried out in limit situations that lie beyond the usual moral framework that operates in human society. Some critics have argued that to give up any information under torture is a betrayal beyond redemption; others have taken a more tempered, empathetic stance toward collaborators, deeming it better to reserve judgment. In her state of absolute abjection, I would argue that Arce reaches a point under torture at which her ability to choose autonomously is called into question. Because she is fully subjected to her torturers' will, the choice to live or die is not hers alone to make, nor is it even remotely a rational decision that emerges after lengthy cerebral reflection. Arce's will to live is instead a purely instinctual impulse that seemingly defies the binary pair rationality/irrationality.

Autonomy and morality are not, however, one and the same. To argue as such would be tantamount to absolving torturers of responsibility based on an erroneous moral relativism. Todorov, careful to avoid such a relativist fallacy, holds that evil, even in the camps, was not unavoidable. Even in the most extreme circumstances, the "possibility of choosing moral values continues to exist" (*Facing*, 43). This is how one can explain those little acts of charity toward others so often reported in testimonial writings—acts akin to those Arce describes at certain points in her own writing, particularly in the case of a young soldier named Rodolfo Valentín González Pérez who, at his own risk, smuggled personal notes to Arce's family while she was interned in the Military Hospital (*El infierno*, 79–81). Yet, at the same time, the camp must be understood as an "artificial situation that tells us only about itself"; as a result, it becomes extremely difficult to judge a collaborator like Arce for actions committed under dire, inhumane conditions (Todorov, *Facing*, 39). Levi echoes this point when he acknowledges the "imprudence of issuing hasty moral judgments" on collaboration (*Drowned*, 43–44). "Certainly," Levi writes, "the greatest responsibility lies with the system, the very structure of the totalitarian state"; collaborators are "vectors and instruments of the system's guilt" (44, 49).[12] So should Arce be blamed for choosing life over death? Toward the end of her book Arce reminds her readers: "Cada ser es por sobre todo una persona con sus propias opciones" [Every human being is, above all, a person with his or her own options] (*El infierno*, 376). She is fully aware of the choices she has made and leaves it to her readers to act as jurors who, individually, can choose to condemn or exonerate.

Diamela Eltit and Nelly Richard, two of the principal critics of *El infierno*, have questioned the extent to which Arce can be forgiven.[13] Eltit, in particular, reads Arce as a chameleonic figure whose identity curiously shifts in tandem with changes in institutional power structures, claiming that her affiliations to the revolutionary Left and later to DINA/CNI reflect a desire to occupy decidedly "masculine" spaces. Although Eltit might agree with Todorov and Levi that Arce cannot be blamed for giving up names under torture, she expresses a profound ethical disturbance toward any person who would accommodate herself blindly to hegemonic powers and, furthermore, finds Arce's eventual acceptance of a salary from DINA/CNI to be morally untenable. Arce, of course, does not see things in this way: she denies she was ever in a position to *decide* her fate and claims that her obstinate will to live guided her every action. According to Arce, her motivation to accept a salary was rooted in a basic material necessity to provide for her child. The projection of a world beyond the camp, coupled with her maternal obligation, she claims, gave her a reason not to die a martyr's death.

Other moments in *El infierno* provide further evidence of Arce's desire to assuage shame. In one scene she fights steadfastly to improve her fellow prisoners' abhorrent living conditions, while in another she recommends to her superior officers that the prisoners' blindfolds be removed. In yet another gesture of altruism, she assumes the role of a nurse who cares for the inmates and administers medications to them. Each of these images stands in stark contrast to accusations leveled against Arce by other survivors that she either witnessed or engaged in the interrogation and torture of prisoners at Villa Grimaldi.

A final attempt at self-justification is linked to Arce's female gender. From the opening pages of her testimony, she presents herself as the "typical" daughter of a lower-middle-class Chilean family who, as a child and adolescent, felt isolated, lonely, and unloved: "Recuerdo mi hambre de afecto" [I remember my hunger for affection] (*El infierno*, 23). She appears as a marginalized girl, racked with guilt, sexually abused as a child and lacking a clear path in life—all crucial details insofar as they permit Arce to establish herself as embroiled from childhood (long before her militancy, captivity, and collaboration) in an identity crisis and struggle for acceptance. As a woman in a *machista* society, how would she ever feel a sense of belonging other than by penetrating masculine spaces? Returning to Eltit's point, time and again Arce seeks acceptance by assuming decidedly masculine roles. First, as a Socialist militant and personal bodyguard to Salvador Allende (GAP), she notes that she will be just "one more 'man' in the regiment" [Sería un "hombre" más de la guarnición] (*El infierno*, 26). Later, as a functionary of DINA/CNI, she alters her physical appearance and comportment in order to seem more masculine, hoping that by masking her femininity she will receive better treatment from the other officers and not be taken as a sexual object (as she was as a detainee). Her strategy, however, is foiled insofar as she continues to be an object of sexual desire for several male officers, especially Rolf Wenderoth Pozo, who eventually establishes an amorous relationship with her and protects her within DINA/CNI. At one point she even becomes entangled in a love triangle with Wenderoth and another young military officer. To complicate matters further, today Arce admits that she felt "gratitude" and "affection" toward Wenderoth both for protecting her and for granting special favors to her son (e.g., paying his school tuition). Her attitude toward this morally complex relationship is neither one of total acceptance nor total condemnation: she understands her affair with Wenderoth as just one more episode in an ongoing struggle for survival and acceptance.

To summarize, then, Arce presents herself as a wayward woman in search of affection, a sense of belonging and a sense of identity.[14] Although she regrets many of her actions, she argues that she was motivated by a desire to survive, to reclaim her dignity, and ultimately to vindicate her usurped name. Clearly, writing is therapeutic for Arce because it permits her to "work through" and justify to herself and others a series of ethically challenging scenarios that for years she was unable to resolve. Given this need for self-justification, a detailed description of her brutal unmaking (and loss of voice through torture) is a necessary prerequisite for the subsequent narration of her self-reparation.

Stage 2. Reconciling with God: Luz Arce's Confession and Conversion to Catholicism

Michel Foucault's lecture on "Christianity and Confession" offers a conceptual framework for thinking about Arce's public act of atonement and conversion to Catholicism.[15] Foucault observes that a fundamental obligation of every Christian is to manifest the truth about herself. From the early days of the Church, the Christian sinner was excluded from participation in many of the communal and sacramental rituals of the faithful. (In a somewhat analogous fashion, Luz Arce has been excluded from participating fully in the national community because she is a "traitor.") Yet the status of penitence—when fully and consciously assumed by the sinner—implied the possibility of reintegration into the community and an end to estrangement. Foucault notes that the writings of various Church fathers (Jerome, Tertullian, Ambrose) refer to a ritualistic, public act of atonement known as *exomologesis*.[16] This dramatic manifestation of "self renunciation" (death or abnegation of one's former self) and "repentance" (the creation of a *new* self) offered the penitent a chance to break free from her former state of sinfulness and forge a new, healthy relationship with God, self, and community. Foucault is especially mindful of the public nature and theatricality of the ritual: although some acts of confession take place in private, Foucault says that Tertullian translates the term *exomologesis* as "publicatio sui" [to publish oneself] ("Christianity," 209). To be reconciled, therefore, the Christian penitent must acknowledge before the community that she is indeed a sinner.

At the same time, Foucault highlights the existence of a related process called *exagoreusis*—the monastic fashion of confession—in which the penitent engages in "an analytical and continuous verbalization of thoughts . . . in a relation of complete obedience to the will of the spiritual Father" ("Christianity," 226). The sinner's job in this ritual is to speak incessantly in order to differentiate "good" thoughts from "bad" thoughts. Moreover, *exagoreusis* typically implied the presence of another (a listener)—an abbot, a spiritual brother or spiritual father—who would represent for the sinner "the image of God" (224). In order to achieve reconciliation or atonement, it was not sufficient for the penitent to confess her sins privately within the confines of her own heart; *exagoreusis*, like *exomologesis*, required the externalization (or public verbalization) of sin.

The relationship Arce forges with God is a prerequisite for verbalizing her shame publicly. It develops gradually over the course of her narrative but can be seen in nascent form early in the text during her internment in the Military Hospital. In a striking section entitled "El capellán y la Eucaristía" [The Chaplain and the Eucharist], she is visited daily in the hospital by a military chaplain who brings her communion. At first, she is skeptical of the chaplain because he is a soldier, but she soon begins to feel a sense of warmth and acceptance toward the "sweet old man" (*El infierno*, 76). Owing to the recentness of her trauma, Arce cannot yet verbalize her shame. She is therefore content to receive communion from the chaplain and watch him pray in silence at her bedside. She ends the section by noting that even though she is not yet capable of viewing Christ as God, Jesus is already becoming an important "friend" and companion in her suffering:

> No tenía muy claro lo que me ocurría. Sólo sentía deseos de recibir la Eucaristía y de que el sacerdote fuera cada día. Lo lindo es que surgió en mi interior algo así como un amigo nuevo, Cristo, pero no lo veía como Dios. En la pared de mi cama había una cruz, y muchas veces en silencio, le dije:
>
> —¿Tú también sufriste, verdad? Y se iniciaron interminables diálogos con Él. . . Me sentía acompañada.
>
> [I wasn't quite sure what was happening to me. I only felt a desire to receive the Eucharist and to have the priest come every day. The beautiful part is that within my being I found a new friend, Christ. But I didn't see him as God. On the wall by my bed there was a crucifix, and many times I said to him in silence:

—You suffered too, right? This was the start of endless dialogues with Him. . . I felt accompanied.] (*El infierno*, 76)

Much later in *El infierno*, Arce briefly narrates her experience as a CNI operative in Uruguay (1978). In this section, she again alludes to her intensifying "friendship" with Christ:

> A pesar de que no me consideraba cristiana por esos días, a diario al acudir a la ciudad vieja, me acostumbré a pasar por la catedral. Ahí en un diálogo con mi amigo, le contaba a Cristo acerca de mis dudas, temores y nostalgias.
>
> [Although I didn't consider myself a Christian in those days, I became accustomed to stopping at the cathedral daily when I went to the Old City. There, in dialogue with my friend, I told Christ about my doubts, fears, and nostalgias.] (322)

Arce's conversion to Catholicism—the centerpiece of her book—transpires shortly after she meets a Dominican priest named Father Gerardo. In their private conversations, the priest orients Arce toward Catholicism, which gives her the strength to verbalize her shame. He administers the sacraments of Extreme Unction and Holy Communion and urges Arce to read the *New Testament* as well as the *Life of Saint Francis of Assisi*. These readings cause a resurgence of repressed memories that drive her to physical illness and leave her bedridden for a short period of time. Desperate in her suffering, she sends her son to find Father Gerardo and her therapist, Anita María, to administer sedation drugs. From there, Arce's conversion, in its textual rendering, occurs quite suddenly. In a narrative gesture similar to Augustine's *Confessions*, Arce's definitive and irreversible orientation toward God occurs as a metaphorical "lightning bolt" from the sky that blindsides the infidel, inspiring her to begin anew: "Fue como empezar de cero" [It was like starting from scratch] (*El infierno*, 339). In *Confessions*, Augustine's conversion occurs suddenly when he opens his Bible and encounters a passage that compels him to break radically with his concupiscence: "I had no wish to read further, and no need. For in that instant, with the very ending of the sentence, it was as if a light of utter confidence shone in all my heart, and all the darkness of uncertainty vanished away" (146). Likewise, Arce's conversion is written as equally miraculous and instantaneous:

> Uno de esos desperté y supe que Dios existía, no podía creerlo. Fue como amanecer en un día soleado, me vestí llena de felicidad y fui a la ventana. Estaba Dios en todo lugar, voceando la maravilla inmensa de su

creación, podía percibir la presencia divina en los árboles, en el cielo lleno de nubes, hacia donde mirara era como un enorme libro hablando de un proyecto de vida, de una vida plena. Conocer a Dios cambió mi vida. Sentir que Dios es Amor, que su Palabra es Palabra de Amor. Que como cristianos somos convocados sobre todo a la obediencia a la Palabra. Me hizo reflexionar acerca de quién fui, quién soy y naturalmente eso implica asumir no sólo en la dimensión personal, también en la colectiva. La tantas veces infiel, la Luz que se sentía miserable comenzó a desear poder decir sí al Señor.

[One day I woke up and found that God exists. I couldn't believe it. It was like waking up on a sunny day. Full of joy, I got dressed and went to the window. God was everywhere, proclaiming the immense wonders of his creation. I could perceive a divine presence in the trees and in the cloudy sky. No matter where I looked I saw a gigantic book speaking of a life project, of a fulfilling life. Knowing God changed my life: to feel that God is Love, that his Word is the Word of Love, that as Christians we are invited, above all, to be faithful to his Word, made me reflect on who I was and who I am, which naturally implied assuming not only the personal, but also the collective aspects. She who had so often been an infidel, Luz, she who felt so miserable, began to want to be able to say yes to God.] (*El infierno*, 338)

Arce's *exomologesis*—the "publication of her-self" through writing—is directly linked to this religious conversion. Thinking that writing will help her externalize her shame and cope with her past more effectively, another Dominican priest named Father José Luis encourages Arce to take up the pen. Writing, however, proves a daunting task and constantly torments her. When she eventually manages to produce one hundred pages, she enters the bathroom, sobs uncontrollably, and burns her manuscript: "El destruir esos escritos llevaba aparejado el deseo de esconder esa parte de mi vida" [The destruction of those writings carried with it a desire to hide that part of my life] (*El infierno*, 341). Yet she perseveres, coming to the conclusion that forgetting is not a viable option: "El olvido no existe" [Forgetting doesn't exist] (341). She pledges to take up the pen again and each day slides her manuscripts under Father José Luis's door. These same manuscripts, in edited form, later become *El infierno*.

The support of priests is important. Their presence in Arce's life (and text) implies that she has the institutional backing of the Catholic Church. She is accepted into Santiago's religious circles as both a theology student and "honorary member" of the Dominican order. Her book, furthermore, opens with a prologue by Father José Luis that legitimizes and frames her discourse, emphasizing yet again her interest in reconciliation, healing, and peace. In Father José Luis's eyes, Arce is clearly a victim, a "martyr" who has traveled a "Via Dolorosa" and whose suffering, in the context of Catholic doctrine, acquires a redemptive quality (*El infierno*, 16). From the Church's vantage point, it would seem, Arce is a sacrificial lamb: she has paid a great price for her freedom and "understands the cross" (16). The priest's prologue suggests that it is not the reader's place to judge Arce; instead we must reserve judgment and focus attention on what is most important, the prosecution of her aggressors: "La cruz no exime de responsabilidad a los soldados; pero es sobre todo a los Herodes y a los Pilatos de turno a quienes enjuicia . . ." [The cross does not absolve the soldiers of responsibility; but it is, above all, the Herods and Pilates of the moment whom we should judge. . . .] (*El infierno*, 16).

In sum, Catholicism affords Arce a framework in which to be "born again," to overcome shame, and reorient her life; it gives her a vocabulary in which to tell her story and free herself from the shackles that chain her to a sordid past. With the Church's institutional backing, Arce is able to speak (and write) with greater confidence because she now has a doctrinal foundation upon which to make her plea for forgiveness. Christianity, in effect, offers Arce a language in which to atone, spurn hatred, ask for empathy, and seek justice, all in the spirit of what she calls "el sueño maravilloso de la reconciliación" [the marvelous dream of reconciliation] (*El infierno*, 352).

Stage 3. Reconciling with the Nation: Scenes of Forgiveness

El infierno details a complex process of reconciliation with self and God that culminates in Arce's reconciliation with the nation. What to this point has primarily been an individual process of coming to terms with shame acquires in the text's final pages a collective/public dimension (e.g., Arce's declarations before the truth commission, her testimony in a number of legal proceedings and the publication of her book). If, as we have seen, the Church was a crucial empathic listener in Part II, in Part III it is the state (or certain representatives of the state) that provides empathy.[17] At the same time, I must add that the three levels on which reconciliation occurs in *El infierno* (self, God, and nation) are not mutually exclusive, isolated, or strictly chronological steps but rather overlapping and organic layers in a complex and ongoing process of integrating trauma.

The legitimization of Arce's testimony takes textual form through a host of symbolically charged images: scenes of granting and receiving forgiveness involving military officials, torturers, members of the human rights community and even government representatives. Notable among these scenes is an encounter with three members of the Truth and Reconciliation Commission (Carlos Fresno, Gastón Gómez and Jorge Correa) who appear at her door one day in late 1990 to solicit her testimony. In her description of the encounter, Arce notes that the men spoke to her at length about "forgiveness, asking forgiveness, and forgiving" and mentions that just as the three men were preparing to leave her apartment, she felt a strange compulsion to embrace them: "Al despedirme de ellos, todavía temblando, sentí el impulso de hacerlo con un abrazo. Sentí calidez y acogida. No eran unos señores que me miraban con asco" [As I said good-bye to them, still shaking, I felt the urge to do it with an embrace. I felt warmth and acceptance. They weren't men looking at me with disdain] (*El infierno*, 347, 344).

This *abrazo*, in symbolic terms, points to a condition of mutual acceptance and sets the stage for Arce's declaration of her political-ideological realignment. In the commission's eyes, Arce is a victim, not a perpetrator, and is therefore granted forgiveness. Moreover, her relationship with the commission's representatives goes well beyond mere formality or professionalism and acquires an intimate, personal dimension: the three men become her close friends, confidantes, and counselors. Her trust of the commissioners, by extrapolation, leads to the formation of an implicit symbolic pact with the government they represent—the Concertación—as well as to an explicit affirmation of her new ideological alignment: "Me di cuenta que me sentía mucho más cercana a la gente de izquierda, a la Concertación, a los sobrevivientes, a las agrupaciones de familiares, que a quienes conocí en la DINA o en la CNI" [I understood that I felt much closer to the people on the Left, to the Concertación, to the survivors and the organizations of family members, than to those I met in the DINA or the CNI] (*El infierno*, 348).

Arce's articulation of her political allegiance to the Concertación seems to serve two purposes. First, it validates her position with respect to the state such that her discourse can be more easily communicated (and received) and her "sin" more readily forgiven. Second, it helps her to resolve further the identity crisis with which she has struggled since the beginning of her book. Here, in an interesting turn of events, Luz Arce—the same woman who earlier announced herself to be engaged since childhood in a constant search for acceptance and affection, the same woman who pledged allegiance to Allende and later to Pinochet—once again allies herself with the regime of the day: the Concertación. Diamela Eltit has suggested, rather provocatively, that Arce's body (her subjectivity) appears as a slate upon which prevailing power discourses inscribe themselves. Eltit reads the collaborator's reiterated ideological morphing in relation to what she calls the "absolute seduction of power": a tendency in certain political bodies (owing either to weakness or a desire for belonging or status) to be swept in the direction of prevailing ideological headwinds (Eltit, *Emergencias*, 51). Acknowledging fully that Arce was coerced to collaborate under torture, Eltit reads her as a chameleonic figure who, seeking stability, perpetually establishes a proximal relationship to hegemonic (and particularly masculine) authority: ". . . parece ser el ansia por participar del poder dominante que llevó [el cuerpo] de esta [mujer] a comprometerse en una empresa fascista, cuya finalidad era la destrucción organizada de los cuerpos disidentes" [. . . it seems that it was a desire to be part of the dominant power structure that drove [this woman] to commit [herself] to a fascist enterprise whose goal was the organized destruction of dissident bodies] (57). Although I find Eltit's reading compelling, I would alter its tenor slightly. To my mind, it is not so much that Arce ever really desired to be a functionary of Pinochet's secret police ("el ansia de participar"), nor that she ever really wanted to be a member of Allende's Grupo de Amigos Personales [Group of Personal Friends]. Rather, her constant ideological morphing—and this is key—was motivated primarily by a desire to survive.

Two things seem certain. First, under dictatorship there is no assured future for a former Allende supporter; second, in democracy there is no assured future for a traitor or collaborator. Consequently, sheer survival necessitated a re-imagining of the self in Arce that had less to do with a premeditated desire for power than with a pathetic, yet human (and perhaps understandable) need to project herself into the future at any cost. Having consciously decided not to die a "martyr's" death (i.e., to remain silent under torture), Luz Arce's pathos lies in that her survival—both in dictatorship and democracy—*required* that she renounce a former version of herself (e.g., the revolutionary, the functionary) in order to assume a new persona. Admitting this, however, does not negate that it is both possible and necessary to debate the ethical implications of the extent—the extremity—of Arce's collaboration.

El infierno details a series of symbolic encounters, all of which focus on acts of forgiveness. In one important scene, Carlos Fresno, at Arce's request, arranges a meeting between Arce and Erika Hennings—wife of Alfonso Chanfreau, a left-wing militant who disappeared in 1974. Hennings, along with Arce, was detained by DINA at Londres 38, but when Hennings was eventually released from custody, she never again saw Arce; she only knew that Arce had become a functionary of the dictatorship's repressive apparatus. This meant that Arce could very well know key information regarding her missing husband's whereabouts. When in 1990 the two women meet in a Santiago café, Arce does not know how Hennings will react to her and is quite surprised when she is treated with respect. Even more surprising is that the two women eventually establish a solid friendship, rooted in their mutually shared condition of victimhood. Significantly, the scene focuses on Arce's being granted forgiveness by a woman who could have easily harbored contempt toward her, but does not: "Gracias a Erika pude recuperar trozos de las conversaciones que, a escondidas de la guardia, sostuvimos estando detenidas en Londres 38. Su aceptación fue como un perdón otorgado gratuitamente" [Thanks to Erika I managed to recover vestiges of the conversations we shared behind the guards' backs as detainees at Londres 38. Her acceptance was like pardon, freely granted] (*El infierno*, 349).

Later in the text, the tables are turned. If in the aforementioned scene Arce was the one asking forgiveness, it is shown to be equally important that others ask forgiveness of her. She recounts the cases of several DINA/CNI officials (her torturers or witnesses to her torture) who in different moments ask her to pardon them. One such passage is particularly compelling for the way in which it symbolically details the perpetrator's shame as well as Arce's radical ability to forgive:

> —Lo que pasa, señorita Ana María [one of Arce's false names], es que si no le pido disculpas, me voy a sentir muy mal para siempre. . . . Por eso quería hablar con usted, y bueno, yo no sé si usted lo sabe. Pero yo estuve ahí. . . . Perdóname. Por favor, diga que me perdona.
>
> Mientras me hablaba estrujaba sus manos con nerviosismo y movía su pie derecho como raspando el piso. Mantenía la mirada baja. Sentí frío. Ira. Siglos de humillación. Inconscientemente alcé mis manos. Me di cuenta que ahora no estaba amarrada como esa noche.
>
> —¡Cabo!
>
> —¿Sí, señorita?
>
> —Cabo, si le hace bien que le diga que lo perdono, vaya tranquilo. Su franqueza de hoy habla bien de usted—logré decir. Estaba temblando.
>
> [—The thing is, Ms. Ana María, if I don't ask your forgiveness, I will feel bad forever. . . . That's why I wanted to talk to you, and well, I don't know if you know it, but I was there. . . . Forgive me. Please, say you forgive me.

> While he spoke, he squeezed his hands nervously and moved his right foot as if scratching the floor. He kept his gaze low. I felt cold. Wrath. Centuries of humiliation. Unconsciously, I lifted my hands. I understood that I was no longer tied down as I was that night.
>
> —Corporal!
>
> —Yes, miss.
>
> —Corporal, if it helps for me to forgive you, go in peace. Your candor today speaks well of you—I managed to say. I was shaking.] (*El infierno*, 380)

Even toward Osvaldo Romo Mena, one of DINA's most notorious and unrepentant torturers, Arce shows compassion.[18] When she sees her former aggressor at a hearing in 1992, she comes to realize that even though he was a brutal torturer and rapist, he should also be considered an "'hombre desechable' que la DINA necesitó para sus propósitos de aniquilamiento" [a "disposable man" whom the DINA needed for its project of annihilation] (142). It is almost as if Arce reads in Romo a magnified version of herself: she, like her torturer, was "used and abused by the DINA" (142). Although it is undeniable that the two collaborated to much different degrees, it is striking that Arce finds common ground upon which to stand with her torturer. Again, she traces a distinction between moral and legal responsibility: she does not deny that Romo is morally responsible for committing many horrible crimes, yet, because Romo was a civilian dragged into the regime's machinery of death and destruction, Arce finds it difficult to believe that he is the one who should ultimately be held accountable for its crimes. Perhaps, she thinks, he should go to jail; but she feels that there are others who should be jailed first: "Me es difícil aceptar que sus jefes queden impunes" [It is difficult for me to accept that his bosses remain in impunity]. The fact that he is ultimately arrested and imprisoned for the regime's crimes makes Romo, in Arce's opinion, a fall guy for other, more serious offenders (Krassnoff, Moren Brito, Wenderoth, Contreras, Espinoza), who turned him into the brutal torturer he was. She emphasizes that Romo, on the occasion of their meeting, asks forgiveness, and she grants it: "Debo confesar que su gesto de pedirme perdón a mí . . . me predispone a perdonarlo y lo he hecho" [I must confess that his gesture of asking forgiveness . . . makes me inclined to pardon him, and I have done so] (142).[19]

Symbolic gestures were crucial in the political sphere as well. In fact, performing reconciliation was a key component of the Aylwin administration's approach to addressing the past. During the first years of democratic rule, for example, the Chilean state sponsored an official funeral service for Allende and erected a monument to the disappeared and executed in Santiago's General Cemetery. At Aylwin's inauguration the wives of the disappeared danced the *cueca* (Chile's national dance) alone as a means by which to mark the absence of their missing husbands. With these and other happenings, the early years of transition were steeped in ritualistic, almost sacramental acts by the government aimed at promoting national healing. Often the religious overtones of these acts were marked.

Particularly prominent among these rituals was Patricio Aylwin's call for atonement at the presentation of the Truth and Reconciliation Commission's final report. In a live television broadcast of 4 March 1991, an emotionally affected Aylwin repented on behalf of the nation for the dictatorhip's crimes: "[M]e atrevo, en mi calidad de Presidente de la República, a asumir la representación de la nación entera para, en su nombre, pedir perdón a los familiares de las víctimas. . . . [T]ambién pido solemnemente a las Fuerzas Armadas y de Orden, y a todos los que hayan tenido participación en los excesos cometidos, que hagan gestos de reconocimiento del dolor causado y colaboren para aminorarlo" [I dare, in my capacity as president of the Republic, to represent the entire nation, in order to ask forgiveness, in its name, of the victims' families. . . . I also solemnly request that the armed forces and all those who may have participated in the excesses committed, make gestures to recognize the pain caused and collaborate to diminish it] (Aylwin, *La transición*, 132).[20]

Chile's president asking forgiveness on national television offers a powerful image: it points to a desire, reiterated discursively time and again from within the government's ranks for a process of atonement that would allow the nation to leave the past behind and "look to the future." In his discourse of reconciliation, Aylwin frequently employed Christian rhetoric. Capitalizing on the predominantly Roman Catholic background of Chileans, the government sought to relate to the citizenry on a personal and spiritual level, hoping to send a moral message that reconciliation was indeed possible. To that end, Aylwin ended his inaugural speech (12 March 1990) with a litany of prayers asking the Almighty to bestow virtues like prudence, energy, knowledge, patience, understanding, justice, and solidarity on the Chilean people (*La transición*, 22). From the very start of his presidency, he made clear that in order to come to terms with the past and forge a brighter future, Chile would have to undergo an intense process of "saneamiento moral" [moral cleansing] (21).

The problem with Aylwin's reconciliatory discourse was that it did not distinguish clearly enough between reconciliation's political meanings (pacts and reparations) and its personal meanings (a true willingness to reconcile on an individual level).[21] The government held out hope that a few well-chosen symbolic rituals, the truth commission's report, and some selective monetary reparations would bring enough "closure" to declare the transition accomplished. Knowing that Chile's traumatic past was a hindrance to the consolidation of democracy and a peaceful national atmosphere, Aylwin on several occasions declared publicly the end of the transition. During a 7 August 1991 press conference, for example, he made the following declaration: "Debemos entender que este gobierno cumple su tarea en los cuatro años de su período. Creo que, por lo demás, no se puede hablar de que es necesario prolongar el período de transición, porque realmente, a mi juicio, la transición ya está hecha. En Chile vivimos en democracia" [We should understand that this government will accomplish its task in the four years it has been given. I think, moreover, that we shouldn't talk about the necessity of prolonging the transition because, in my opinion, the transition is over. In Chile we live in democracy] (Aylwin qtd. in Otano, *Crónica*, 190). Shortly thereafter, the government would realize that neither national reconciliation nor the end of the transition could be wishfully imposed by political decree, and even more important, that the "theme of human rights" was not something that would go away easily.[22]

How could there be any hope for "real" reconciliation if different sectors of Chilean society remained—as they do to this day—firmly entrenched in irreconcilable memory narratives? In the Chile of the early 1990s (and well beyond), the necessary *conditions for dialogue* between victims and victimizers simply did not exist.[23]

In January 1991, following her testimony before the truth commission, Luz Arce decided to leave Chile to start what she thought would be a new and better life for her family in Europe. Upon arriving in Germany, she began to concentrate intensely on writing her book, and it was in the process of writing and self-exploration that she made a vitally important decision: her personal journey toward reconciliation and personal healing could not occur in exile (*El infierno*, 353–354). If she were ever to understand her past in a meaningful way, Arce knew it would be necessary to return to Chile to confront her fellow countrymen in a public act of atonement. This would mean not only admitting the shame she felt for having collaborated but also a willingness to participate fully and without reservation in the process of bringing the regime's perpetrators to justice. Public atonement also meant facing any possible consequences that might arise from her testimony (e.g., threats against her life or even judicial convictions). Having weighed the costs and benefits carefully, in January 1992, exactly one year after her arrival in Germany, Arce packed her bags and returned to Chile.

Luz Arce's ritual of public atonement reached its culmination in November 1993 at the launch of *El infierno*, organized by Editorial Planeta. The launch provided a public forum in which Arce could cast off her old image (the traitor, the collaborator) and adopt a new one (the repentant Christian mother). It is a quintessential scene of *exomologesis*.

According to articles published in *La Época* and *La Tercera*, the audience assembled at the Galerías Hotel in downtown Santiago consisted of family members, friends, journalists, members of the clergy, members of the Rettig Commission, and at least one of the regime's victims, Erika Hennings—Arce's close friend and wife of Alfonso Chanfreau (detained-disappeared). This diverse audience represented, in symbolic terms, an important legitimization of Arce's act of atonement by different sectors of Chilean society: Church, family, the government, the victims, and the press. The article that appeared in *La Época* notes specifically the presence of a "Jesuit priest" who spoke on Arce's behalf and goes on to observe that the "nucleus of her book," in the opinion of presenters Carlos Orellana and Rafael Otano, centered on "acts of forgiveness and forgiving."

Arce's own discourse at her book launch played out as a mise en scène of ritualistic atonement. Seated before such a diverse public, she formally asked forgiveness for her collaboration and dedicated her book to the victims' memory. The article that appeared in *La Tercera* bore the title "Luz Arce lloró al presentar *El infierno*" [Luz Arce Cried when She Presented *El infierno*]; it began by setting the scene in which Arce's plea for atonement took place: "Luz Arce no pudo contener sus lágrimas. Cuando se dirigió a los presentes, su voz se quebró, pero luego se repuso para continuar con su discurso. . . . [Luz Arce couldn't contain her tears. When she spoke to the audience, her voice cracked, but soon she composed herself in order to continue her speech. . . .] ("Luz Arce," 6).

Claudia Feld, in her study of the spectacle of the Argentine military trials, emphasizes the importance of what she calls "escenarios de la memoria" [scenes of memory] for giving meaning to the past. Informed by theatrical discourse, Feld notes that acts of memory are often staged events that seek to lead spectators toward the construction of specific meanings. In their performative

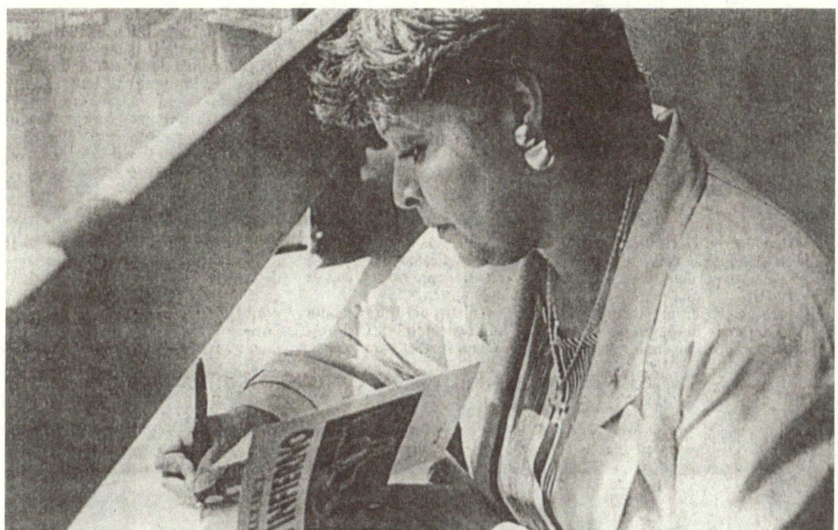

Figure 1. Luz Arce signing books at the launch of *El infierno. La Época*, 18 November 1993, page 22.

dimension, the words and physical gestures used in public discourses as well as the visual elements that "set the scene" are particularly noteworthy (*Del estrado*, 5–6). A photograph of Arce that appeared in *La Época* (in conjunction with the article mentioned above) brought the Chilean nation face-to-face with the "new" Arce: a middle-aged, middle-class, Christian woman, dressed conservatively, looking like a "typical" Chilean mother and wearing a metal cross around her neck. Arce's appearance in the photograph made her look the part of the penitent and perhaps even sought (on some level), whether consciously or unconsciously, to influence public perception. She clearly wanted to be seen as an average Chilean woman seeking forgiveness, not as a criminal of DINA/CNI. As if to say "You could have been me," Arce, as the image of the penitent mother, hoped to strike a chord with spectators, to convince them that she, the collaborator, was not so different from them. Furthermore, her maternity lent credence to her voice because it forced the public to see her (and, she hoped, accept her) as a mother, not a monster.

This new public image—the repentant mother—stands in stark contrast to Arce's previous image as a dark functionary of DINA. One particularly unflattering picture appeared in a special edition of *El Siglo* entitled "La DINA hoy" [DINA Today] in February 1992. *El Siglo* notes that in her testimony before

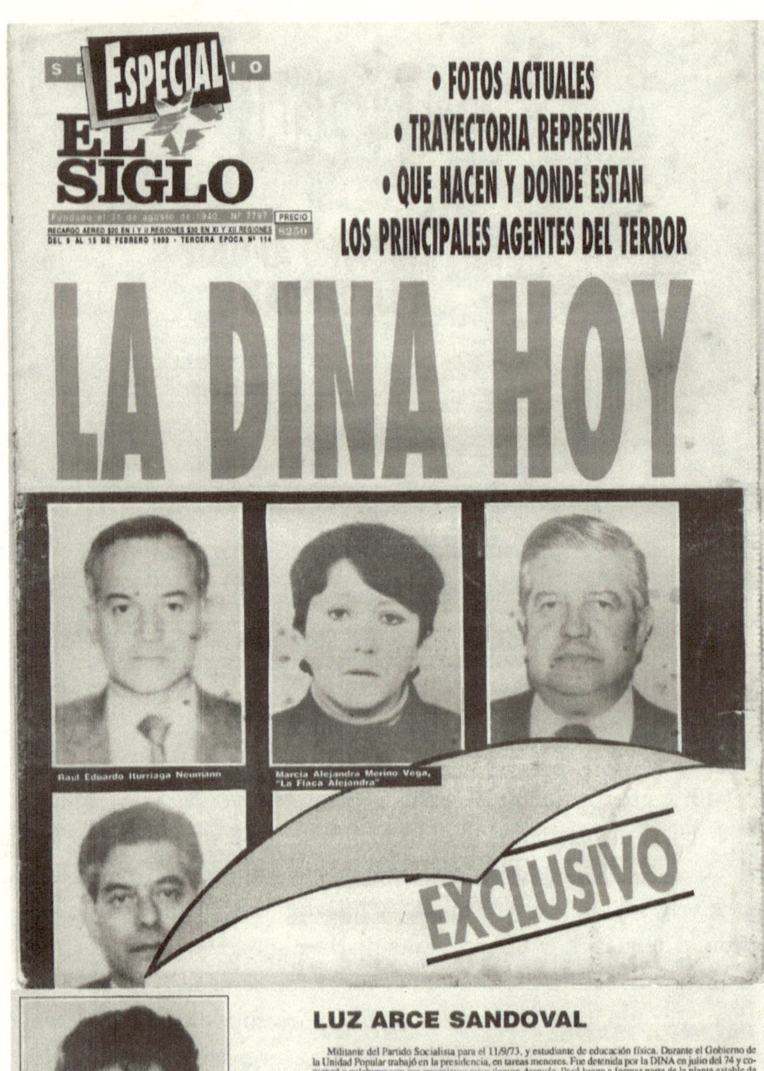

ESPECIAL

EL SIGLO

Fundado el 31 de agosto de 1940. Nº 7797

RECARGO AEREO $20 EN I Y II REGIONES $30 EN XI Y XII REGIONES

DEL 9 AL 15 DE FEBRERO 1992 · TERCERA EPOCA Nº 114

PRECIO $250

• FOTOS ACTUALES

• TRAYECTORIA REPRESIVA

• QUE HACEN Y DONDE ESTAN

LOS PRINCIPALES AGENTES DEL TERROR

LA DINA HOY

Raul Eduardo Iturriaga Neumann

Marcia Alejandra Merino Vega, "La Flaca Alejandra"

EXCLUSIVO

LUZ ARCE SANDOVAL

Militante del Partido Socialista para el 11/9/73, y estudiante de educación física. Durante el Gobierno de la Unidad Popular trabajó en la presidencia, en tareas menores. Fue detenida por la DINA en julio del 74 y comenzó a colaborar con ese organismo poco tiempo después. Pasó luego a formar parte de la planta estable de la DINA, así como de la CNI en su tiempo. En la DINA fue informante y participó en detenciones, secuestros, trampas, seguimientos y también sesiones de torturas. Ella verificaba personalmente si los prisioneros torturados decían la verdad o no. Prisioneros sobrevivientes la recuerdan en Villa Grimaldi, Londres 38 y Cuatro Alamos. Las investigaciones de la Comisión Rettig, la sindican como involucrada en las desapariciones de Oscar Manuel Castro Videla, Joel Huaiquiñir Benavides, Sergio Alberto Riveros Villavicencio, Sergio Emilio Vera Figueroa. El año 76 pasó a cumplir funciones en el Departamento de Análisis de la CNI. Fue amante del miembro del estado mayor de la DINA Rolf Wenderoth Pozo. El año 1990, apareció como uno de los testigos más importantes ante la Comisión Rettig y su testimonio fue difundido por la prensa nacional. Sin embargo, muchos de los que la conocieron y supieron su historia por dentro, han señalado que en ese testimonio la ex agente de la DINA-CNI no dice toda la verdad y que distorsiona algunos datos para ponerse a salvo a sí misma de las responsabilidades que le cabe en la muerte y desapariciones de numerosos chilenos. Se desconoce su paradero actual.

Figure 2. Photo and biographical sketch of Luz Arce as they appeared in the special edition "La DINA hoy." *El Siglo*, 9–15 February 1992. By permission of *El Siglo*, Santiago de Chile.

the truth commission Arce "distorted the facts" in order to absolve herself of personal responsibility for the deaths and disappearances of many Chileans. Arce's photo, strikingly akin to a mugshot, clearly portrays her as a criminal.

The two photographs suggest radically different iconographies: on one hand, the image of Arce as an evil perpetrator, pictured alongside other villains of DINA; on the other, the "new Arce," the Christian penitent seeking forgiveness in a dramatic scene of *exomologesis* staged before the nation.

On the Possibility of Reconciliation: Images from beyond El infierno

Do apologetic discourses strive to restore a harmony that, in reality, cannot be restored? In other words, do such discourses, full of excuses and justifications, though proffered with all good intentions, offer a convenient space—perhaps too convenient—in which to reconcile discursively tensions that are exceedingly difficult, if not impossible, to resolve?

Shoshana Felman strikes an important cautionary note about confessionary texts when she claims that they are "all too readable" (Felman and Laub, 151). Confessions, because of the gamut of excuses they present to explain the motivations behind human actions, partake of the "continuity of conscious meaning and of the illusion of the restoration of coherence" (151). Confessionary writing, in Felman's opinion, tends to "reduce historical scandals to mere sense and to eliminate the unassailable shock of history by leaving the very assumption of intelligibility unquestioned" (151). It is precisely for this reason that we must interrogate a text like *El infierno*. Certainly, we can wonder about the extent to which Arce's confessionary and reconciliatory tone resolves too quickly, or too easily, the profundity of trauma and the ethically challenging nature of collaboration.

On one hand, it seems that reconciliation discourse offers great possibilities for liberating individuals and nations that have suffered extended periods of violent repression. On the other hand, it seems that the language of reconciliation (with its attendant concepts of healing, forgiveness, confession, apology, pardon, and closure) should place us on guard for the way in which it risks masking wounds that continue to bleed long after the traumatic moment has passed. In that vein, the very idea of reconciliation begs certain questions: Can "radical evil" be forgiven? If so, what does it mean to forgive? Who has the right to forgive, and in whose name? Are truth and justice necessary prerequisites for reconciling, or can we imagine reconciliation in a society like Chile where truth and justice remain ongoing, unfinished business?

Reconciliation can indeed be a dangerous concept. Heidi Grunebaum raises this point eloquently when she warns against its "sanitizing vocabulary." Mindful of the perils of a reconciliation imposed from above by political elites, Grunebaum argues that "all conditions, terms, modes and vocabularies of possible endings, healings and closures . . . have to be made by the historically victimized" ("Talking," 309). Jacques Derrida, in a similar line of argumentation, offers the idea that political reconciliation is a pragmatic and purely symbolic process that societies undergo in order to move beyond historical trauma (*On Cosmopolitanism*, 51). "Pure forgiveness" is different: it takes place as a "lateral," freely assumed interaction among individuals, not as a "top down," politically crafted solution (58).[24] It is a "forgiveness without power, unconditional but without sovereignty," a monumental gesture of absolving a wrong that is at its core unforgivable, a forgiveness that defies our sense of logic: it is "the madness of the impossible" (45, 59).

My interest here centers on reconciliation as narrative utopia in both the personal and political spheres. I would hold that in trauma's aftermath there is a pressing need for symbolic resolution to trauma so that individual victims (and fledgling democracies) can survive into the future. Both individuals and nations seek to "master" trauma by constructing narratives that permit them to integrate the traumatic episode and "gain control over the occurrence of intrusive memories" (Brison, *Aftermath*, 53–54). Narratives are powerful, and shared narratives (fictions), notwithstanding their exclusions, have the potential to provide stable foundations on which to imagine harmonious futures. The language of reconciliation, as one possibility, can offer a forcefully symbolic (even if unrealized) liberation of bodies (and the body politic) from feelings of rage and vengeance.

Arce's entire textual project hinges on the possibility of setting aside deep-seated resentments.[25] She stresses repeatedly that she does not "hate" her victimizers, even if as a detainee she did feel animosity toward her aggressors. Toward the end of her book, she mentions how a quotation from Augustine of Hipona—"¿Cómo odiar al que mañana puede ser mi hermano?" [How can I hate someone who tomorrow could be my brother?]—helped her to understand that hating her enemies was not in accordance with Christian doctrine (*El infierno*, 381). Thus hatred and resentment have no place in Arce's project of reconciliation, and the radical nature of her conversion inspires her to believe that others, too, can experience a change in attitude toward her.

Without discounting the possibility that the kind of real reconciliation that Arce proposes—what Derrida calls the "madness of the impossible"—can be achieved by some people in some circumstances, I would like to pose two rejoinders for further consideration:

Operating outside a Christian or religious framework, Jean Améry posits reconciliation as highly problematic for the survivor. In "Resentments," Améry grapples with the question of what attitude he should take toward his victimizers, noting that neither revenge, nor force, nor atonement, seem to be historically viable options. Atonement, Améry writes, "has only theological meaning and is therefore not relevant for me" (*At the Mind's Limits*, 77). Reconciliation amounts to forgetting the egregiousness of the offense or, at the very least, to risk smoothing over traumas so deeply rooted in the social fabric that they cannot be eliminated by a sheer act of will. A conciliatory approach to his victimizers is therefore dubious at best. In the alternative, Améry feels that victims must necessarily harbor resentment toward their victimizers in order to assure that the past remains an open question. Victims must be the "incorrigible ones," true antihistorical reactionaries: those who guarantee that the horrors of the past do not slip into oblivion or become neutralized by the tides of history (*At the Mind's Limits*, 80). To forgive (and forget) is to defuse potential political efficacy.

Second, we can recall Hannah Arendt's comment in *The Human Condition* that societies, in certain situations, need to forgive wrongs deemed "irreversible" if they are to have any hope of surviving into the future. "Without being forgiven, released from the consequences of what we have done," Arendt claims, "our capacity to act would, as it were, be confined to one single deed from which we could never recover; we would remain the victims of its consequences forever, not unlike the sorcerer's apprentice who lacked the magic formula to break the spell" (237). On the surface, Arendt's statement seems to support Arce's method of framing her experience: Arce recognizes the necessity of freeing herself from trauma and uses Christian confession as a way of doing so. But there is a caveat. For Arendt, forgiveness carries with it an important prerequisite: the ability to punish. Since forgiveness is a conscious decision made by one who has been wronged, one can only freely choose to forgive if punishment can be rejected in the alternative. What one cannot punish, one cannot forgive; forgiveness must be asked for if it is to be granted, and this necessarily begins with an admission of responsibility by the perpetrator.[26] In Chile, where perpetrators have been extremely reluctant to assume responsibility for human rights violations and where justice has been quite slow in coming, it is therefore debatable whether reasonable conditions exist in which reconciliation can occur.

Commenting specifically on the Chilean context, sociologist Tomás Moulián, too, has expressed serious doubts about the viability of Chile's official discourse of reconciliation, offering particular criticism of all governmental attempts to put "closure" to the problem of human rights violations in a "top-down" or authoritarian fashion. He worries about the consequences of pardoning perpetrators of heinous crimes in the interest of social and political stability:

> Me parece que hay que oponerse a cualquier intento de igualar víctimas y victimarios en la escena de la culpa repartida y que también debemos sospechar del discurso de la reconciliación con su reino de la armonía que responde a una idea mística de la sociedad y a un sueño de orden religioso: las sociedades son siempre sociedades de la división más que de la armonía y su tarea es construir reglas que garanticen la tolerancia cívica, asegurar que no se va a eliminar ni destruir al enemigo, lo que no quiere decir que haya que amar al enemigo para vivir con él.
>
> [It seems to me that we must resist any attempt to equate victims and victimizers in a scene of shared guilt, and that we should also remain suspect of the discourse of reconciliation, with its reign of harmony that responds to a mystic conception of society, a dream of a religious nature. Societies are always societies of division more than of harmony, and their job is to establish rules that guarantee civic tolerance and assure that one's enemies will not be eliminated or destroyed. However, this does not mean that one has to love his enemy in order to live with him.] (Moulián, "La liturgia," 25)

Luz Arce—the convert—speaks of her traumatic past from a relatively "comfortable" position. The Christian discourses of forgiveness and reconciliation provide her a language for coming to terms with a limit experience that might otherwise be beyond conceptualization, and her new Christian belief system helps her to stabilize her identity, her "I," within the autobiographical act. In opposition to Moulián's "societies of division," Arce embraces and promotes the utopian possibility of achieving reconciliation in Chile and echoes in her book's narrative construction the government's forward-looking rhetoric of forgiveness. Despite the admirable nature of Arce's optimism, however, the reader remains skeptical of her project's feasibility. Conscious of the absence of any real possibility for a conversation between perpetrators and victims, forging a space of reconciliation arguably remains, beyond *El infierno*, a kind of utopia to be achieved at the levels of both individual and society.

As a point of contrast to the utopia of reconciliation that Arce's book projects, I would like to conclude by presenting two images, both found in recent Chilean documentary films, that emphasize reconciliation's difficulty and raise important questions that shed light retrospectively on Arce's text.

The first scene, from Carmen Castillo and Guy Girard's documentary *La Flaca Alejandra: vidas y muertes de una mujer chilena* [*Skinny Alejandra: Lives and Deaths of a Chilean Woman*] (France, 1994), shows Marcia Alejandra Merino, Chile's other symbolic figure of betrayal and collaboration, engaged in a discussion with former militants Alicia Barrios and Carmen Castillo about the reasons for her collaboration. The filmmaker and narrator, Castillo, herself a torture survivor, assumes the role of a journalist trying to understand the experience of collaboration as "objectively" as possible. Castillo's attitude toward Merino is one of confusion, but more importantly, of forgiveness and understanding. Castillo admires the tremendous risk Merino assumes by telling her story publicly. She asks "What right do I have to reject her?" and proves willing to enter into a dialogue with Merino. Castillo opts for empathy.

Alicia Barrios, on the other hand, is more resistant to dialogue and unwilling to compromise her position that Merino is a "traitor" beyond redemption. The scene opens with Barrios claiming that she is tired of listening to justifications for collaboration: "¡Llevan horas hablando de la misma huevada y ya hace 20 años de todo esto!" [You've spent hours talking about this same shit that you've been talking about for twenty years!] The documentary goes on to dramatize an intense interchange between Merino and Barrios and ends with Merino at an impasse, struggling to say something—anything—to Barrios that might make her see her point of view: "No podrás comprenderlo porque no lo viviste" [You will never be able to understand because you didn't live it yourself].

The second scene, from Tony Comiti and Manolo D'Arthuy's *Chili: des bourreaux en liberté* [*Chile: Torturers at Large*] (France, 1999), shows Luz Arce confronting one of DINA's top officials, General Marcelo Moren Brito, in the parking lot of a Santiago grocery store. Moren Brito is seen in a common, everyday situation: he is out buying groceries with his family. With the camera hidden from view, Arce approaches her former victimizer and acts as if she is going to greet him. Moren Brito seems not to recognize Arce and motions to give her a kiss on the cheek. Suddenly, Arce stops him in his tracks and accuses him in a loud voice of having tortured her. Moren's strategy is to ignore Arce. He tells her, in whispered tone, that he thought she was simply going to "greet him," to which Arce replies: "¿Ud. cree que yo puedo saludarlo?" [Do you think I would be able to greet someone like you?] The scene ends with Moren Brito being whisked away in his family's Mercedes, while Arce sobs uncontrollably before the camera asking why Moren will not "show his face" and account for those who disappeared at Villa Grimaldi.

The two documentary scenes share something important in common: they emphasize a lack of *conditions for dialogue* about Chile's traumatic past. In the first scene, the conditions seem to be in place: three former militants get together to talk about their conflicts. But the conversation breaks down when one of the parties is unwilling to listen or is incapable of empathy. In the second scene, the conditions are markedly absent: Moren Brito maintains a haughty attitude rooted in the belief that he is untouchable. The scenes foreground the difficulty of achieving reconciliation and leave a question mark hovering over Arce's textual project. Arce wrote her book in 1993 in a political moment when words like "reconciliation" and "consensus" dominated public discourse (as they still do). Six years later, in 1999, despite the space of encounter she tries to open up in *El infierno*, she discovers, through the metaphor of her failed meeting with Moren Brito, that attainment of mutual forgiveness and atonement remain (at least in the collective dimension) distant ideals.

A final image comes to mind: Arce today (2006) lives in a tiny pueblo outside Mexico City where she struggles to support her ailing husband and her two sons. She has established a small business selling handmade jewelry that affords her family barely enough money to survive. On a personal level, she continues to struggle with her past, but considers herself reconciled with herself and, to the extent possible, with others. She hopes to move back to Chile someday soon, though many Chileans still reject her outright. I am left contemplating this image of Luz Arce—the "traitor," the "convert"—shunned, estranged from Chile despite her strikingly dramatic ritual of reconciliation, despite her gut-wrenching confessionary text, unable to find work in her native country, forced into a life of self-imposed exile. This image, too, speaks volumes about Chile's arduous journey to come to terms with its past.

3

Presence and Absence (On Art and Disappearance)

Cuando hoy hablamos de violaciones a los derechos humanos, se simboliza el tema en los desaparecidos, los ausentes siempre presentes.

[When today we speak of human rights violations, they are symbolized by the disappeared, the ever-present absent ones.]

Pamela Pereira

It is the case with "disappeared" people that even though we know no hope remains, we still wait.

Marcel Proust

Absent Voices, Absent Bodies: On Narrative and Disappearance

It is impossible to reflect on the poetics and politics of memory after Pinochet without considering the ramifications of disappearance for narrative telling. The *desaparecidos*—those "vanished" victims whose deaths have consistently been denied or covered up by the military—offer a particularly salient problem with regard to narrating the past precisely because their voices have been silenced forever.[1] To employ a Benjaminian term, they are the *expressionless*: spectral presences who haunt the post-dictatorial scene and who have been denied not only language and a voice, but also a visage, a *human* face (Felman, *Juridical Unconscious*, 13). Because they are dead, they will never bear witness to the abominable horrors they suffered, nor will they tell of how their bodies were tortured, mutilated, disposed of in common graves or dropped from military planes into the sea. To be certain, they are the dictatorship's most obstinate legacy: they stand as a marked *narrative void* in the history of the regime. Although, with the passage of time, forensic analysis has allowed some unearthed remains to be identified and reburied with dignity, the locations of more than one thousand bodies remain shrouded in mystery owing to the military's unwillingness to share information. Where there are no bodies, no real proof of death and no "closure" for family members, the disappeared persist in a kind of limbo *between* life and death—like specters haunting the living, wanting to be heard, acknowledged and remembered.

Several questions arise from these preliminary observations. What are the consequences of disappearance for the construction of post-dictatorial memory? How have those left behind recognized, accounted and/or compensated for the voices of the "drowned" (Levi, *The Drowned*)? And what role can art play in restoring expression to the expressionless dead?

As was the case in previous chapters of this study, Giorgio Agamben's theorization on the *Muselmänner*—the "complete witnesses" to the horrors of the Nazi concentration camps—again offers a helpful point of departure.[2] The *Muselmänner*, Agamben indicates, were the prisoners who "touched bottom," who "saw the Gorgon" and never returned to tell of it. Dehumanized humans, they were pushed to the brink of their very humanity, stripped entirely of their dignity. Their specters are inscribed within every act of witnessing as a "lacuna," a void that marks not only an impossibility of testifying because of the *Muselmann*'s irrevocable absence, but also, paradoxically, an unforgettable presence "with whom we must reckon" (Agamben, *Remnants*, 81).

Agamben is particularly concerned with the inhumane way these "complete witnesses" died in Auschwitz. Auschwitz stood for a death that was not really a death at all but rather a *non-death*, a death without dignity: "In Auschwitz, people did not die; rather, corpses were produced: corpses without death, non-humans whose decease is debased into a matter of serial production" (Agamben, *Remnants*,72). Citing Heidegger, Agamben refers to the "fabrication of corpses" as a way of signaling the bureaucratic inhumanity and anonymity of the mass murders carried out (73). Because the *Muselmänner* did not die with dignity or receive a proper burial, these ultimate victims haunt the living like ghosts (*larvae*) demanding witnesses, demanding recognition. At this juncture, the writer-witness acquires a special role. If the *Muselmänner* attest to a new form of life that "begins where dignity ends," it is Primo Levi (the survivor to whom Agamben's theory is most indebted) who will speak in their stead, by proxy. Levi, the narrator, appears in Agamben as the "cartographer" of a "new terra ethica, the implacable land-surveyor of Muselmannland"; his testimony signals and probes the void left by those deprived of voice, face and dignity (Agamben, *Remnants*,69).

Extrapolating these ideas, I would like to propose the figure of the *desaparecido* as a locus for articulating a series of tensions—tensions among presence and absence, visibility and invisibility, life and death, humanity and inhumanity, speech and silence, memory and forgetting. It seems possible to argue that absence (even more than presence) characterizes post-dictatorial experience. I say this because the reality of state sponsored repression has left us to deal with considerable gaps in the collective archive that cannot (and will not) ever be filled. We have no photographs of Chile's death flights, nor do we have images of people being tortured or disappeared. Left, then, to face the irreversible absence of what has "disappeared" from view (or was never recorded as an image), our ability to perceive the void, to sense absence, becomes all the more important. Consequently, I would hold that art is crucial to the construction of post-dictatorial memory insofar as its unique ability to incorporate silence and the "unsayable" permits a fuller, more direct engagement with absence than other representational modes. Artistic signifiers have the ability to stand in semiotic juxtapositions so that what is missing, although it is not really there, is what we "see" or sense. Likewise, a poetic device like metonymy—whereby a shoe, a ring, a pair of eyeglasses, or some other personal object belonging to a "disappeared" victim might, by its presence, allude to the stark absence of a real body—can also function in art to help us *feel* what is not there.

Of course, when I speak of "feeling," I speak of *affect*, which raises a related question regarding the role affect can or should play in historical reconstruction. Though some might argue that history (as distinct from memory) relies on our ability to form linear, chronological accounts based on factual evidence and identifiable relations of cause and effect, traumatic experience appears to defy our ability to reconstitute it in linear fashion. Because there are certain aspects of trauma that cannot be fully apprehended through acts of pure cognition, I am convinced that that affect does have a place in the construction of post-dictatorial narratives. I want to make clear, however, that by affirming this I am not in any way diminishing the importance of cognitively conceived, factual accounts (which indeed have crucial ramifications for both history and legality); rather, I am acting as an advocate for affect's role in reconstructing the past and its ramifications for future generations. Affect, I think, can serve as a tool for placing us *in relation to* the void, for rescuing *something* from oblivion even when cognition fails us.

Beyond the issue of affect, Chilean legal language, too, has dealt with the perennial tension between presence and absence. Because of the 1978 Amnesty Law left in place by Pinochet to absolve the military of its crimes, human rights attorneys have had to invent a legal fiction known as *secuestro permanente* [permanent kidnapping] in order to bring a small number of perpetrators to justice. The term "permanent kidnapping" evokes a paradox insofar as it refers to a disappeared person for whom there is no real possibility of return. Whereas kidnapping normally implies the possibility of reappearance, the idea of "permanence," in this case, points to an irrevocable finality—death—though a death that, in a matter of speaking, has not finished dying. As Felipe Victoriano notes, disappearance is a "total suspension of death," a death without conclusion: he who has "disappeared" has not fully died because his death has neither been claimed by the living nor by history ("Lo desaparecido," 39). Disappearance thus refers to a loss without an object, an absence that, at the same time, points to a presence that exists and persists only in the realm of memory. Moreover, the concept of *secuestro permanente*, in its linguistic configuration, alludes metaphorically to the unfinished and interminable state of mourning suffered by victims' families: the long wait for a return that will never come. The living are therefore left *in suspense*, left to grieve without ceasing for relatives whose bodies, in many cases, have not been found or received a proper burial. They are left immersed in a perpetual tension between mourning and melancholia.

My goal in this chapter is to probe the narrative void left by the disappeared and to understand some of the strategies artists have employed to either mark or fill that void. My conviction is that Chilean artists have confronted disappearance by employing two primary strategies that coexist in a profound dialectical relationship, and that, in the final assessment, cannot be separated from one another: *marking the presence* and *marking the absence*. Where the expressionless cannot show their faces or speak for themselves, Chilean artists have made them "reappear" and have carved a place for them in the national imagination, either by speaking on their behalf (Levi/Agamben) or by offering to the public eye concrete images that remind us at once of their presentness as well as their irrevocable absence. In other instances, artists have evoked the disappeared not by marking their presence (via reappearance) but, conversely, by signaling the void left by their violent extermination.

To emphasize these strategies, I will survey four artistic projects that span literary prose, poetry, documentary film, and public art. As examples of marking the presence, Silvio Caiozzi's documentary film *Fernando ha vuelto* [Fernando Returns] (1998), Claudio Pérez and Rodrigo Gómez's *Muro de la memoria* [Wall of Memory] (2002) and Marjorie Agosín's poetic cycle "La Desaparecida" [The Disappeared Woman] in *Las zonas del dolor* [Zones of Pain] (1988) attempt to rescue the disappeared from oblivion by granting them recognizable voices and faces or by rendering visible the materiality of their absent bodies. In these works, the artists speak on behalf of the absent dead, restoring to the expressionless living, human characteristics. In a different, though related, narrative gesture, Carlos Cerda's novel *Una casa vacía* [An Empty House] (1996) evokes the memory of the disappeared by marking their absence, and, in so doing, implores us to heed their silent (silenced) voices. The novel, in allegorical mode, offers a radical critique of many Chileans' unwillingness to acknowledge the specters that haunt the nation.

Laying the Dead to Rest: Silvio Caiozzi's *Fernando ha vuelto* (1998) and the Task of Mourning

If, as I have proposed, we understand disappearance to be a state located somewhere *between* life and death—a state that does not permit psychological closure for friends and relatives left to do the work of mourning—it seems, then, that those who have suffered loss are placed at tremendous risk. This risk has to do with the fact that disappearance, as a disavowal of death, prohibits carrying out the rituals associated with dying and burial that are crucial to completing the task of mourning. Where there are no bones, no ashes, no material traces to confirm that a disappeared person has really died, the living risk becoming fixated on the object of their loss and of being rendered unable to move forward. The scenario I describe, of course, concerns the classic Freudian distinction between mourning and melancholia. In Freud's conceptualization, mourning designates a process of coming to terms with loss, of "working through" loss, in order to make possible a future free from or lessened of mental anguish. Melancholia, in contrast, refers to an unresolved, interminable process of mourning from which the mourner cannot break free and which prohibits the projection of the self into a viable future.

But even when some degree of closure is achieved, the task of mourning is, in fact, never really finished. Even if the mourner manages to discharge his libido successfully into a surrogate object (e.g., a symbol of the lost loved one) or, in the best case scenario, to bury his or her remains, "mourning is never simply completed" (Avelar, *The Untimely Present*, 5). Idelber Avelar points out that the task of mourning always leaves behind some "remainder" that the living continue to mourn interminably. Burying a body is therefore only a beginning (though a vital beginning) to the process of laying the dead to rest. In addition to carving out a niche in the earth in which to inter bones, it becomes equally important to keep the dead alive in memory. Martine Déotte notes that "la desaparición programada de los cuerpos es insoportable para los sobrevivientes. Para aquellos que quedan no hay duelo posible sin que el sufrimiento pueda anclarse *en un lugar y en relatos*" [the programmatic disappearance of bodies is intolerable for the survivors. For those who remain, there is no possible mourning unless their suffering can anchor itself *in a place and in stories*] (Déotte, "Desaparición," 95) [emphasis mine]. Narrating the dead is a way of keeping their memory alive or affirming their existence. When someone dies, there is a basic human need to tell stories about that person, to remember individual uniqueness, to utter the deceased's name over and over.

For more than thirty years, various Chilean organizations of family members of the disappeared have worked tirelessly, both in the public and the private spheres, to keep the memory of their disappeared relatives alive. They have fought unceasingly for truth and justice, unwilling to compromise either goal, in an atmosphere of indifference, amnesty, and cover-ups. Viviana Díaz, former president of the Agrupación de Familiares de Detenidos Desaparecidos, once told me that at its founding in 1974, the organization's main mission was to search for the families' missing loved ones. However, during the dictatorship, this search was constantly frustrated by the military's lies and denials. In response to their incessant and impassioned inquiries, the family members were told that their "subversive" loved ones never existed or had left Chile to live in exile without notifying anyone. The truth about the disappeared was an official state secret and only rarely did Pinochet allow news of human rights abuses to reach the public as a tactic for cowing the citizenry.[3] Over many long years of waiting and searching, Díaz told me, the families have accepted that they will never again see their loved ones alive, though this has not quelled their desire to continue searching.[4] In some cases, thanks to the small successes of efforts like the Mesa de Diálogo (1999–2000)—a government initiative aimed at acquiring information from the military about the disappeared—the remains of some of the regime's victims have been returned to their families for burial. Nevertheless, the military has also acknowledged that some bodies will likely never be recovered because the remains were disinterred and thrown into the sea or otherwise destroyed.[5] According to some human rights activists, the regime even unearthed certain bodies, incinerated them, and mixed the ashes with birdseed to be spread around the city of Santiago. The destruction of bodies (a practice that some believe continued even beyond the 1990 transition) has therefore left many families at an impasse, unable to obtain information and unlikely ever to have an opportunity to bury their loved ones properly. Their only recourse is to call attention publicly to the crime of disappearance via the little media attention they receive.

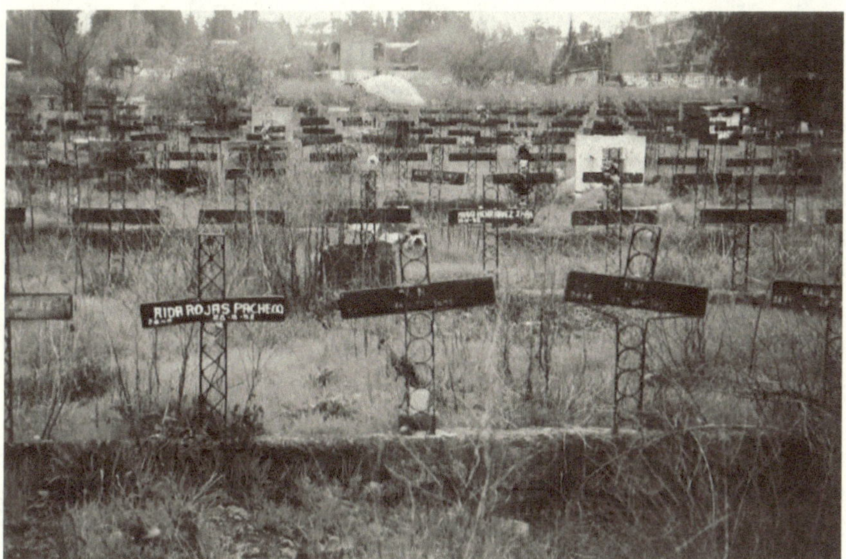

Figure 3. Patio 29, General Cemetery, Santiago de Chile.

Silvio Caiozzi's documentary project *Fernando ha vuelto* (1998) follows one case in which a body has, in fact, been positively identified.[6] The documentary is a moving mise-en-scène of an individual family's process of mourning and of the reconstruction, identification, and, perhaps most important, rehumanization of the remains of one of Pinochet's victims. Caiozzi's circumscribed focus, his emphasis on the case of one disappeared man, Fernando Olivares Mori, an activist in the MIR [Movimiento de Izquierda Revolucionario/Leftist Revolutionary Movement] who disappeared in 1974 and whose bones were interred in the General Cemetery's infamous Patio 29, makes the film poignant and personal. The documentary opens in the Identification Unit of the Instituto Médico Legal [Medical-Legal Institute], where two doctors, Isabel Rebeco (an anthropologist) and Patricia Hernández (a forensic specialist), demonstrate the scientific techniques they have used to identify and reconstruct Fernando's physical remains. Fernando's case, as the doctors explain, is one of the most dramatic among the disappeared because it was one of the lengthiest and most difficult to resolve. The doctors began working on Fernando's reconstruction in 1991 when, following the return to democracy, a number of bodies were discovered at Patio 29. They met his family in 1994, and thanks to both the family's help and the advances of science (DNA testing and matching dental records), were able to identify Fernando definitively in late January 1998.

In addition to DNA analysis and dental records, the forensic team also employed a technique known as *superposición fotográfica cráneo-facial* [craneo-facial photographic superimposition] whereby photos of Fernando provided by his family were used to identify the victim's bone structure. At this early point in the film, the filmmaker's desire to rehumanize the victim is made clear: Caiozzi wants to show Fernando to be more than a skeleton, more than bones, and he does so by portraying him as a real man with affective familial ties. To that end, as the scientists offer their explanations of how Fernando died, wedding and family photos appear intermittently on the screen. Before the viewer's eyes, an x-ray of Fernando's skull (scientific and impersonal) gradually morphs into a human face. Fernando's teeth, almost magically, come to match the smile of a living photo.

The combination of reconstructive imaging with the use of personal, family photographs dramatically emphasizes the tension between presence and absence. Fernando's physical bones serve as a reminder of his absent life, brutally stolen by the dictatorship; at the same time, the familial (affective) images conjure his ever-present memory in the hearts and minds of the living. I am reminded of Roland Barthes's observation that "[e]very photograph is a certificate of presence" (*Camera*,87). The juxtaposition of a corpse (a stark reminder of the realities of loss and death) with photographs of a living man authenticates and provides evidence for "what has been." Caiozzi, in the Barthian sense, employs the photograph as a kind of "evidential force" that refers to a life whose existence "can no longer be denied." For years the military dehumanized the disappeared, labeling them subversives and enemies of state, denying their very deaths. Now, through a trick of the camera, and thanks to the insights of forensic science, one who was disappeared and dehumanized can reappear. Through visual superimposition, the invisible becomes visible; the faceless is given a human face. On screen, the bones of the dead recover their humanity and dignity.

Reconstructing a dismembered body, in tandem with the process of laying that body to rest, are shown by Caiozzi to be complex and painful processes. In fact, *recognition* (identifying and naming the skeleton) and *ritual* (waiting for the arrival of the body to be waked, burial) are the driving forces behind the documentary's narrative emplotment. In a moving scene of identification, the doctors escort Fernando's widow, Agave Díaz, into the operating room and describe to her the condition in which her husband was found: naked, in a box, with his clothes lying beside him. They point out the lesions in his skull and the trajectory of the bullets that killed him, noting the bullet holes that penetrated his clavicle and spinal column. More than fifty-five fractured bones that "were probably a product of torture" resulted from blows received while Fernando knelt submissively before his aggressors. All those involved in the ritual of identification (doctors, orderlies, and Fernando's wife) appear emotionally stricken. As the doctors speak, Díaz lays her hand gently on top of her husband's skull. She remains mute. Tears (again we note the presence of affect) are her only recourse as she is led from the operating room to an adjacent office.

The verbalization of pain (so vital to the process of mourning) is shown by Caiozzi to be premature in the presence of the deceased body. The viewer notices Fernando's widow's *speechlessness* and is moved by the overwhelming presence of her pain. Her lack of speech stands in stark contrast to other family members' verbal testimonies that are interspersed throughout the documentary to compensate (partially) for Díaz's muteness. As I noted in previous chapters, Elaine Scarry writes about how pain under torture is so intense for victims that it causes them to lose control of their voices. As an extension of Scarry's argument, Agave Díaz's mute pain might be read as a further iteration of the impossibility of bearing witness after trauma, here extrapolated to the realm of the mourner.

Toward the end of *Fernando ha vuelto*, Caiozzi once again emphasizes the link between trauma and speechlessness by including a scene in which Señora Juana Mori, Fernando's elderly mother, also performs for the camera her inability to articulate pain. The old woman, who has awaited her son's return for nearly three decades, has lost her ability to speak clearly due to time's passage and the natural aging process. She tries desperately to bear witness, but her speech act transmits as broken and unintelligible. And because of its unintelligibility, her testimony requires that a family member "translate" her feelings for the viewer. What I find significant about this scene is that Señora Mori's pain is so strong that her depth of feeling cannot be articulated from the *inside*. Pain, for those directly immersed in it, manifests as a moment in which "all possibility of speech ceases" (Kofman, *Smothered Words*,9). Consequently, if it is to be articulated at all, it must be spoken from the *outside*, by a translator. The elderly mother's grandson Mauricio and other family members assume this role in the film by attempting to voice the pain Señora Mori cannot. Aware of how deep pain has destroyed his grandmother, Mauricio reminds the spectator: "My grandmother was like another disappeared woman who was not on the list. She suffered a lot. There are various ways of disappearing."

We are told, too, by another family member that "pain is pain." It is clear that Caiozzi wants the viewer to understand pain and loss as eminently human conditions independent of political ideologies. He wants us to contemplate the cruelty and barbarity of disappearance, to consider its effects on the living and the dead as well as its consequences for narrative. To watch Caiozzi's documentary is to share in the pain of those who remain and to be stricken by their speechlessness. Many, in fact, are the audiences—both in Chile and abroad—that have literally been left mute in the initial moments following a screening of the film.[7] From there I would hypothesize that to comment on this or other post-dictatorial films that treat horrifying acts of violence and appeal to the viewer's affect requires a *coming into language* that emerges only gradually out of a temporal and physical *distancing* from the material traces of pain (i.e., the remains of Fernando's body, a photograph of the living man, Caiozzi's film). In *Fernando ha vuelto*, human suffering causes a break, a rupture with language (and within language) that can only hope to be restored with time. The process of speaking about the dead, as the documentary suggests, originates from the *outside*: it starts with those who stand at a mental or physical "arm's length" from the immediacy of the deceased, beyond the intimate presence of his reappeared body. Material remains, Caiozzi shows, inspire only muteness, tears, and reverence. In order to speak (to narrate), it becomes necessary to step back, to gaze upon the bones of the dead from the perspective of an outsider looking in (like the filmmaker himself or the spectators who watch his film). In short, Caiozzi's representation of the grieving wife and mother offers a compelling manifestation of the presence/absence duality by dramatizing the perennial tension (born out of pain) between the possibility of speech and the absence of words to describe monumental human loss.

As the documentary draws to a close, the burial rite is prepared. Fernando's extended family gathers around his bones and touches him, as if to verify his existence, as if to burn his material presence into their somatic memories. They place objects to aid the ritual at his feet: an angel and a cross. Flowers are cut, music is selected, a coffin is built, and Fernando's remains are delivered to his mother. The homecoming (the return, *la vuelta*) signals an end to the absence of a body and the beginning of a new stage in the mourning ritual: the possibility of an escape from melancholia toward a more advanced kind of "working through."

22 April 1998. Friends and relatives gather at Santiago's General Cemetery to give Fernando a proper burial. Members of the Agrupación de Familiares are on hand, each wearing a photo of his or her disappeared relative as a certificate of presence, an evidential force of what has been. In the background, we hear Joan Manuel Serrat's "Elegía" [Elegy]: *tenemos que hablar de muchas cosas/compañero del alma, compañero* [we still have many things to talk about/ comrade of the soul, comrade]. At the funeral, the mourning ritual that was at first exclusively private and personal now becomes a ritual for the broader community. The public/communal dimension of mourning is shown to be a vital step in the process of "working through" insofar as it re-inscribes the disappeared body within society and the nation. The graveyard represents a space of inscription into culture, history, and memory. Moreover, through the funereal rite, the "expressionless" one is given a voice. Friends and relatives offer eulogies, and although we cannot hear what they are saying because of the music playing in the background, the documentary visually emphasizes the importance of *speaking* for and about the dead. Iván Trujillo Correa has written: "Ante el desaparecido la retórica es el cien por ciento de lo que hay. La verdad forense no viene a reemplazar a la retórica sino sólo a añadírsele" [With respect to the disappeared, rhetoric is all there is. Forensic truth cannot replace rhetoric; it can only add to it] ("La construcción"). Memory is therefore much more than just identifying a body: it implies creating a narrative. To remember, Caiozzi wagers, means keeping Fernando's voice present and active through the voices of the living (and through the artistic act).

Bones are little more than ruins if no one is there to name them.

Images of the Living Dead: Claudio Pérez and Rodrigo Gómez's *Muro de la memoria* (Puente Bulnes, 2002)

. . . *that* is dead and *that* is going to die. . .

Roland Barthes

To remember is, more and more, not to recall a story, but to be able to call up a picture.

Susan Sontag

The family members of the disappeared have employed many strategies to keep the memory of their lost loved ones alive: public protests including chaining their bodies to the fence outside the National Congress (18 April 1979), hunger strikes, pilgrimages, and statements in the media.[8] Each of these strategies has had as its goal to challenge official silences and draw public attention to the family members' plight. Within the families' epic struggle, photographs have played a key role. I would argue that today it is practically impossible to think of the Chilean Agrupación de Familiares (or Argentina's Mothers of the Plaza de Mayo) without simultaneously conjuring an image of ghostly photographs hanging from their necks, coupled with the words *¿Dónde están?* [Where are they?]

It is true, as Susan Sontag points out, that to remember often means to "call up a picture" (*Regarding*, 89). Likewise, Saint Augustine, in *Confessions* X, refers to the "imagistic" nature of memory. Undoubtedly, human beings remember through images, and when we are somehow unable to recall a face, we are left feeling anxious and empty.

The dictatorships of the Southern Cone not only sought to eliminate their subversive and revolutionary enemies but also the very evidence of their crimes. Bodies were made to disappear in many ways, in multiple phases: through torture, through murder, through official silences regarding the victims' whereabouts, and through the physical destruction of remains. Because of this erasure of bodies and evidence, family members strove in their public protests to mark the absence of a living body and a human face. One particularly moving example is the *siluetazo* [silhouette protest].[9] In this act of defiance, families cut out black, life-sized, cardboard human figures and inscribed them with the names of the disappeared and their dates of disappearance, proceeding to parade the silhouettes through Santiago and Buenos Aires like faceless ghosts returning to haunt the nation. The *siluetazo* was at once an affirmation of presence in ghostly form (*revenant*) and of the disappeared's absence from official history. And its drama and impact had to do, precisely, with the fact that the images employed were *not* photographic in nature. Unlike photographs that permit us to see real human faces and refer us to concrete biographies, the faceless silhouettes symbolically evoked the victims' *anonymity* as well as the magnitude of loss, state terror, and unfinished mourning.

If the silhouettes marked a ghostly absence that, as I have said, is always also a presence, photographs, in contrast, constituted a poignant and personal affirmation of existence, a certification and proof of "what once was." In *Camera Lucida*, Barthes affirms that the photograph "does not necessarily say *what is no longer*, but only and for certain *what has been*. . . . [T]he photograph's essence is to ratify what it represents" (85) [emphasis mine]. Photographs authenticate: they attest to an undeniable reality of something or someone who once existed. Faced with images of the living dead, we are reminded of lives—often young lives—cut short by the violence of dictatorship. Yet photographs of the disappeared are not just reminders of lives torn asunder. They have something much more dramatic to tell us about the tension between the "then" of their living presence and the "now" of their physical absence (their ghostly presence). Barthes notes that photographs capture the "defeat of time": "*that* is dead and *that* is going to die" (*Camera Lucida*, 96). Pictures therefore not only affirm the existence of a real flesh-and-blood human being at some anterior moment but also announce the catastrophe of impending death. All photographs of human visages, in this sense, bear within them the marks of a death-to-come. What could be truer when we look at the youthful, vibrant photos of the disappeared? We know they have already passed on, yet we are moved by the dramas they are about to live: torture and death. Therein lies their *punctum*, their sting.

Claudio Pérez and Rodrigo Gómez's *Muro de la memoria* [Wall of Memory] (2002) is an attempt by two visual artists to reappear the disappeared and remind Chileans that, thirty years later, their drama continues.[10] Located at Puente Bulnes, just above the Mapocho River (a symbolically charged site because of bodies found floating there during the dictatorship), the *Muro de la memoria* consists of 950 photos fired onto individual ceramic tiles.[11] Significantly, the monument does not stand in isolation but is semantically connected to other important sites of memory located nearby. Immediately adjacent to the photographs we find a memorial to Father Juan Alsina, a priest executed by the military in 1973 at Puente Bulnes, whose body was dumped into the Mapocho River.[12] Across the street stands a mural, also depicting Alsina, bearing the inscription "Mátame de frente porque quiero verte para darte el perdón" [Kill me directly because I want to see you so I can forgive you]. These different reminders of Chile's dictatorial past enter into a complex dialectic with each other and with the neoliberal, urban landscape surrounding them.

The photos used for the project, carried out through a 1999 grant from the Chilean Ministry of Education, were obtained by Pérez and Gómez from various sources: the archives of the Vicariate of Solidarity, the Agrupación de Familiares, the Instituto Médico Legal, the Rettig Commission, and the family members themselves. The project was originally intended to include photos of all 1,192 *desaparecidos* named in the *Informe Rettig*; however, the artists were unable to locate 242 photos as some family members could not be contacted, had passed away, moved out of the country, or simply did not possess any pictures of their loved ones. Empty spaces have therefore been left in the monu-

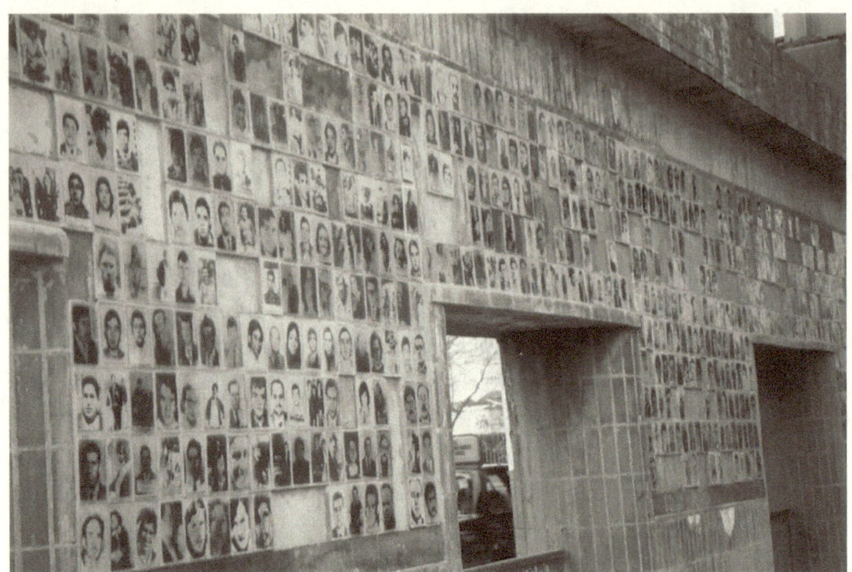

Figure 4. *Muro de la memoria*, by Claudio Pérez and Rodrigo Gómez. Puente Bulnes, Santiago de Chile, 2002.

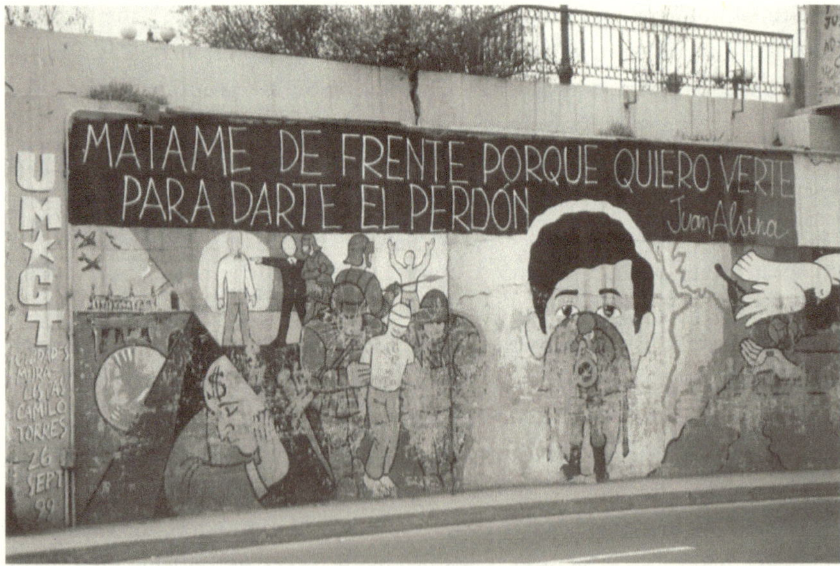

Figure 5. "Mátame de frente porque quiero verte para darte el perdón" [Kill me directly because I want to see you so I can forgive you]. A mural dedicated to Father Juan Alsina, murdered by the military regime on 19 September 1973. Father Alsina's body was abandoned in the nearby Mapocho River. Puente Bulnes, Santiago de Chile, 2002.

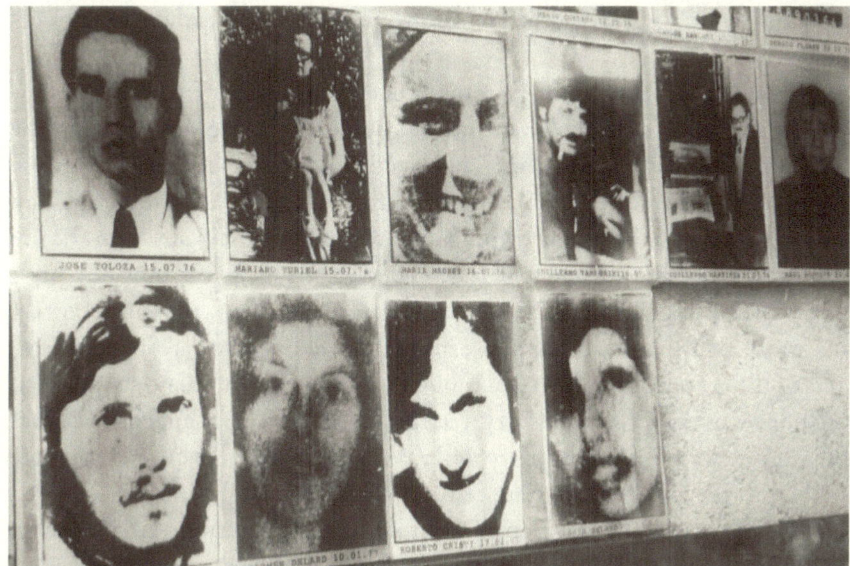

Figure 6. *Muro de la memoria*, close view. The monument draws attention to the absent photos of the disappeared.

ment for the 242 missing photographs in the event that they someday surface. The artists, however, are convinced that their project will always remain incomplete.

Because of its unfinished nature, the *Muro de la memoria* is a "countermonumental" space that resists any impulse to petrify the past (Young, 1993). Given its fragmented aesthetic, the project announces the writing of history to be a work in progress. Yet despite its counter-monumental, fragmented, and dynamic appearance, the *Muro de la memoria* paradoxically exudes a desire to *fix* in time and space images of the disappeared. Pérez and Gómez achieve this end by listing under each photograph the name of the person depicted and the date of his or her disappearance. (The photos, like materials in an archive, appear in chronological order by date and alphabetically by last name.) If the faces of the disappeared (on posters, on the lapels of family members) have historically been mobile images—that is, images that manifest themselves dynamically and sporadically in different situations and at different historical junctures (e.g., in protests, and on occasion in the media)—Pérez and Gómez attempt to give these images a permanent place. Their artistic project seeks to grant the disappeared a *context* in which to reside: to inscribe them permanently upon Santiago's urban landscape using strong, weather-resistant ceramic tiles.

When Cathy Caruth defines trauma, she proposes that traumatic memories do not surface in a coherent mental, textual, or historical context. The traumatic moment remains somehow outside the traumatized individual's life narrative and therefore must be incorporated into that narrative through an ongoing process of "working through." So too, one might claim, with the life of a nation. The disappeared have remained, to a certain extent, outside Chile's official historical narrative. The *Muro de la memoria* is an attempt to correct this problem by reminding all Chileans that the disappeared are indeed members of the great "Chilean family," though members who, until now, have been excluded from the victors' history. For this reason, it is not happenstance that the photos we see are not the typical *fotos-carnet* (state ID cards) that were so vital to the apparatus of state terror. (We recall that detainees were often rounded up in public squares and asked to produce their state-issued ID cards. The institutional, bureaucratic-looking ID photos erase the personalities and the humanity of those they depict, turning them, in the Foucauldian sense, into subjects of state vigilance.) Pérez and Gómez, instead (like Caiozzi), include family photographs: personal photos of weekends at the beach, of fathers playing with their sons and daughters, wedding photos, and photos taken at birthday parties. By doing this, they hope to evoke an anterior life, a happy life, a life before the disaster that allows passers-by to see the victims not as subversives or revolutionaries, but as human beings, as Chileans like themselves. It is also not coincidental that the photographs are sepia toned—a detail that refers us to a lost time, but which simultaneously evokes violence to come. Viewed holistically, I think that Pérez and Gómez's monument offers a reading of the military coup as a histrionic event that produced an irrevocable fissure within Chile's national fabric (the "Chilean family"). By reincorporating personal family photos of the disappeared into the "album" of the nation (and using the city as a site of inscription), the *Muro de la memoria* urges passers-by to identify with them.

(I am reminded that these moments of identification, of the possibility of *punctum*, are what make a photograph—and a monument, for that matter—more than just inert material. A personal anecdote comes to mind. Once, while looking through some photographs I had taken of the *Muro de la memoria* with a Chilean friend who had not seen the monument herself, my friend recognized in my snapshots the image of a disappeared person she had known personally. As one would expect, she was quite emotionally impacted. The experience was an important one for me because it reminded me that what one reads in a photograph cannot be preordained. Rather, as Barthes instructs, a photograph provokes a different reaction in every person who sees it. Perhaps, then, Pérez and Gómez's only wager in the case of the *Muro de la memoria* is that their project will elicit *some* reaction in the spectator, that it will produce something more than indifference. Therein may reside the monument's political efficaciousness.)

The daring of Pérez and Gómez's project lies in its not being afraid to show the naked faces of those whom the dictatorship brutally tortured and killed. In *Regarding the Pain of Others*, Susan Sontag writes, "With our dead, there has always been a powerful interdiction against showing the naked face" (70). What concerns Sontag is the reluctance of any nation's citizens to acknowledge the faces of their own dead. She maintains that we often deem it acceptable to gaze voyeuristically at the suffering of others in far-off lands, for when pain is of the Other, it is somehow less real, less imminent, more estranged, more distant. However, when it comes to admitting the suffering of one's own countrymen, of people who dress and look the same as oneself, there is indeed a tendency (and perhaps a natural one) to look away.

I feel that the *Muro de la memoria*'s radical effect is that it forces the gaze. The faces on the wall, in all their vitality and human uniqueness, demand that we look them in the eye and own up to their existence. This is why the monument's context is vital: its location in a highly traveled, urban thoroughfare signals the artists' hope that the *desaparecidos*' presence (the materiality of their physiognomies staring out from the photographs) will interrupt the hustle-and-bustle of urban life, alter the trajectories of pedestrians crossing Puente Bulnes, and compel them to look, to *see*. In a city that every day moves at a faster pace thanks to the neoliberal economic policies put in place by Pinochet and continued by the transition governments, the artists seek to remind us of a historical moment in sepia, ever more remote, yet ever more relevant to the present.

Making the Dead Speak: Prosopopoeia in Marjorie Agosín's "La Desaparecida" Poems

An essential change took place that day I finished my interviews with a group of detained-disappeared in Chile in 1983. It was a misty afternoon, like most afternoons

> *in Santiago, and a group of women approached me holding little photographs, tokens and clothes belonging to their children. They were gifts for me from ghosts outside of time and space. I felt my body covered with wounds, and knew that my challenge was to make the dead speak, not to elaborate on an empty space, on the absence of the disappeared.*
>
> Marjorie Agosín

When one thinks about the way the dictatorial state dehumanized its victims—deprived them of voice and face, usurped their identities, labeled them, numbered them, denied them—one can begin to understand something about the human impulse to speak on behalf of the dead. Aharon Appelfeld once wrote that one of the functions of art in the wake of the Holocaust is "to attempt to make the events speak through the individual and in his language, to rescue the suffering from huge numbers, from dreadful anonymity, and to restore the person's given and family name, to give the tortured person back his human form, which was snatched away from him" (92). The machinery of state terror turned the disappeared into anonymous corpses, subversives whose very identities were denied to families desperate for information. Chilean artists, from the very early years of dictatorship, began to mark this absence in their artworks. In 1977, for example, visual artist Eugenio Dittborn, hoping to call public attention to torture and disappearance, collected a number of anonymous photographs of victims and put them together in an installation entitled *Fosa común* [Common Grave]. His project focused on the absence of bodies; its power stemmed from its reference the machinery of state terror—to the "fabrication of corpses" (Heidegger/Agamben)—and from its emphasis on disappearance's anonymity (Richard, *La insubordinación*, 21).

Marjorie Agosín—a Chilean exile, poet, essayist, and novelist currently teaching at Wellesley College in the United States—has, following Appelfeld's insight and contrary to Dittborn's "Fosa Común," marked the presence of the disappeared by speaking on their behalf through her poetry. In this regard, Agosín's 1988 collection *Las zonas del dolor* [Zones of Pain], a bilingual edition with translations into English by Cola Franzen, offers a radical example of literature's power to make present the voices of the expressionless. The collection consists of sixty-two poems that refer to the realities of torture, disappearance, and the mourning of family members; the most powerful among them are a few in which the lyric voice speaks in the first person via *prosopopoeia*, a poetic device whereby absent persons or things who cannot speak for themselves are afforded a voice. Derived from the Greek *prosopon* ("face," "person") and *poiein* ("to make"), prosopopoeia dramatically gives face and voice to the anonymous.

In Book III of his *Rhetoric,* Aristotle mentions prosopopoeia specifically as a technique that promotes vividness in discourse—a technique that allows human beings greater emotional access to the object of representation. Agosín's poetic cycle, "La desaparecida," allows us to hear the ghosts of the disappeared calling from beyond the grave. Out of poetry, the shades implore the living to hear them and heed their call, to bury them "como Dios manda" [as God commands] (Agosín, *Las zonas*, 31).

Before referring to Agosín's "desaparecida" cycle, however, it first is necessary to say something about the poet's relationship to the shades. Toward the end of *Las zonas del dolor*, Agosín's poem "Los ojos de los enterrados" [The Eyes of the Interred] places the writer in the position of mediator among ghosts, of one who hears their cries and serves as a channel between them and the living. Like the disappeared whom the living refuse to hear and acknowledge, the poet, too, demands to be heard:

Los ojos de los enterrados,
como en una lejanía inquieta,
nos amenazan
óyen*los*, óyen*me*.

[The eyes of the interred,
as in a restless distance,
threaten us
listen to *them*, listen to *me*.] (59–60) [emphasis mine]

The lyric voice is haunted by the ghosts of three female victims whom she names specifically: "Ana Frank," "Milena," a Jewish woman (a detail that indirectly alludes to Agosín's own Jewish heritage), and "Lila Valdenegro. Desaparecida. Carnet 353, olvidada en la/ memoria que no desmiente" [Lila Valdenegro. Disappeared. I.D. number 353, forgotten/ in a memory that does not deny] (59–60). As the lyric voice writes (note that here the lyric voice is a writer figure), she sits in the position of one transfixed by the absences she perceives. Turning these absences into presence, into verse, into words, becomes a guiding force behind the whole of *Las zonas del dolor* and forms the very core of Agosín's aesthetic. It is not coincidental that the act of writing figures so prominently in the final stanza of the poem:

. . .
Los ojos de los enterrados
nos acusan

se acusan,
escribo, me miran
y me atraviesan
las ausencias.

[...
The eyes of the interred
accuse us,
accuse themselves,
I write, they watch me
and the absences
transfix me.] (59–60) [emphasis mine]

This poetic expression of the writer's position as *mediator* between the living and the dead serves to echo the sentiments Agosín expresses in her brief "Prologue" to the collection:

> Las desaparecidas se deslizaron entre los sueños. Me vigilaban, a veces me despertaban acariciándome, más que nada me pedían que no las olvide. Así fueron creciendo estas Zonas del dolor. Ellas, las mujeres enterradas pero siempre vivas, fabricaron las urdimbres de mis palabras que en la humildad de la impotencia buscaron claridades y voces.
>
> [The disappeared women slipped in among dreams. They would watch me, at times they would wake me up caressing me, more than anything else they would ask me not to forget them. That's how these Zones of Pain kept growing. The women buried but still alive wove the fabric of my words that in the humility of helplessness sought for clear places and voices] (1–2).

The "Prologue" goes on to register a complaint about the general tendency (of Chileans? of human beings?) to ignore the pain of others. Agosín's writing emerges from a desire to enter into a relation of solidarity with her "dead sisters" who continue to "wander" in search of someone to hear and bury them.

In "La Desaparecida I" [Disappeared Woman I], the lyric voice announces:

Soy la desaparecida,
en un país anochecido,
sellado por los
iracundos anaqueles

de los desmemoriados.
¿Aún no me ves?
¿Aún no me oyes
en esos peregrinajes
por las humareadas
del espanto?
Mírame,
Noches, días, mañanas insondables,
cántame
para que nadie me
amenace
llámame
para recuperar
el nombre,
los sonidos,
la espesura de la piel
nombrándome.
No conspires con
el olvido,
derriba al silencio.
Quiero ser
la aparecida
y entre los laberintos
regresar, volver
nombrarme.
Nómbrame.

[I am the disappeared woman,
in a country grown dark,
silenced by the
wrathful cubbyholes
of those with no memory.
You still don't see me?
You still don't hear me
in those peregrinations
through the dense smoke
of terror?
Look at me,

nights, days, soundless tomorrows
sing me
so that no one may
threaten me
call me
to give me back
name,
sounds,
a covering of skin
by naming me.
Don't conspire with
oblivion,
tear down the silence.
I want to be
the appeared woman
from among the labyrinths
come back, return
name myself.
Call my name.] (27–28)

We are confronted in the poem with the lyric voice of a disappeared woman who tries forcefully (note the reiteration of commands) to assert her identity, to call attention to her existence within a context where "los desmemoriados" (those in power or simply all those people who have participated either directly or tacitly in the forgetfulness of the post-dictatorship) have refused to acknowledge her. She wants to "recover her name," to have her story told because she cannot tell it herself. The poem, in effect, is a demand for a witness.

Yet the poem presents a dilemma insofar as it refers us to a fundamental impossibility. Clearly, a disappeared woman cannot speak for herself. Agosín's poem thus acquires a utopian character: it becomes a space in which the impossible becomes possible and where, simultaneously, the impossibility of the poetic gesture itself (the dead speaking) is brought into relief. When one hears the disappeared woman speak, what one really hears is not just an imagined ghostly voice, but a profound silence, a gap in the very possibility of expression. Agosín intentionally dramatizes a linguistic lack, the *desaparecida*'s nonlanguage, through an act of verbalization; she dramatizes that which cannot be said except by proxy (Levi). An infinite subtext—always potential, unrealized and unheard—speaks from between the lines of her verse.

When Adorno warned against the "barbarity" of writing poetry after Auschwitz, he did not say (as many critics have mistakenly claimed) that it is *impossible* to write poetry after Auschwitz. Indeed, the breadth of poetic expression generated in the wake of the twentieth century's concentration camps has been significant. Instead, by referring to poetry's "barbarity," Adorno uncovered a fundamental tension between the ethical and the aesthetic that is always at stake in the type of cultural production I am examining in this study. He offered two reasons for his concern. First, he worried that post-Holocaust art might allow the reader to extract some kind of sadistic (or voyeuristic) pleasure from his engagement with the artistic object. Second, he saw a certain risk in art's capacity to render intelligible the horror of events that should remain, in his opinion, beyond the realm of intelligibility. Adorno worried that artists, in the wake of the Holocaust, would attempt to redeem the disaster or turn the Holocaust into a commodity to be bought and sold.

Writers like Agosín defy Adorno outright. Agosín writes her poetry and speaks for the dead out of an ethical exigency *not* to remain silent or participate in the pact of the "desmemoriados," who themselves are linked to the world of capitalist consumption. Yet her poetry, in some sense, would allay Adorno's fears insofar as it brings us closer to the disaster without fully rendering it comprehensible. When Agosín speaks for the dead, she does so with no pretension to render transparent the realities of Chile's torture chambers or to make us understand what it was really like to disappear. Her poetry, instead, is born out of a plea to the living to recognize the ethical consequences of not heeding the voices of the dead. I would argue that the power of Agosín's "La Desaparecida" cycle comes not just from the politically and ethically significant action of speaking *for* the dead, *about* the dead, and in solidarity *with* the dead, but from the collection's gesture toward embodying poetry's *failure* to render the reality of disappearance fully legible.

Susan Gubar notes that poetry after Auschwitz "matters" precisely because of its power to show us snippets of experience, without engaging in totalizing or redemptive discursive practices. Poetry, Gubar writes, "abrogates narrative coherence and thereby marks discontinuity." "By so doing, it facilitates modes of discourse that denote the psychological and political, ethical and aesthetic consequences of the calamity without laying claim to experiencing or comprehending it in its totality" (*Poetry*,7). Marjorie Agosín's "Desaparecida" cycle, in this sense, never seeks to transcend the realm of the partial and the subjective. Her poems are simply a cry to the living from the specters of the dead. They seek a place to reside; they wish to have their names spoken, for only through speech (through naming) is their memory possible. For the moment, Agosín's writing is their space to inhabit, a temporary burial ground, a makeshift home for spirits set adrift on history's tides.

The Voice and the Wound: Carlos Cerda's *Una casa vacía* (1996)

In her book *Unclaimed Experience*, Cathy Caruth offers a theory of trauma, based in Freud, whereby trauma is understood as a catastrophic wound inflicted upon the psyche whose depth and gravity can only be assimilated over time, via a process of "working through." Trauma, for Caruth, is a wound that is inflicted "too soon, too unexpectedly, to be fully known and is therefore not available to consciousness until it imposes itself again, repeatedly, in the nightmares and repetitive actions of the survivors" (4).[13] The traumatic moment is therefore an unbearable, elusive event that has an incalculable and endless impact on the victim's life. This becomes even more evident when we think about how trauma victims often find it exceedingly difficult to free themselves from the torment of recurring nightmares. Victims are haunted, Caruth tells us, not just by the reality of the traumatic event itself, but also by "the reality of the way that its violence has not yet been fully known" (*Unclaimed Experience*, 6). This observation leads her to question whether the real "wound" inflicted by trauma actually occurs at the moment of the catastrophe itself or rather, later, in the tormenting aftermath of its unassimilated pain.

In her introduction, Caruth cites Freud's reference in *Beyond the Pleasure Principle* to the Tancred story (found in Tasso's *Gerusalemme Liberata*):

> . . . Tancred unwittingly kills his beloved Clorinda in a duel while she is disguised in the armor of an enemy knight. After her burial he makes his way into a strange magic forest which strikes the Crusaders' army with terror. He slashes with his sword at a tall tree; but blood streams from the cut and the voice of Clorinda, whose soul is imprisoned in the tree, is heard complaining that he has wounded his beloved once again. (*Unclaimed Experience*, 2)

Caruth reads Tancred's double-killing of Clorinda not only as a metaphor for the way in which traumatic events are reenacted (or reenact themselves), but also for the emphasis the story places on Clorinda's voice emanating from the tree. The girl's voice cries out to Tancred from the punctured traumatic wound. It wants to be heard and recognized, yet at the same time is a voice "that witnesses a truth that Tancred himself cannot fully know" (*Unclaimed Experience*, 3).

What I would like to emphasize here is the *otherness* of Clorinda's voice, that within it which is, and always will be, unknowable. Tancred, in Caruth's example, is traumatized by the wound he inflicts (both on Clorinda and on himself) and continues, in the aftermath of the disaster, to be haunted by her voice. However, despite his desire to know it, the voice of the dead Clorinda remains radically Other to him.

Caruth finds attractive how Freud turns to literature (Tasso) to say something about traumatic experience. In literature, Freud sees a parallel to psychoanalysis insofar as both disciplines desire to understand the complex tension between "knowing" and "not knowing." For Caruth, life after trauma (both for survivor-victims and family members) is ultimately defined by this tension. After reading Caruth, one cannot help drawing a parallel with the case of the family members of the disappeared. Their lives have been guided and defined at once by their interminable search, their need to know, but also by their very inability to know everything with certainty. Their role as historical witnesses is characterized by the simultaneous exigency to remain always attentive to the voices of the drowned (to make them present), but also to point out the absence (the void) left behind in the disaster's aftermath.

Carlos Cerda's (1942–2001) novel *Una casa vacía* [An Empty House] (1996) can be read as a literary dramatization of this exigency to heed the voice that emanates from the wound. Written during the transition to democracy, the novel is set precisely at the historical juncture (post-1983) where Pinochet's fall looks imminent. The main characters, Manuel and Cecilia, struggling to piece together their failing marriage (a kind of personal trauma), are given a house by Cecilia's father, Don Jovino (a rigid, controlling businessman), with the hope that the couple can "turn the page" and begin anew. But as the novel's action unfolds, the characters discover that the beautiful house in which they live was once a torture center for political dissidents under Pinochet. Upon moving in, they find the house in terrible disrepair: there are red stains on the walls and burn marks on the floors, and the property's exterior is overrun by vegetation. Unable to imagine how such a charming house could have deteriorated so badly, Manuel and Cecilia unwittingly ignore the physical marks of the disaster and proceed to beautify the house cosmetically. At first, the house appears to be a "house of forgetfulness." Who would have suspected that such a charming Ñuñoa home, located in a quiet residential neighborhood, could have such a dark and terrible past? And furthermore, who could have suspected that Cecilia's own father would be capable of complicity in the shady business practice of buying "houses of torture" from the military in order to expunge the marks of the disaster and resell them in renovated condition? It gradually becomes clear that Cerda's "empty house" is a metaphor for the nation and a staging ground for dramatizing the dilemmas of memory and forgetting, exile and return, dictatorship and transition.

To inaugurate the house, Manuel and Cecilia throw a party for a group of their friends. Two of the guests are particularly memorable: Andrés, a returned exile and prior owner of the house (pre-1973), who struggles throughout the novel to understand his place in a country that has become for him "el único territorio definitivamente extraño del planeta" [the only definitively foreign territory on the planet], and Julia, a torture survivor currently working for the Vicariate of Solidarity and who, as part of her work, is in charge of recording and transcribing the testimonies of other survivors like herself (Cerda, *Una casa vacía*, 41). I would like to focus for a moment on Julia's particularly central role in the novel.

During the party, Cecilia and Manuel show their guests around the house and Cecilia tells everyone about a strange dream she had in which the noise of a tree branch scratching at her bedroom window "se transformaba en una voz humana, un quejido, algo que arrastraba con mucho dolor y que parecía a punto de morirse, o desaparecer en el abandono más completo" [became a human voice, a cry, something dragged along in great pain and that seemed on the verge of death or disappearance into the most complete abandonment] (Cerda, *Una casa vacía*, 115). She then tells her guests that on her second night sleeping in the new house, the same experience repeated itself in reality. She remembers "ese roce, ese raspar la ventana, ese movimiento de las ramas, que al verlo esa noche me pareció el esfuerzo de un cuerpo, de un brazo, de algo humano, de algo que sólo tendría salvación si finalmente terminaba abriendo esa ventana" [that brushing, that scratching at the window, that movement of branches, that when I saw it that night seemed like the effort of a body, of an arm, of something human, of something that would only find salvation if I wound up opening that window] (Cerda, *Una casa vacía*, 116–117). Soon thereafter, while touring the basement, Julia has a strange premonition that she has been in that very place before. She, like Cecilia, hears "human voices" crying out from within the walls and is moved to sickness when she touches their "cold and rough consistency" (120). She further notes that there are exactly eight stairs leading to the basement. Her tactile memory suddenly transports her back to her days as a prisoner of DINA and she remembers how, blindfolded, she would take note of otherwise inconsequential details like the number of stairs or how the walls felt. Sickened, she quickly extricates herself from the tour of the house, encloses herself in the bathroom and vomits uncontrollably from the depths of her being.

While Julia is in the bathroom, the narrative recounts her process of recording the oral testimony of a woman named Graciela Muñoz Espinoza—"La Chelita"—who, years earlier, was imprisoned with her at the torture center and who now tells her story for the Vicariate's archives. The scene emphasizes Julia's role as listener and recorder of the Other's testimony. Hearing La Chelita's voice causes Julia to experience flashbacks to her own time in detention. The traumatic memories of the two women thus appear intricately intertwined. Later in the novel, in a gripping scene, Julia sees La Chelita staring at her from within the bathroom mirror (Cerda, *Una casa vacío*, 191). She tries to wipe her image away, but is unable to do so. Inasmuch as she wants to ignore the image she sees, as a victim of trauma subject to recurring episodes, she cannot escape the wound: when she stares into the mirror, she sees herself in La Chelita. Of all the characters in the novel, Julia is perhaps the one most violently forced to heed the voices that emanate from the wound (the wound within herself and the wound within other tortured women like Graciela Muñoz). As much as she would like to forget the past, she cannot escape the image she sees in the mirror. She is unable to turn a deaf ear to the *desaparecidos*' ghostly cries.

The novel's penultimate section bears the title "Último grito de las olvidadas" [The Last Cry of the Forgotten]. Written in italics and in the first person plural (*nosotras*), the verses we read (a generic break with the prose form of the novel) evoke the absent voices of the disappeared. As in Agosín's poetry, via prosopopoeia, disappeared voices are now suddenly made present and the reader is forced to hear the cries that emanate from the wound. Significantly, Cerda's novel ends on a question: *¿Habrá un corazón abierto a las voces de la casa?* [Will any heart be willing to hear the voices in the house?] Ultimately, Cerda shows the destinies of each individual Chilean (like the destinies of his characters) to be bound to the house's (the nation's) fate. Will the house remain empty and abandoned forever in a state of blissful forgetfulness, or will the citizenry admit its ghosts and listen to their voices?

Una casa vacía is an invitation to probe the wound and acknowledge the silent, silenced voices of the dead.

The presence/absence dialectic that these Chilean artists (Caiozzi, Pérez and Gómez, Agosín, and Cerda) foreground in their works calls to mind a final cultural image that poignantly re-emphasizes the simultaneous marking of the void and the desire to fill it that I have explored in this chapter: the *cueca sola*. At Patricio Aylwin's 1990 inauguration, the wives of Pinochet's disappeared victims marked the absence and presence of their loved ones by dancing the *cueca* (Chile's national dance, meant for two people) alone. Their gesture, like the gestures of these artists, called public attention to the missing and served as a moving testimony to lives, homes, and a nation torn asunder by seventeen years of political violence. The *cueca sola*, like Cerda's novel, was a way of asking if anyone would be willing to heed the mute cries of the disappeared, to acknowledge the lacuna left in their absence—in a word, to *name* them.

4

Lenses of Memory (On Narrating Villa Grimaldi)

Hay cuerpos y experiencias que son desaparecidos físicamente y, luego o simultáneamente, un relato extinguido en la palabra común.
[There are bodies and experiences that have physically disappeared but also, simultaneously, a narrative that has been expunged from the vernacular.]

Guadalupe Santa Cruz

A criminal always tries to cover his tracks, as if eliminating evidence could somehow erase the crime itself. Santiago, in the post-dictatorship, is like an immense crime scene where a number of important political actors (the military, the *pinochetista* political right, big business) have entered into a kind of tacit agreement to expunge from the urban landscape any symbols of the dictatorship's human rights violations. The ruins of political violence are indeed hard to map in the city's modernized, neoliberal urban space. Today, a visitor would be hard-pressed to identify specific sites of repression since very few have been formally marked or memorialized.[1] Notorious locations like the "Houses of Torture" at 1367 José Domingo Cañas Street or Londres 38, for example, despite persistent attempts by human rights activists to turn them into officially recognized "sites of memory," remain anonymous buildings in a city that everyday brims with more malls and fast-food restaurants.[2] Even the fissures, cracks, and bullet holes in the walls of La Moneda have all been filled. Encrusted ammunition has been extracted and a fresh coat of white paint now eclipses the strangely charming, dingy façade that older Chileans remember.

As I stood in front of La Moneda in July 2001, noticing how it looked with respect to the buildings around it, I could not help sensing a profound irony. If the government *whitewashed* the presidential palace so that it could stand as a symbol of a new, modernized Chile, its stark alabaster would simultaneously clash with the urban landscape around it, where many edifices still maintain their dingy tone. It occurred to me that sometimes attempts to whitewash the past can backfire. When there is an intentional smoothing over of trauma (in this case, by the state), the fact that something important has been forgotten or eclipsed—especially for those attuned to its importance—can be all the more salient. For those who remember La Moneda as it was before President Ricardo Lagos's 2001 renovation, there will always be something about this new and "improved" landscape that is, to say the least, unsettling.[3]

Santiago's geography—in subtle, but telling ways—has changed in the post-dictatorship. Important memory sites have been altered significantly, ignored outright, or expunged by parties disinterested in preserving them for future generations.[4] Often ruins of the past remain, but as history has taught us time and again, if they are not vested with meaning by human actors, each day they are doomed to become ever more estranged, ever more temporally disconnected from the traumatic history they embody. The problem is even more egregious when we consider that memory work is often inspired by place; physical ruins, in fact, frequently serve as a point of departure for narrative construction. Quite simply, ruins matter: they mark the ever-presentness of the disaster and invite us to consider our relationship with the past as well as the past's importance for the future. When our physical connections to the past are severed, we are left with an irrevocable sense of loss. And because of this, we must question the long-term consequences of leaving physical memory sites permanently altered or unmarked.[5]

Yet to preserve a site physically is not enough. For a site to have meaning, it must also be narrated. James Young, in his groundbreaking work on Holocaust memorials, reminds us that monuments do not relieve people of the work of memory. Monuments need to be activated, "experienced internally," so as to avoid becoming "exteriorized forms" devoid of significance (*The Texture of Memory*, 5). Nietzsche knew this all too well when in *The Use and Abuse of History* he cited the danger of petrified, invisible monuments that states create to propagate univocal readings of history. For Nietzsche, memory is not at all stagnant, but rather a dynamic and critical activity. Memory is an ethical battleground upon which multiple senses of the past compete for viability. Consequently, memory sites should be understood as palimpsests that are constantly invested and reinvested with symbolic meanings by the human imagination.[6]

How, then, to narrate the ruins of the past, to restore to language what has been irrevocably lost?[7] In an illuminating chapter on trauma and post-Holocaust landscape photography, Ulrich Baer writes about how the empty spaces left where certain Nazi concentration camps once stood offer no "proof" of the horrors that occurred there. The *nothingness* displayed in the photographs alludes to a radical "absence that cannot be undone," a void "so extreme that it seems to swallow up the possibility of ascribing meaning to it, even though it is indisputably significant" (Baer, *Spectral Evidence,* 84, 80). Not only, in certain cases, was every physical manifestation of the camps destroyed, but the vast majority of those who passed through them (those who could have testified to their existence) were killed as well. The erasure was therefore double: on one hand, materiality was eradicated in the world; on the other, a void was created in memory itself because of the lack of testimony. As a result, in the disaster's aftermath, it becomes impossible to comprehend fully what we see.[8] The aesthetic object places us *in relation to* the void, allowing us to sense the catastrophe without ever mastering it; it facilitates critical reflection without engaging in totalitarian or erroneously wishful narrative gestures. As Baer explains, the empty landscape photos "preempt closure and instead beckon us—without hinting at redemption or restitution—toward thought and language with which to reach from within the Holocaust's imploded sites to a place beyond it" (*Spectral Evidence,* 84).

Perhaps no modern thinker sensed more keenly the difficulty of narrating ruins than did Walter Benjamin. In a little known vignette entitled "Excavation and Memory," Benjamin offers a powerful and complex metaphor in which he compares the process of remembering to an archaeological excavation:

> He who seeks to approach his own buried past must conduct himself like a man digging. . . . He must not be afraid to return again and again to the same matter. . . . For the matter itself is only a deposit, a stratum, which yields only to the most meticulous examination what constitutes the real treasures hidden within the earth, severed from all earlier associations, that stand—like precious fragments, or torsos in a collector's gallery—in the prosaic rooms of our later understanding. (Benjamin, *Selected Writings*, 576)

Benjamin depicts remembrance as a process of "digging" through the layers and strata of memory, of unearthing the buried fragments that lie within. Like an ancient city interred beneath centuries of built-up sediment, human memories become trapped under multiple layers of subsequent experience whose thickness and solidity determine the extent to which it is possible to access those memories and the condition in which memory traces will be found. Temporality is a key element in Benjamin's metaphor, since memories are always recast and reframed with respect to later experiences such that they become meaningful (or understandable) in the present. Ruins, once unearthed, must be activated, woven into a narrative context. Just as the archaeologist unearths fragments of a shattered past, he who remembers must decide what to *do* with the fragments of memory, how to use them, what *form* to give them.

But narrating absence—or, creating presence rooted in absence—is profoundly difficult when material links to the past are gone. Sites in ruins whose meanings cannot be easily shown or "proven" thus become malleable slates upon which meanings can be inscribed; they are subject to multiple interpretations, to conflicting narrative constructions that depend on the speaker and his motivations for speaking.

My aim in this chapter is to explore the relationship between *ruins* and *subjectivity* by focusing on one specific site that has generated intense debate in Chile's post-dictatorship: the former detention center at Villa Grimaldi.[9] Through my analysis, I hope to show how markedly different memory narratives—both in real life and in the realm of fiction—have been inscribed upon the torture center's ruins toward very different ends.

Within the geography of Chile's sites of memory, Villa Grimaldi occupies an important place. From mid-1974 to 1978, it served as one of the military regime's primary sites of repression. There, more than 5,000 Allende supporters were brutally interrogated and tortured. Of those 5,000, today it is known that at least 240 were killed or disappeared, while the remaining survivors returned to society with the difficult task of remaking themselves and confronting the traumas they suffered.

During the dictatorship, there were more than eighty torture centers in the Chilean capital alone. Today, although more than a decade has passed since the beginning of the transition, very few of these sites have been formally marked or acknowledged.[10] In the case of Villa Grimaldi, the last director of CNI, General Hugo Salas Wenzel, sold the property in 1987 to a construction company of which he was part owner. The company intended to level all the buildings on the site to make way for a modern condominium complex. A *politics of destruction* thus began so that no vestige of the former torture center would remain.

By 1990, most of the buildings that once stood at Villa Grimaldi had been eradicated by the construction company's bulldozers. All that remained were ruins, fragments of what had been one of the most notorious symbols of Pinochet's repression. However, thanks to a sustained effort between 1991 and 1995 by a diverse constellation of social actors who did not want Villa Grimaldi to become a condominium complex—among them the Agrupación de Testigos Sobrevivientes de Villa Grimaldi [Group of Survivor-Witnesses of

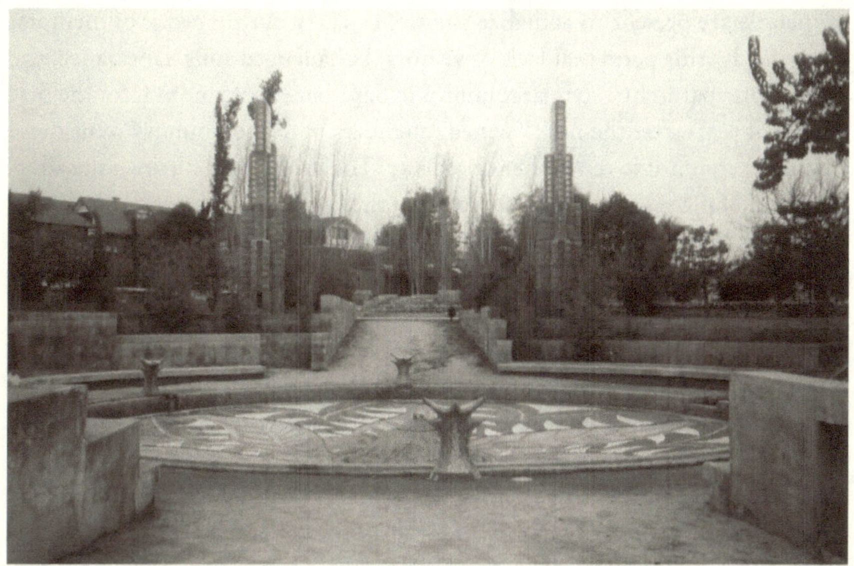

Figure 7. Villa Grimaldi, Park for Peace (1997). The park's center, El Patio Deseado [The Desired Patio], features a fountain for gathering and intimate reflection.

Villa Grimaldi]; then-Minister of Housing and Urban Development Alberto Etchegarray; certain community-based organizations in the neighborhoods of Peñalolén and La Reina; and certain voices linked to the Catholic Church and Chilean human rights organizations—today a Park for Peace [Parque por la Paz] stands on the site. Approved by the Chilean legislature after years of intense debates, the park was inaugurated in 1997 to serve as a "space of encounter" for remembering the victims and reflecting more generally on the dictatorship's human rights violations. Through guided tours, commemorative acts organized by family members, personal pilgrimages, and massive ceremonies held every 11 September (the date of the coup) and every 10 December (the International Day for Human Rights), the park, as a territorial marker of repression, serves to challenge the transition governments' politics of forgetting.[11]

Notwithstanding the park's important symbolic value as a memory site, Villa Grimaldi strikes me as a remote, semiforgotten place on Santiago's map. Located on the periphery of the city, it is not at all well marked. In fact, if one did not know of its existence in advance, it would be easily passed by without one even realizing it was there. Each time I have visited Villa Grimaldi, it has impressed me as a ghostly place, a place where ruins linger but where virtually no people are present to actualize the site or carry out the work of memory. Intrigued by this perpetual lack of visitors, I challenged Luis Santibáñez, the park's principal architect, to account for it. Santibáñez told me that for the first couple of years after the park opened, members of the community went there frequently, but not to remember or reflect: "The park would fill up in the afternoons and on weekends, but just like any other park, not as a park of memory. There was also a great deal of looting and graffiti, and this forced us to place limits on visitation."[12] Santibáñez also mentioned that the park is often used for soccer matches by neighborhood children. These other (forgetful) uses of the park undermine the conscious memory acts that occur there and not only remind us that memory sites serve multiple functions but also that they must be activated (narrated) continuously if they are to have meaning.

The most frequent visitors to Villa Grimaldi today are foreigners—mostly American and European professors and students with a particular interest in human rights. Though a number of Chilean school groups (both at the secondary and university levels) have organized field trips to the Park for Peace, the relative scarcity of Chileans visiting the site begs asking how successful the project has really been for recovering and actualizing the memory of human rights violations in Chile. One cannot dispute that it has been an important project in symbolic terms (a project whose worth will hopefully become even more apparent as time goes on), yet I cannot help feeling that the park also dramatizes the crisis of memory Chile has faced in the transition. This crisis, as we shall see, is brought into relief through the aesthetic strategies used in the park's design and through the profound irony of a memory park that, because of its lack of visitors, is constantly on the verge of becoming a *non-place*.[13]

In the interest of exploring some of the lenses through which Villa Grimaldi has been seen and narrated, I will offer three "tours" of the site. The first tour is my own personal narrative that seeks to understand the political and ethical consequences of the park's aesthetic design. My analysis, offered from the perspective of a critic who approaches Villa Grimaldi as an aesthetic object that deploys specific representational strategies, will suggest that the park's design can be read as an extension of the consensus-based politics of reconciliation that have dominated official state discourse during the transition.

The second tour will focus on the narrative of Mr. Pedro Alejandro Matta Lemoine, a Villa Grimaldi survivor and one of the principal activists in preserving the site. Matta frequently returns to Villa Grimaldi to give tours of the park, during which he describes to his audience the brutal tortures he and his *compañeros* suffered. His discourse offers a compelling example of how one survivor enters into contact with ruins and uses them as a surface of inscription for a memory act.

The third and final tour will focus on the experiences of the narrator of German Marín's novel *El Palacio de la Risa* [The Palace of Laughter] (1995). The novel tells the story of an exile who returns to Chile after the dictatorship, encounters the ruins at Villa Grimaldi, and faces the extreme difficulty of narrating what happened there. By comparing Pedro Matta's discourse to that of the narrator of Marín's novel, I hope to reveal how subjects speaking from different positions can elaborate surprisingly dissimilar narratives (one closed and polished, the other open and tenuous) upon the ruins of a single site. In Matta's case, the survivor offers his discourse as uncontestable truth with clear pedagogical motivations; in the case of *El Palacio de la Risa*, literature offers a reflection on the difficulty, if not the impossibility, of accessing and narrating the past.

First Lens: The Park for Peace as Aesthetic Object

How would it be possible to preserve the weight of torture and death in the Park for Peace without recreating the original space of repression? How could the park be "encoded" in order to lead the visitor toward a desired reading of the site? And what, for the designers, would be that desired reading? These questions were at the center of the debates that preceded the inauguration of the Park for Peace on 22 March 1997.

Between 1991 and 1995 an intense polemic ensued among the survivors of Villa Grimaldi and the family members of the disappeared about how best to preserve the ruins left behind by the military. In the course of the debate, three conflicting proposals emerged: (1) the ruins of Villa Grimaldi could be left just as they were found and a simple sculpture dedicated to the victims' memory could be placed on the site; (2) Villa Grimaldi could be restored to look exactly as it did when it functioned as a detention center; or (3) the site could be totally redesigned as a Park for Peace so that it would cease to stand as a symbol of death and destruction but rather be resignified as a symbol of life and hope. The third proposal was the one that ultimately prevailed, not only because it had the most support among families and victims but also because the park's designers—logically in need of government funds to carry out its construction—understood that a park conceived as a space of reconciliation (of life, of hope, of unity) would be most in keeping with the government's political agenda and therefore more likely to receive financial support from Chile's legislature.

According to Luis Santibáñez, the greatest challenge the designers faced was deciding how to respect the desire of the vast majority of survivors and family members to "hacer un parque de reencuentro con una simbología que recordara lo que en ese lugar sucedió y rendir homenaje con la vegetación al triunfo de la vida" [make a park for gathering, with symbols that embodied what took place there and to use vegetation to pay tribute to the triumph of life]. Such a park that deliberately focused on Chile's present and *future* rather than "dwelling excessively on the past" would undoubtedly be most acceptable to different sectors of Chilean society. Furthermore, as a reflection of the government's politics of *consensus* and *reconciliation*, such a park would not endanger the relatively recent and still unstable Chilean democracy.[14]

Even the speeches delivered at the park's 1997 inauguration had a reconciliatory tone. Carlos Gho, then-president of the Park for Peace/Villa Grimaldi Corporation, spoke the following words at the dedicatory ceremony: "La Corporación Parque por la Paz Villa Grimaldi recibe este parque con alegría, con esperanza, con entusiasmo: con alegría y esperanza porque en este lugar, donde en otro tiempo, los señores de la muerte cometieron crímenes bestiales y negaron todos los derechos a sus prisioneros, hoy florecerá la vida" [The Park for Peace/Villa Grimaldi Corporation receives this park with joy, with hope, with enthusiasm: with joy and hope because in this place, where in another time "men of death" committed beastly crimes and denied their prisoners every right, today life will flourish].[15] Gho's comment constitutes a clear public acknowledgment that the park's designers fully intended to resignify the site, to make a *new* space that would be markedly different from the former site of horror. The guiding principle behind the aesthetic design, it seems, was to create something positive out of the ruins of the disaster.

Spatially, the park's design in the shape of a cross (or an "X") invites the visitor to think of it as a symbol of reconciliation. Two diagonal pathways converge upon a central fountain covered with brightly colored mosaic tiles. One of the pathways originates at the current entrance gate and compels visitors to begin their pilgrimage toward the center. The other pathway originates from the park's opposite corner at the Portón Metálico [Metal Doorway] through which political prisoners entered the camp. Since Villa Grimaldi was locked for years following the dictatorship, the front gate became an important symbol of the need to access the past, to re-enter and reclaim the site. At the park's

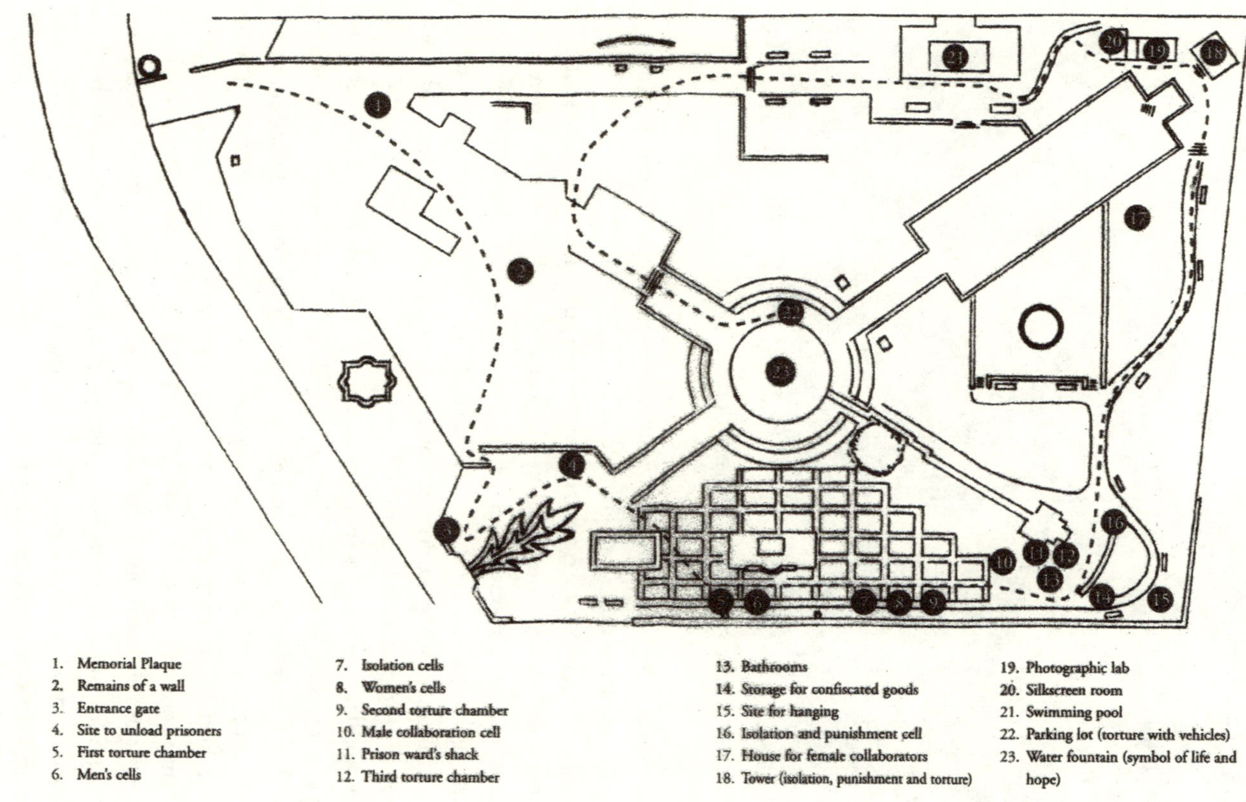

Figure 8. Park for Peace Map in Pedro Alejandro Matta's *Villa Grimaldi, Santiago de Chile: A Visitor's Guide* (2000). By permission of Pedro Alejandro Matta, Santiago de Chile.

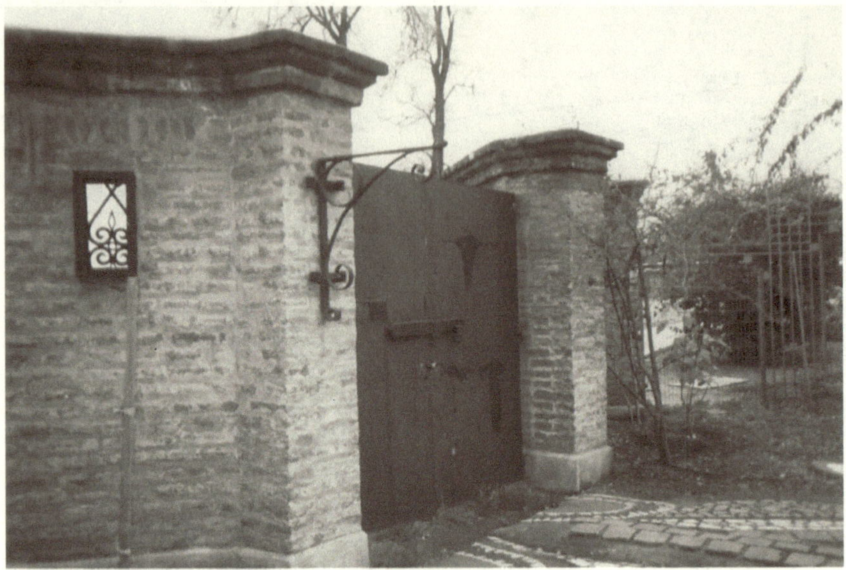

Figure 9. El portón metálico [The metal door].

inauguration, however, the door was intentionally sealed forever so that the horrors committed therein might "Never Again" occur.

The park's architecture suggests at least three possible readings. First, it calls to mind the "+" sign often used by Chileans as an abbreviation when writing "Nunca Más." Second, it serves to mark the site as worthy of distinction in Santiago's urban landscape. Third, it recalls the religious symbolism of the cross. This last reading, curiously, was the one emphasized in the guidebook written for the park's inauguration. Rodrigo de Arteagabeitía writes: "Con su doble significado, muerte y resurrección, el cruce de los dos ejes, al centro del parque, acoge una fuente la cual es un lugar de encuentro y orientación donde es posible entrar en contacto con el agua" [With its double meaning, death and resurrection, the cross with two axes at the center of the park encompasses a fountain that is a place of encounter and orientation where it is possible to enter into contact with the water] (*Corporación*, 38). This "redemptive" reading begs certain questions. What does baptism in the fountain's waters signify? And for whom is it intended: victims, perpetrators, family members, all Chileans, humanity in general? Who must repent to be "washed clean"? And is redemption even possible after the horrors that occurred at Villa Grimaldi? These questions, admittedly, remain open for debate. What is important is that the fountain never ceases to be an ambiguous symbol: not at all clear to the visitor is exactly *who* is meant to be cleansed, or *why*.

If it is true that the Park for Peace hopes to project, through its design, the possibility of redemption and reconciliation, there are at least four contradictory elements in the park that, to my mind, challenge this possibility. First, on one side of the park we find a swimming pool that, during the dictatorship, was used to torture and kill a prisoner. One perceives the pool's waters to be contaminated (probably as a result of the rainwater that collects in it), and these dirty waters create an inevitable contrast with the purifying and redemptive flow of the fountain. Second, despite the designers' attempts to adorn the park with beautiful vegetation, remnants of the barbed wire that once surrounded the detention center are still in place. Though the barbed wire was meant to serve a purely functional purpose—to keep loiterers and vandals out—its symbolic significance is obvious. Third, when I visited the park in July 2002, I noticed a new addition that had not been there on my previous visits. To my surprise, a wooden replica of the tiny isolation cells where prisoners were held had been placed on the site where the original cellblock once stood. The model cell offered a striking contrast to the relatively benign, beautified landscape around it, and, as I later came to learn, the placement of the model was a conscious—although belated—attempt to interrupt the park's serene landscape. As Luis Santibáñez told me, he took advantage of the political opening and resurgence of memory that came after Pinochet's 1998 detention to challenge an aesthetic design that was "negotiated" with the government in the early 1990s. Somehow unsatisfied with how the park "silenced the truth," he felt that a visible marker of violence would allow that truth to be told more overtly. Finally, in 2003 yet another interruption of the park's beautified landscape was added: a replica of the infamous "Torre de los Suplicios" [Tower of Cries] where prisoners were held for long periods in complete isolation and darkness. Given these four contradictory elements, I would propose that the park, which in general confronts the visitor with an aesthetic of "smoothing over" or "beautifying" the rough surfaces of the past, also contains subtle details that permit us to consider the horrors committed there.

The *beautification* and *smoothing over* that dominate the park's aesthetic configuration are brought into relief by the small mosaic plaques we find on the ground to designate the detention center's main areas. These mosaics, on which are inscribed the names of different spaces within the park ("The Tower," "The Pool," etc.), are significant because they are made from fragments of tiles

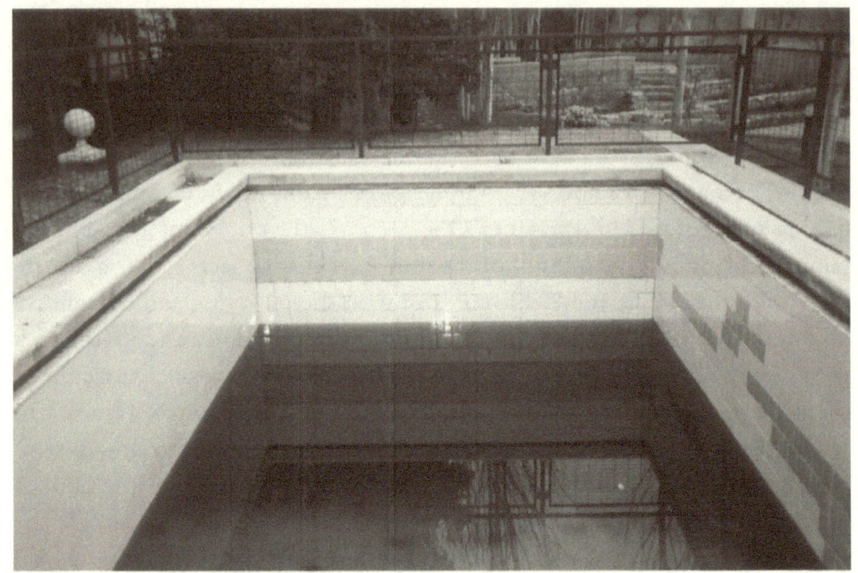

Figure 10. La piscina [The pool].

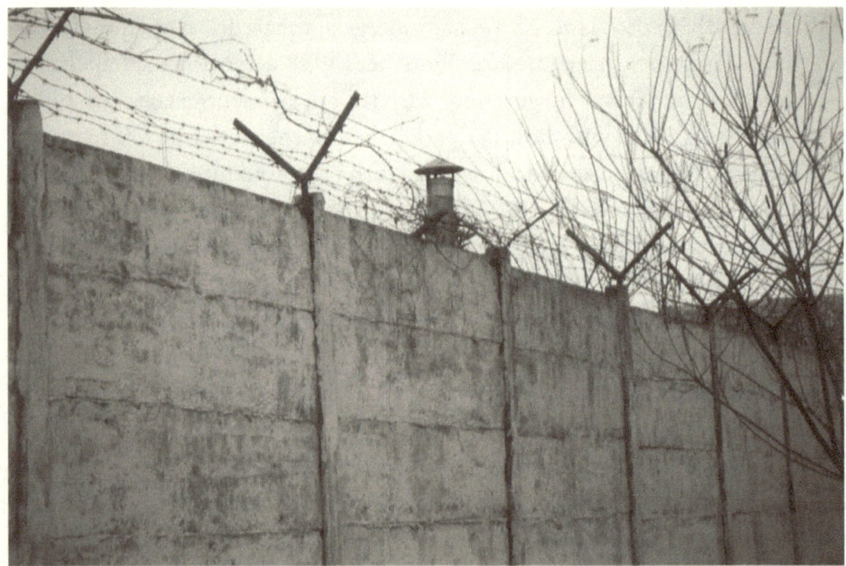

Figure 11. Remnants of barbed wire surrounding the Park for Peace.

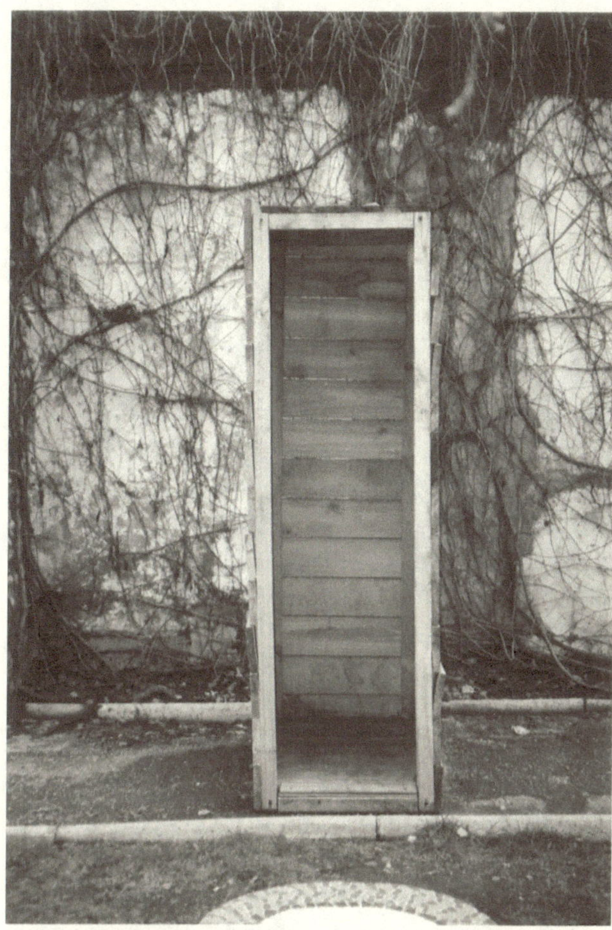

Figure 12. Isolation cell.

that were part of Villa Grimaldi's main building and that were likely visible to prisoners when they peered beneath their blindfolds.

Do these colorful sculptures, in their attempt to "piece together" fragments of the past, enter into direct contrast with the victims' fractured lives? The mosaics require us to reflect, yet again, on Adorno's famous dictum about the "barbarity" of art after Auschwitz. Adorno highlights a fundamental tension between the aesthetic and the ethical insofar as certain aesthetic procedures, like the reconfiguration of fragments within the mosaics, may try to render too intelligible that which is, in fact, unintelligible. The very idea of a former torture center turned into a beautiful park full of trees, flowers, and multicolored mosaic sculptures should leave us questioning the consequences of converting

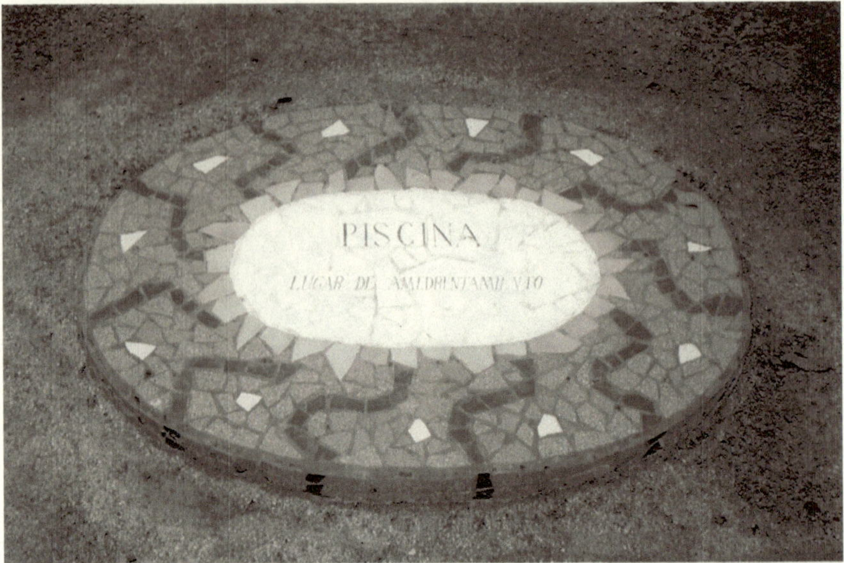

Figure 13. Descriptive mosaic made out of tiles from the original construction at Villa Grimaldi. The prisoners could sometimes see these tiles from beneath their blindfolds.

a former site of repression into a type of art that can be construed through the lens of the "beautiful." Innumerable testimonies have established that the prisoners' world was one of darkness, extreme fear, and unspeakable violence. If the Park for Peace is supposed to tell us something about that world, I fear that it has, on some level, failed at its attempt. I say this because the site in no way offends our sensibilities. It does not shock. It does not allow us to really sense the barbarity of the horrors perpetrated there. One might even say that, without the assistance of a guide, it unwittingly permits complacent spectatorship. This, I feel, is its greatest shortcoming.[16]

Second Lens: Pedro Alejandro Matta, an Ex-detainee of Villa Grimaldi

On the battlefield of memory, Elizabeth Jelin writes, there are always *memory entrepreneurs* [*emprendedores de la memoria*] "que pretenden el reconocimiento social y de legitimidad política de una (su) versión o narrativa del pasado, y que también se ocupan y preocupan por mantener visible y activa la atención social y política sobre su emprendimiento" [who strive for the social recognition and political legitimacy of a (their own) version or narrative of the past, and

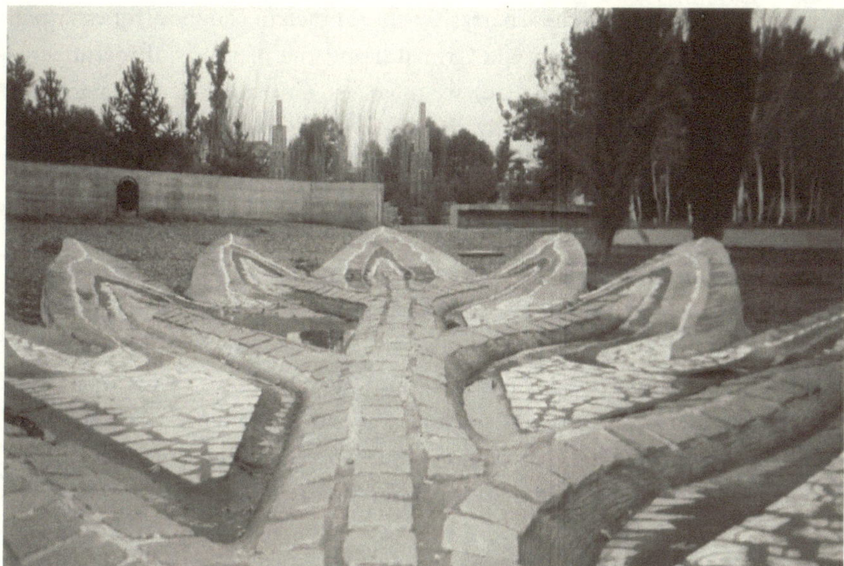

Figure 14. *La llama* [The Flame], by Mexican artist Nora Domínguez, marks the entrance to the park.

who work to keep social and political attention visible and active around their enterprise] (Jelin, *Los trabajos*, 49). In the case of Villa Grimaldi, Mr. Pedro Alejandro Matta, an ex-detainee, has been one of the most active memory entrepreneurs.

A former leader of the Socialist Youth Movement during Popular Unity, Matta was detained and tortured first at La Venda Sexy and later at Villa Grimaldi in 1975. After spending thirteen months in Pinochet's prisons, he was granted political asylum by the United States government and lived in San Francisco and New York until Chile's return to democracy. Since returning to Chile in 1991, Matta has dedicated much of his time to reconstructing the history of repression under Pinochet. As a central aspect of his work, Matta organizes guided tours of the Park for Peace for interested individuals and student groups.

To highlight Matta's voice as "exemplary" among the victims who regularly offer guided tours of the Park for Peace does not mean that he has been the only person to promote a narrative about repression at Villa Grimaldi. Indeed, a number of family members and other survivors offer their own tours of the park and tell, from their own unique perspectives, their personal experiences of torture. And although these narratives share much in common(for example, references to the history of Villa Grimaldi and the methods of torture employed by Pinochet's secret police), we must also remember that the narrative of one victim need not necessarily coincide with that of another.[17] Nevertheless, Matta's voice, in my opinion, seems to warrant special attention for its salience and wide-ranging influence. Because Matta is one of the park's only English-speaking guides, his voice has resonated strongly among foreign visitors. On certain occasions, Matta has also given tours to former detainees who, because they were blindfolded as prisoners, could not get a sense of the topography of the site. In addition, he has given interviews on PBS, has appeared in documentary films produced by local and foreign filmmakers, and has spoken at a number of U.S. universities and academic conferences. Owing to his public prominence, Pedro Matta has come to be viewed by many not only as the primary historian of Villa Grimaldi but also as a kind of "representative" survivor.[18]

Given that the purpose of Matta's tours is to explain in detail how torture was carried out, how much students know about the general historical and political context of Villa Grimaldi becomes a vital part of how they will assimilate the experience. With what memory narratives do Matta's audiences come to his tours? And who propagates these narratives (books, the media, university professors, the students' host families)? Without a doubt, how much one knows about the dictatorship and its context plays a key role in determining how Matta's discourse will be received. From my personal experience accompanying Matta's tours, I am well aware that the contextual information students bring varies widely. Some have spoken at length about the Pinochet years with their professors and host families, while others seem grossly underprepared to comprehend what they are hearing with any degree of sophistication.

During his tours, the park provides Matta a metaphorical stage upon which to carry out a *performance* of memory.[19] Using a minimalist backdrop dotted with ruins and absences, he establishes an intimate relationship with physical space as a trigger for narrating the tortures he and others suffered at Villa Grimaldi. With his hands, he gestures toward the sites where the prisoners' cells and the DINA agents' offices once stood. He sits on the edge of a low brick wall and describes how torturers forced prisoners to sit and consume their meals in a matter of minutes. He stands upon a block of cement—a ruin of the Villa's stately main house—and points out the comfortable conditions in which DINA's agents lived relative to the prisoners' misery.

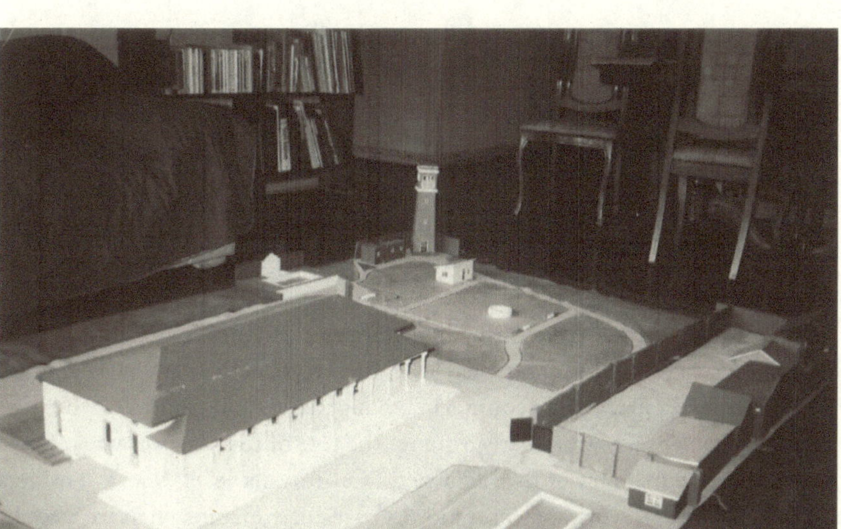

Figure 15. Pedro Alejandro Matta's scale model of Villa Grimaldi.

Matta's narrative, which emphasizes the tortures suffered by prisoners, promotes a specific vision of Villa Grimaldi's history. He guides visitors step-by-step along the typical trajectory of a detainee. In the context of his narrative (which is almost always in the third person, although sometimes the first person does surface unexpectedly), Matta even physically demonstrates the mechanics of a torture method like the *Pau de arara* ("The Perch"). At the halfway point of his tour, he crouches down in the place where this method was employed and, using his own body, shows how prisoners' hands and ankles were tied together so they could be hung upside-down from a wooden perch, thus leaving their genitalia exposed for torture. In these moments, Matta's reenactment of torture complements his oral narrative, shocking visitors and leaving them horrified. This evocation of shock seems a central part of Matta's didactic mission: it is clear that he wants to impress upon his audiences the sheer barbarity of repression.

Thanks to Matta's sustained efforts, his tour has traveled beyond Chile's borders to reach a broader audience comprising mainly U.S. academics. At the 2001 meeting of the Latin American Studies Association (LASA) in Washington, D.C., Matta presented a publication of his own authorship entitled *Villa Grimaldi, Santiago de Chile: A Walk through a 20th Century Torture Center*

(A Visitor's Guide). The book, which contains sketches that permit the visualization of torture methods, allows English speakers to participate in his tour remotely, via the act of reading, and to follow a detainee's trajectory with the aid of a numbered map. At LASA 2001, Matta simulated his memory tour for the academic community using a scale model he had built. Before beginning, he invited all those present to abandon their seats and come forward so as to experience more fully, and more personally, the impact of what was about to take place.

When I asked Matta about the importance he ascribes to his tours, he answered on two levels. On a personal level, he considers the park to be a "lugar de encuentro" [a space for encounter] with his friends and comrades who died there. In this sense, Matta clearly assumes the role of the *survivor* whose job is to preserve the memory of the "drowned." On another level, Matta considers himself a *historian* working to promote a particular memory narrative about what happened at Villa Grimaldi. As he begins each tour, he expresses his desire to contribute to the construction of a broader, more "universal" memory of human rights violations in the contemporary world:

> Yo quiero mirar a la transición chilena como un período bastante efímero dentro de un contexto histórico global y a largo plazo. Por lo tanto, si bien trato de aportar a que esta transición sea la menos desmemoriada posible, es mucho más importante mirar lo que fue Villa Grimaldi y el actual Parque por la Paz en una perspectiva de largo plazo y como mensaje y experiencia a las generaciones de chilenos y latinoamericanos que yo no alcanzaré a conocer, pero que, a través de la reconstrucción histórica y de la preservación del lugar, puedan tener una mejor visión y entendimiento de las increíbles capacidades de causar daño que como especie llevamos dentro de nuestra naturaleza humana.
>
> [I want to look at the Chilean transition as a rather ephemeral period within a global, long-term historical context. Therefore, if it is true that I am trying to help this transition be the least forgetful it can be, it is much more important to look at Villa Grimaldi and the Park for Peace in long-term perspective, as both message and experience for the generations of Chileans and Latin Americans I will never know, but who, through the preservation and historical reconstruction of the site, can gain a better vision and understanding of the incredible capacity to cause harm that is part of human nature.]

Despite his desire to present Villa Grimaldi in a global context, however, it is clear that Matta's tours, in practice, focus almost exclusively on the local and the particular. In the final assessment, his descriptions of torture prevail above all else. And although his strategy, it would seem, is to transform the "literal"—the concrete experiences of real victims like himself—into something more "exemplary" and universal, Matta's audiences are only able to derive implicitly connections between Villa Grimaldi and other genocides in the modern world.

Third Lens: German Marín's Returned Exile in *El Palacio de la Risa* (1995)

> *The exile exists in a median state, neither completely at one with the new setting nor fully disencumbered of the old, beset with half-involvements and half-detachments, nostalgic and sentimental on one level, an adept mimic or a secret outcast on another.*
>
> Edward Said

El Palacio de la Risa, by Germán Marín, offers a profound reflection on the extreme difficulty of narrating ruins.[20] If in Pedro Matta's case the survivor used ruins as a palimpsest for elaborating a pedagogically oriented discourse about the horrors of torture, in the case of Marín's unnamed narrator, the very possibility of narrating ruins becomes tenuous.

After seventeen years living abroad, the novel's protagonist returns to the ruins of Villa Grimaldi in a historical moment that predates the construction of the Park for Peace (sometime between 1990 and 1995). Before going into exile in 1973, the narrator had extensive contact with the site. As a child, he spent countless weekends as a guest of a friend whose family owned the old aristocratic mansion constructed there by the Egaña family in 1835. As an adolescent during the Popular Unity years, when Villa Grimaldi became a discotheque called "El Paraíso" [Paradise], he continued to go there on dates with his girlfriend Mónica. Because of his intimate involvement with the site pre-1973, the narrator—post-exile—harbors memories of a beautiful mansion filled with fountains, gardens, and ornate sculptures. However, this imagined space is clearly at odds with the "desolación" [desolation] and "escombros menores" [bits of rubble] he now sees before him (Marín, *El Palacio*, 97, 100). Consequently, he is a man embroiled in the difficulties of reintegration into a country he once called home, but which he now finds completely changed, almost unrecognizable. At once a stranger among his countrymen and a man estranged from his country's history, he is caught in a profound temporal disconnect between Chile's pre-dictatorial past and the present, post-dictatorial moment:

> Yo no venía del extranjero, sino del pasado, el que al parecer nadie quería, pues, de acuerdo a lo que ya había captado, aquel tiempo ya no representaba nada en la vida de los chilenos. . . . Era un extranjero en mi propio país. Desde la orilla opuesta de este destierro . . . proseguía al ver con una historia escindida que no encajaba con el presente.
>
> [I hadn't come from abroad, but from the past, a past which it seemed no one wanted, since based on what I understood, that time now meant nothing in the life of Chileans. . . . I was a stranger in my own country. From the opposite shore of this exile, I forged ahead, faced with a fragmented history that didn't meld with the present.] (Marín, *El Palacio*, 192–193)

Standing upon the ruins of what had been one of DINA's most notorious detention centers, the narrator faces an existential dilemma: How can he restore to language a fractured history from which he himself was absent? How can he come to know the truth about what happened at Villa Grimaldi if the physical traces of that past are gone forever? Narrating the story of Villa Grimaldi is presented as a daunting task. Even though the narrator can see some of the detention center's physical remnants (e.g., the barbed wire, the swimming pool, the oil stains left behind by automobiles used to torture prisoners), he cannot "señalar a ciencia cierta lo que había sucedido" [prove with certainty anything that had happened] (Marín, *El Palacio*, 107).[21]

The central enigma the narrator wants to resolve is the mysterious disappearance of his ex-girlfriend Mónica. While in exile, he occasionally heard rumors that Mónica fell into DINA's clutches just after the coup and later became a civilian collaborator. (Interestingly, Mónica's character seems loosely based on other prominent collaborator-figures like Luz Arce and La Flaca Alejandra, both of whom are mentioned by name in the text.)[22] He wonders how a woman he once knew so well could have become a traitor. He finds no logical explanation. The history of what happened to Mónica after 1973, and more precisely, of where she is now, remains shrouded in mystery:

> La realidad proseguía imperturbable frente a mí, depositaria en su seno de la verdad acerca de Mónica que no podía descubrir. En cualquier

> caso, ninguno de los indicios, aunque se entrecruzaran, me señalaba como pistas dónde permanecía ella en ese minuto. ¿Es que desaparecida no estaba en consecuencia en ningún lugar?
>
> [Reality continued undisturbed before me, containing within its bosom the truth about Mónica that I couldn't discover. In any case, none of the clues, even though they overlapped, suggested leads concerning her current whereabouts. Is it that "disappeared" meant she was nowhere?] (Marín, *El Palacio*, 159)

The novel casts the narrator as both a historian and a detective who turns to every imaginable source to reconstruct Mónica's story. He consults history books, written memoirs, paintings, and oral testimonies; he looks for information in the archives of Santiago's National Library and the Vicariate of Solidarity, yet no written documentation leads to the truth he desires. Written sources allow him to trace only the Villa's *remote* past (roughly from the time of its construction in the mid-nineteenth century, until 1965, when it was sold and converted into a discotheque); they tell him nothing about the period from 1973 to 1990. Quite literally, the dictatorship is a void in the archive.

The narrator's desire to know brings him, at last, to the doorstep of a woman named María del Carmen Posada: a forty-two-year-old survivor who, like Mónica, collaborated with the regime.[23] Much to the narrator's dismay, María del Carmen is not quick to divulge information about Mónica and instead uses the encounter therapeutically as an opportunity to talk about her own experience of torture. Racked by shame, alienated from society, and suffering from extreme depression and alcoholism, María del Carmen is glad to have found an empathic listener in the returned exile. She evades the topic of Mónica and even says at one point that she does not remember her at all. But the narrator persists, and his persistence ultimately leads to a confirmation of his worst fears about his ex-girlfriend:

> Fue así como esa noche tormentosa me confirmó [María del Carmen] que la había conocido [a Mónica], a poco de empezar ella en Peñalolén, luego de ser reconvertida en el campo de detención de Cuatro Álamos. Mónica se había trocado en una colaboradora gracias a cierto capitán de ejército de apellido Salazar, quien después de liberarla de ciertos cargos, en una historia que no dejaba de ser una más en aquel ambiente, se había ido a vivir con ella luego de abandonar a su mujer. Una historia vulgar me soltó concisa María del Carmen, aunque golpeado por la información le pregunté qué sabía, ansioso de indagar hasta dónde había alcanzado la

iniquidad de Mónica. Si bien las actividades que desarrollaba en la DINA eran diferentes de las suyas, María del Carmen sabía, a pesar de la compartimentación de las tareas, que trabajaba como analista de la oficina dedicada en el segundo piso a asuntos internacionales. . . . Según rumores, la pareja vivía ahora en Buenos Aires, retirada aparentemente de los caminos secretos del tirano, después de que Mónica tuviera un hijo. Vaya, me sorprendió. Fuera de esto último no disponía de más antecedentes y, al terminar su cuento suspiró, Dios es injusto, acercándome la botella de whisky. Me dijo, mejor bebamos, mi negro.

[On that tormenting night she confirmed that she had met Mónica just after starting in Peñalolén, having been part of the restructuring of the Cuatro Álamos detention camp. Mónica had become a collaborator thanks to a certain army captain named Salazar who, having freed her of certain responsibilities (a story that was just one among many in that environment), had gone off to live with her after abandoning his wife. María del Carmen revealed, concisely, a vulgar story. Though I was battered by the information, I asked her what she knew, anxious to discover the limits of Mónica's iniquity. Although Mónica's activities in the DINA were different from her own, María del Carmen knew that, despite the compartmentalization of labor, she worked on the second floor as an analyst in the international affairs office. . . . According to rumors, Mónica had had a baby and the couple now lived in Buenos Aires, far from the tyrant's secret paths. Damn, I was surprised. Aside from this, she had no more information. And upon finishing her story, she sighed "God is unjust," pushing the bottle of whisky toward me. She said, "Better that we drink, my negro."] (Marín, *El Palacio*, 189–190)

Although the narrator has partially come to understand Mónica's fate, he is aware that this partial truth is based solely on the testimony of one fragile woman whose words are infiltrated with "rumors." María del Carmen's character thus suggests that even the survivor's testimony can be given to hearsay. Her speech act is almost exclusively about her personal confession; regarding Mónica, she is clearly evasive and, when she is not, her memory is, at best, incomplete. The narrator's frustration only exacerbates his melancholy and alienation.

El Palacio de la Risa, therefore, establishes a profound narrative tension between the *desire to narrate the past* and the *difficulty of accessing that past*. Toward the end of the novel, standing once again upon the ruins of Villa Grimaldi, the returned exile reiterates his irrevocable uncertainty:

> De mi parte estaba en un punto, luego de haber pasado la mañana en aquel erial, en que sólo cabía dar todo por aceptado y marcharse. Abrigar alguna esperanza de restituir la existencia a la antigua casa era quimérico, asimismo devolver a Mónica a su vida anterior.
>
> [For my part, I had reached a point, having spent the morning in that wasteland, at which the only fitting thing to do was to accept everything and leave. To harbor any hope of bringing the old house into existence was chimerical, and so was restoring Mónica to her former life.] (Marín, *El Palacio*, 192)

What is important, though, is that the narrator does not leave his comments there. Yes, he resigns himself to the enigma, but not to oblivion. Although he is tempted at many points to forget the past and move on with his life, he knows that forgetting is not an option. Instead, he affords the past the status of an open book (a narrative *in process*), resisting the notion that trauma can be resolved. It is significant that he concludes by calling his own narrative a "provisional" text, necessarily in need of revision and editing: "El dios solitario del yo me hacía dar cuenta que, viejo como me sentía para recibir esos imprevistos, tampoco estaba en condiciones de asimilar el pasado o, al menos, de cerrarlo. Era un ayer trabado por mi propia mano" [My solitary god made me realize that, old as I felt to receive these unforeseen occurrences, neither was I in a position to assimilate the past or, at least, to close it off. It was a yesterday written by my own hand] (Marín, *El Palacio*, 197).

This last sentence—*Era un ayer trabado por mi propia mano*—reveals yet another reason it is so important that the narrator not put closure to his narrative: he must not do so because his personal experiences at Villa Grimaldi as well as the part of its history that he "missed" are vital for constructing his own identity. The ruins at Villa Grimaldi allow the narrator to imagine himself, to narrate himself, to understand how his past self connects to his present self. In short, connecting with physical space permits him to reflect at length on the questions *Who am I?* and *What is my place in this radically changed society?*[24] Indeed, the exile's condition always stands in relation to the dictatorship. He is who he is—an exile—precisely because of who he is *not*: one who stayed behind or one who perished. By returning to Villa Grimaldi, he seeks to understand a destiny (death, disappearance, torture, betrayal, collaboration) that could have easily been his own.

El Palacio de la Risa is noteworthy for the healthy skepticism it maintains regarding any memory narrative that purports to offer uncontestable truth. From the space of literature, Marín reflects on the danger of narratives that appear too "clean" or too "polished," privileging instead the fragmentary nature of memory and the multiplicity of truths that circulate in the post-dictatorship.

The Lenses of Memory

The three lenses of memory I have explored point to the problematic and complex relationship among *site*, *subjectivity* and *narrative*. In each case, a different subject engages with physical space and attempts to offer a narrative built on ruins and absences.

The critic's lens emphasizes the perspective of someone who approaches the Park for Peace without a guide and attempts to comment on its architectural and aesthetic configuration. It posits the park's geography as a "text" to be read and seeks to question the political, ethical, and aesthetic risks that stem from its reconciliatory and beautifying gestures.

The case of Pedro Alejandro Matta foregrounds the personal narrative of *one* survivor who chooses to stress the methods of torture employed at Villa Grimaldi and the details of daily life in the camp. Matta's tours are valuable insofar as they offer his audiences familiarity with details of repression that remained silenced for many years. Yet ruins, in Matta's case, are not at all malleable: his scripted discourse does not vary from one tour to the next (though I cannot presume to say that it should necessarily be expected to). To the contrary, he is interested in teaching specific lessons about what happened at Villa Grimaldi. He wants to promote the politics of "Nunca Más" [Never Again] for the next generation.

Matta's "fixed" narrative can be productively contrasted with that of Germán Marín's narrator in *El Palacio de la Risa*. If it is true that Matta offers an unmalleable memory text, Marín's novel, from literature, posits memory as conflictive and uncertain terrain. The comparison offers a compelling example of how literary writers tend to focus on the problematic nature of memory construction, while living survivors do not feel at liberty to admit communicative ambiguity lest they be rendered unable to effect political or social change in the "real" world. Although Marín's returned exile wants to know everything about Villa Grimaldi's sordid past, his attempts lead only to frustration and doubt. This, however, does not stop him from trying. He does not resign himself to oblivion but rather recognizes the writing of history and the (re-)formulation of identity as always unfinished works in progress.

On the ruins of Villa Grimaldi, radically different memory narratives have been written and will continue to be written. Each of these narratives is born of different motivations and evidences different degrees of narrative "closure." It is only by understanding the variations among memory texts—only by understanding the prisms through which they are written—that we can begin to ask necessary questions about the personal, intellectual, or political agendas that motivate them and about the place(s) of enunciation of the subjects who speak to us about the past.

Epilogue

The Politics and Ethics of Form

El Pinochet histórico está desacreditado. El Pinochet biológico está muriendo.
[The historical Pinochet has been discredited. The biological Pinochet is dying.]

José Zalaquett

This book, at its core, has been about *form*. By now two things should be abundantly clear: first, post-traumatic scenarios yield a diverse array of narrative configurations, and second, these configurations have important political and ethical consequences. The discursive gestures I have studied range from fragmentary aesthetics that resist closure and defy totalitarian meanings (Eltit, Marín, Pérez and Gómez) to personally or politically programmatic discourses that seek either to communicate clear, unambiguous pedagogical messages (Matta's "Nunca Más") or to assuage cognitive dissonance in post-traumatic subjects (Arce). At the same time, I have concerned myself with the silences and lacunae implicit in every testimonial act, seeking to show how art, through its complex operations, either marks or fills the void such that the expressionless can speak and the "drowned" can reappear (Caiozzi, Agosín, Cerda).

If one considers holistically the works examined in this book, the debate on *modes of narrating* the disaster might best be characterized by two opposed concepts: "open" versus "closed" forms. By the former, I refer to narrative configurations that challenge facile resolutions to trauma and evidence some degree of metatextual reflexivity in their construction; by the latter, I refer to narratives that are non-self-reflexive, that operate from a desire to smooth over ambiguity and establish narrative harmony. Having defined these terms, I appeal to an anecdote to illustrate the conflict more concretely.

During one of my trips to Chile, I asked Pedro Matta if he had ever read Marín's novel on Villa Grimaldi. Not knowing what to anticipate and eager to hear a survivor's comments about how the novel's protagonist deals with the difficulties of narrating ruins, I was surprised by Matta's quickness to dismiss the novel as a mere "fiction" that, according to him, contributes little or nothing to the reconstruction of a historical site where real people suffered greatly. Matta's deployment of the word *fiction* (as opposed to reality) carried with it a series of negative overtones linked to the idea of falsehood. How could a novelist presume to make *literature* out of Villa Grimaldi? What gave him—a fiction writer who was never tortured himself—the right to speak about the site? What worth did his novel have if it could not contribute new names, dates, or "facts" to the historical archive?

Matta's reaction to Marín's fiction made me realize that when it comes to post-dictatorial memory, it is necessary to talk about different types of truths. On one hand, one might speak of factual truth, whose goal is the accrual of names, times, dates, and numbers that are undoubtedly essential to the construction of a historical archive and to the pursuit of justice. Particularly in a context where countless details about life under Pinochet are still unknown, establishing factual truth remains a pressing concern. However, factual truth is only part of the story; it does not exhaust our inquiry into the past. We know that often the facts of one testimony do not align with those of another. Contradictions abound. Likewise, we know that truth utterances are malleable, that they are crafted in the present based on a speaker's motivations and perceived outcomes. The same survivor, for example, can tell her story in many ways: to promote reconciliation, to achieve justice against a military official in court or to promote democratic tolerance among the next generation. In each case, she will necessarily alter her emphasis or reconfigure memory traces to elicit a desired response in her addressee. Given these problems, post-authoritarian truth-telling has to be more than a simple summation of denotative facts. Post-authoritarian truth-telling, I feel, is the aggregate of discourses—official and unofficial, factual and fictional, written and performative—that have the capacity to transform society and help it imagine a better future, without forgetting its past.

Truths are constructed over dinner tables and in popular culture, just as they are in political speeches, university debates, or in the realm of high art. And sometimes, as I have shown, the truth in discourse stems not from *what is told*, but from the emphasis a given textuality places on the very *difficulties of telling* or on the impossibility of establishing transcendental meanings.

One might argue, then, that the axis of post-dictatorial memory debates does not lie primarily in the distinction between fact and fiction (which, as we know, is always ambiguous), but in what different textualities can contribute to our constructive engagement with the past. Truth-telling is as much about understanding affect and questioning epistemological limits as it is about compiling data or pursuing justice. Because of this, I feel that literature has a place in post-dictatorial debates precisely because it contributes to a more complete conceptualization of truth. Literature, unlike other modes of expression, places us *in relation to* the void; it permits us to probe silences and examine our very ability to know. With that said, however, I want to stress that admitting diverse textualities into the archive does not relieve us of our perennial duty to read all memories—notwithstanding their origins, genres, emphases, and motivations—with a keenly critical and deconstructive eye.

In my examination of the *lenses of memory*, I have returned frequently, perhaps obsessively, to the relevance of *impossibility* for memory debates. Here, I want to reemphasize the complexity of this concept without closing the debate. The term's finality and apparent defeatism may at first give us pause—and rightly so—for to resign ourselves to witnessing's impossibilities appears tantamount to admitting silence or fomenting denial. In other words, to acknowledge that bearing witness is, on any level, "impossible" carries with it the inherent danger of muteness or of fueling negators. (I refer here to those who would argue—shamefully—that torture in Chile never occurred or that Hitler's gas chambers were a figment of survivors' imaginations.)

Simultaneously, impossibility leads to other problems. If, for example, it is impossible to bear witness to trauma because of testimony's mediated character, or because of memory's fallibility, or because of the fundamental lacunae bound up in every witness's utterance (Agamben), then why attempt to bear witness at all? The question is at once completely ludicrous and theoretically challenging: ludicrous because of the existence of so many attempts to bear witness through music, films, memoirs, novels, poems, or other representational modes; challenging because it forces us to consider impossibility's theoretical utility.

I would hypothesize that to acknowledge testimony's impossibilities should not be taken as a defeat but rather as a challenge, not as a call to silence but as a call to arms, a point of departure for acts of historical revisionism (if we take this term in its most positive sense). The notion of the impossible foregrounds, forcefully, the pressing need within post-traumatic societies to bear witness insistently and incessantly because of the disaster's sheer magnitude and inexhaustibility. By their nature (and I say this warning of testimony's ability to slip into ideological dogmatism), testimonial utterances, no matter their modes of transmission, invite further telling: they invite implicit and explicit dialogue and debate, complementarity as well as refutation. Therein, perhaps, resides testimony's anti-authoritarian potential, its democratic impulse, its dynamism.

My investigation of post-traumatic textualities has taught me that political and ethical desire is implicitly bound to narrative form. Luz Arce's testimony, for example, expresses its politics (and ethics), its wish for reconciliation and closure, through its most basic images and narrative operations. In contrast, Eltit's *El padre mío* and Marín's *El Palacio de la Risa* are eminently anti-reconciliatory in their formulations. These latter texts work with fragments of meaning that resist totalitarian recastings. They do not arrest the sign *a priori*; they do not seal off meaning, but keep it in play. Their subversion comes from their ability to question correspondences, to intervene signifiers that in other instances appear naturalized.

Thinking about the political and ethical potential of form, Francine Masiello wonders if the fragment, as a textual strategy deployed by post-dictatorial artists, is "sufficient" in and of itself (*The Art*, 13). The question is important insofar as fragmentary aesthetic procedures, like those of Eltit and others, constitute sites from which to interrogate and undermine authority. Yet, Masiello notes, the fragment is not effective simply because it is "scandalous," but rather because it compels us to conceptualize our world in ways that open space for rebellion and counter-hegemonic thinking. The fragment paves the way for readers to take the "necessary conceptual leaps for the practice of politics" (13). Because, under both dictatorship and democracy, state institutions (or structures like the neoliberal market) seek to influence and control thought and actions, the anti-authoritarian impulse of some artistic discourses becomes all the more relevant. I would extrapolate Masiello's idea from the realm of art into the broader realms of the textual and the cultural in order to pose a question for future consideration: Without discounting the important contribution of any textuality that engages productively with the past, might it be true that those discourses and cultural practices that resist closure or the imposition of meaning are the ones that can best stand up to the epistemological challenges facing post-dictatorial societies?

In Chile, the work of memory remains unfinished. Although some justice has been obtained, many criminals walk the streets unpunished. More than one thousand *desaparecidos* still haunt the nation, and countless survivors live in anonymity, struggling to piece together their shattered lives. Stories go untold because of fear, shame, or indifference. Repentance by perpetrators has been slow in coming, and the gloss of neoliberalism has turned Chile's traumas into just one more news item that ebbs and flows according to the tides of public interest. Although President Lagos has taken significant and concrete steps to address Chile's traumatic past, an attentive reader notices that his discourse regularly shows signs of the same futuristic tenor that characterized the preceding transition governments. (It remains to be seen how Chile's newly elected president, Michelle Bachelet, will handle the memory issue.) Moreover, the question of how memory is being transmitted to and created by the next generation proves salient in a context in which many young Chileans have been socialized to adopt their parents' ideologies without receiving necessary tools to think critically about the convulsive experiences of the 1970s and 1980s.

Still, despite these negative aspects, there are also many positives. The *Informe Valech* has opened Chileans' eyes to the practice of torture in ways that, until now, were completely unfathomable. And Pinochet's detention in London, coupled with the recent Riggs Bank scandal and his loss of judicial immunity in certain prominent human rights cases, has caused the ex-dictator and his family to fall into deep disrepute. For a considerable number of once-fervent *pinochetistas*, the ninety-year-old general is now a dead political body, a nonentity, a "murderer *and* a thief." Yet the most significant advancement of all has been the destruction of the dictatorship's institutional legacy. In 2005, Chile's legislature passed a landmark series of reforms to the 1980 Constitution that largely eliminated long-standing authoritarian enclaves within the government.

The unfinished business of memory invites a reexamination of the archive, in all its breadth and complexity, and challenges us to think critically about the politics and ethics of its diverse textualities. Only by gaining a clear sense of the past, and of the operations that guide its telling, can Chile or other post-authoritarian societies begin to imagine a more democratic future.

Notes

Prologue: Two Angélicas, Two *Onces*

1. The dates of Chile's transition, both its beginning and its end, have been a great source of debate among analysts. While it is true that the transition was already taking place behind the scenes following the October 1988 plebiscite that ousted Pinochet, Patricio Aylwin, Chile's first transitional president, did not take office until 1990. Recognizing the complexity of the issue, for the purposes of this study I will designate 1990 as the transition's official start. I would argue that the transition will remain ongoing until greater degrees of truth and justice are achieved.

2. Support for Pinochet, as Marcela Said's recent documentary *I Love Pinochet* (2003) effectively illustrates, was not limited only to the upper classes but was expressed by a large number of the poor as well.

3. The origin of this cultural mythology is the sixth stanza of the first "Canto" in Alonso de Ercilla's epic poem *La Araucana* (1569): "Chile, fértil provincia y señalada/ en la región antártica famosa,/ de remotas naciones respetada/ por fuerte, principal y poderosa;/ la gente que produce es tan granada,/ tan soberbia, gallarda y belicosa,/ que no ha sido por rey jamás regida/ ni a extranjero dominio sometida" [Chile, fertile province, famous/ In the vast Antarctic region,/ Known to far-flung mighty nations/ For her queenly grace and courage,/ Has produced a race so noble,/ Dauntless, bellicose and haughty,/ That by king it ne'er was humbled/ Nor to foreign sway submitted](33).

4. Steve Stern aptly observes that "loose" individual memories are frequently narrated within "emblematic" collective frameworks that help give them meaning and make them understandable to both self and others. More than a question of memory versus forgetting, he adds, the memory debate in Chile is a question of "competing selective remembrances" (*Remembering,* xxvii).

Introduction: The Poetics and Politics of Memory

1. Constable and Valenzuela offer the following perception in their prologue to *A Nation of Enemies: Chile under Pinochet*: "Often we were struck by the vast psychological and cultural gap between these two Chiles—the winners and losers of the Pinochet years. The coup had frozen society at a point of great trauma and divisiveness, and all sectors—right and left, rich and poor, military and civilian—remained locked within separate microcosms, nursing their mutual fears and private dreams. Chile had become a nation of enemies. Not until the late 1980s did this hostility begin to thaw, as debate challenged propaganda and a spirit of reconciliation began to replace the climate of war" (10). Despite my general agreement with Constable and Valenzuela's characterization, I wonder about when and *if* the hostilities they mention actually "thawed." I

would argue that this thawing has only recently become overtly perceptible in society, and that in the late 1980s and early 1990s, animosities among Chileans still ran deep. I would ask: To what extent have the patent divisions so visible in the 1970s and 1980s become, in the transition, tacit, yet still existent, masked behind the rhetoric of reconciliation?

2. Adorno, sensing something insidious behind the idea of "coming to terms," asked the question "What Does Coming to Terms with the Past Mean?": "'Coming to terms with the past' does not imply a serious working through of the past, the breaking of its spell through an act of clear consciousness. It suggests, rather, wishing to turn the page and, if possible, wiping it from memory. The attitude that it would be proper for everything to be forgiven and forgotten by those who were wronged is expressed by the party that committed the injustice. . . . One wants to get free of the past: rightly so, since one cannot live in its shadow, and since there is no end to terror if guilt and violence are only repaid, again and again, with guilt and violence. But wrongly so, since the past one wishes to evade is still so intensely alive" (115). A reading of the Chilean transition, following Adorno, begs asking: How can Chile come to terms with its past as long as the forces and causes of the initial disaster remain present, potential, alive, or active in society? Traces of the dictatorship are ever-present in Chilean democracy today. In fact, many of Chile's most prominent politicians have careers that predate the military coup. As the thirtieth anniversary of the coup approached, the media pressured a number of these politicians to offer perspectives on the Pinochet years. Were they for or against the dictatorship? Where did they stand on human rights? Would they participate in the government's tribute to Allende, scheduled for 10 September 2003? Andrés Zaldívar, then-president of the Senate, prominent Christian Democrat and political opponent of Popular Unity, stated in an interview on TVN's *Medianoche* news program (25 August 2003) that he would not participate in the government's homage to Allende: "Los partidarios del Presidente Allende tienen todo el derecho a hacerle todos los homenajes que quieren, pero lo que no le pueden pedir a uno es no ser consecuente con lo que dijo y lo que hizo" [President Allende's supporters have every right to pay him all the tributes they want, but they have no right to ask me to be inconsistent with what I've said or done in the past]. Zaldívar's refusal to attend President Ricardo Lagos's tribute to Allende raised questions in the media about whether the Concertación should have a "unified" politics regarding the past.

3. First delivered as a lecture at the Sorbonne in 1882, Ernest Renan's "What Is a Nation?" is an attempt to think through the crisis of French national identity brought on by France's defeat in the Franco-Prussian War of 1870–71. Writing in the complex historical context of the postwar, Renan was aware of the threat German imperialism and the consolidation of the Second Reich posed to Europe's stability. What would "nationhood" mean in this new context where geographical boundaries within Europe were shifting? He argues that the basis for nationhood does not hinge on race, religion, language, geography, or even common interests. Instead, he defines the nation as "a soul, a spiritual principle"—"a large-scale solidarity" whose inhabitants voluntarily consider themselves citizens. Renan's essay is an important forerunner to later concep-

tualizations of nationhood like Benedict Anderson's idea of "imagined community." At the heart of Renan's essay lies the conviction that a "national idea" is based on the shared memory of a heroic past. Grief, Renan admits, binds citizens together, but if a nation is to survive into the future and solidarity among its citizens is ultimately to be strengthened, memories of "common glories" are essential. Consequently, forgetting what divides is crucial to the formation of nations.

4. Benjamin critiques the historicist tendency to empathize with history's "victors," claiming that such a tendency only benefits those in power. In his "Theses on the Philosophy of History," he defies a blind acceptance of the victors' history as legitimate and true, and he challenges the historical materialist to "brush history against the grain" (*Illuminations*, 257). History should not be perceived as a "continuity" whose parameters are laid down by the oppressors but rather as "discontinuity." The historian's charge is therefore to rescue from oblivion the voices of the expressionless.

5. I employ the term "expressionless" as it is used in (Felman, 2002).

6. In an interview with *Qué pasa* magazine on 23 August 2003, Marco Antonio Pinochet, Pinochet's son who is now implicated in the Riggs Bank scandal, offered the following statement about the military government's responsibility for human rights violations. His words reveal the typical *pinochetista* desire to "contextualize" the violations and to shift the burden of responsibility away from Pinochet to his secret police organizations:

"El gobierno está compuesto por muchas personas. Tampoco fueron las Fuerzas Armadas. Creo que fueron los sistemas creados para la seguridad del país que sobrerreaccionaron. . . . Se cometían excesos, pero, aunque sea fregado decirlo, hay que entender que gracias a esos organismos no había más terrorismo, más muertes. Tal vez habría sido mejor que no cometieran excesos y sufriéramos más muertes y más atentados, pero eso hubiera traído costos más grandes para el país. Es una hipótesis. No estoy justificando nada, no justifico ningún exceso, ninguna muerte. Tendría que estar mal para hacerlo. Estoy tratando de entender por qué actuaron así en una situación y una época histórica distinta a la de hoy" [The government was made up of many people. It wasn't just the armed forces. I think the national security organizations were the ones who overreacted. . . . Excesses were committed, but, even though it's tough to admit it, we have to understand that thanks to those organizations (DINA, CNI), there was not more terrorism and more death. Maybe it would have been better if there were no excesses, if we suffered more deaths and more terrorist attacks. But that would have had great costs for the country. It's a hypothesis. I'm not justifying anything. I don't justify any excess, any death. I would have to be crazy to do so. I am trying to understand why the military acted as it did in a different situation and historical time].

7. Cheyre's greatest desire is to end the "desfile de militares por tribunales" [the parade of military officials through the courts] and create a new, modern military, dissociated from Pinochet's legacy. This has been difficult to do, however, as loyalties within Chile's armed forces have splintered into an "old guard" (Pinochet's inner circle) and a "new guard" (those faithful to the project of renovation).

8. The *Concertación de Partidos por la Democracia* refers to a center-left coalition

of political parties that formed to oust Pinochet in the October 1988 plebiscite. This realignment of Chile's traditional tripartite system was decisive for overthrowing the regime. To date, the Concertación has produced two Christian Democratic presidents (Patricio Aylwin and Eduardo Frei) and one Socialist president (Ricardo Lagos). Michelle Bachelet, also a socialist and a former victim of Pinochet's repression, recently won the 2005 presidential election for the Concertación.

9. The definitions of these terms are elusive. What does it mean to achieve "national reconciliation"? Is reconciliation possible? On what levels does it occur? I will explore these questions more fully in Chapter 2.

10. Wilde's conception of historical events that "irrupt" into national memory reads as a theory of social trauma. Keeping with Freud's idea that traumatic memories break into individual consciousness suddenly and unexpectedly, Wilde's essay shows how Chile's traumatic past (also subject to unbidden, unexpected recurrences) is not a singular event or even a series of events in the past, but the ever-present, inescapable recurrence of that past in the present.

11. On reconciliation in Chile, Azún Candina Polomer has written: "Para que el concepto de reconciliación tenga sentido debió haber antes conciliación. Es decir, debe haber un *qué* (ese vínculo perdido, que antes existía y que ahora no está, pues se ha quebrado) y, podríamos agregar, también debe existir un *quién*: como expresara la hija de un detenido desaparecido, ella no puede reconciliarse con alguien que no conoce y que no le ha dicho nunca si se arrepiente o no de lo hecho. En el caso chileno parece faltar el *qué*, y también el *quién*. No había conciliación antes del '11' de 1973: tampoco la hubo después. Tampoco llegó en democracia. La reconciliación, entonces, se revela como un deseo, como un lugar común necesario, pero con contenidos contradictorios" [In order for the concept of reconciliation to make sense, there has to have been a prior conciliatory state. That is, there has to be a *what* (a lost link that existed before, but that is no longer because it has been broken) and a *who*. As the daughter of a *desaparecido* said, she cannot be reconciled with someone she does not know and who has never told her if he repents for what he has done. In Chile, the *who* and *what* are missing. There was no conciliation before 11 September 1973, nor was there conciliation after that date, nor did it come with democracy. Reconciliation, therefore, appears as a desire, a necessary commonplace, but full of contradictory meanings] (Polomer, "El día," 44).

12. Moulián evokes the metaphor of the *iceberg* sent by Chile's government to the 1996 Expo-Sevilla: "El iceberg representaba el estreno en sociedad del Chile Nuevo, limpiado, sanitizado, purificado por la larga travesía del mar. En el iceberg no había huella alguna de sangre, de desaparecidos. No estaba ni la sombra de Pinochet. Era como si Chile acabara de nacer" [The iceberg represented the societal debut of the New Chile: clean, sanitized, purified by the long crossing of the sea. There were no traces in the iceberg of blood or of the disappeared. There wasn't even a shadow of Pinochet. It was as if Chile had been born again] (*Chile Actual*, 35).

13. The National Stadium was used as a detention and torture center in the days

following the coup. In September 2003, the Lagos administration decided to turn the site into a national monument with artworks and a memorial.

14. It would be interesting to study the *Informe Rettig* as a memory text that offers and legitimates its own version of the past.

15. For a detailed history of the difficulties faced by the transition governments, see Loveman and Lira (*Las ardientes* and *El espejismo*) and Otano (*Crónica*).

16. It was on the occasion of the Mesa de Diálogo, for example, that the military first admitted having carried out its infamous "death flights." At the time of the Mesa, the armed forces divulged that they had dropped 151 bodies from airplanes into the sea. It has since come to light (November 2003) that this number, contrary to the military's conservative estimate, likely exceeded 400.

17. Pinochet's detention in London caused the military to put its "modernizing" mission on hold and shift its attention back to the Pinochet issue temporarily. Upon Pinochet's return (3 March 2000), an event that coincided with the appearance of the Mesa de Diálogo's final report, the military staged a hero's welcome for the ex-dictator at Santiago's Pudahuel airport. The armed forces' pomp and circumstance was a brazen demonstration of institutional support for Pinochet and ultimately served to aggravate improving civilian-military relations. Regarding the impact of Pinochet's return on the Mesa de Diálogo, Gregory Weeks notes: "The meetings advanced in fits and starts. There were core disagreements over such things as the military's assertion that the country had been at war. The president of the Chilean Commission on Human Rights, Jaime Castillo Velasco, rejected that interpretation as well as the idea that force was the only remaining solution in 1973. By March 2000 the Mesa had produced a general document that contained the points of consensus reached by the group, but the ceremony and surrounding controversy of Pinochet's return prompted many in the civilian contingent to refuse to sign it" (Weeks, *The Military*, 146).

18. Elizabeth Jelin refers to commemorative dates as "fechas in-felices" [unhappy dates]: "En la medida en que existen diferentes interpretaciones sociales del pasado, las fechas públicas mismas se convierten en objeto de disputas y conflictos. ¿Qué fechas deben ser conmemoradas? O, en otras palabras, ¿quién/es quiere/n conmemorar qué? Pocas veces hay consenso social al respecto. Y las mismas fechas tienen sentidos diferentes para actores políticos diversos que enmarcan sus memorias en los sentidos de las luchas políticas del ahora, del presente" [Insofar as different societal interpretations of the past exist, public dates themselves become objects of dispute and conflict. What dates should be commemorated? Or, in other words, who wants to commemorate what? There is seldom social consensus about that. The same dates hold different meanings for different political actors who frame their memories within the political struggles of the present] (Jelin, *Las conmemoraciones*, 1–2).

19. Pablo Longueira is one of Chile's most controversial political figures. In an interview on Televisión Nacional's *Medianoche* (19 August 2003), he expressed "una satisfacción ética-moral" [a moral and ethical satisfaction] with the UDI's response to the family members. He noted how grateful the families were to the party for bringing

their concerns to the national agenda. Yet, in the same breath, Longueira expressed the UDI's desire to "darle un sentido de futuro a estos treinta años y no seguir anclados al pasado" [give a sense of future to these thirty years and not remain anchored to the past]. When asked directly whether or not he knew in the 1980s that human rights violations were occurring, he became physically and verbally evasive: "Yo tenía quince años recién cumplidos para el 11 de septiembre. . . . Entré en política el año 80/81, pero no me dediqué intensamente" [I had barely turned fifteen for 11 September. . . . I entered politics around 1980–81, but I didn't dedicate myself intensely]. Longueira insinuated that those who today decry the dictatorship's human rights violations were also partially responsible for the breakdown of democracy. It is therefore, in his opinion, not easy to assign blame.

20. The officials who signed were Hermán Brady Roche, César Benavides Escobar, Carlos Forestier Raensgen, Washington Carrasco Fernández, Santiago Sinclair Oyaneder, Sergio Covarrubias Sanhueza, Jorge Lucar Figueroa, and Jorge Zincke Quiroz.

21. For the victims and their families, Lagos's failure to propose legislation that would eliminate the 1978 Amnesty Law was his proposal's biggest drawback. Lagos, however, insisted that the courts be left to interpret the law and make decisions about the legal responsibilities of perpetrators on trial. He has been reluctant to exercise executive pressure in judicial matters of human rights.

22. Though there has been much talk of "closure" in Chile, it remains an open question whether trauma victims can really achieve such a state. In reference to posttraumatic scenarios, the idea of "closure" needs to be defined more rigorously. I am reminded of Jean Améry's observation that "whoever was tortured, stays tortured. Torture is ineradicably burned into him, even when no clinically objective traces can be detected" (*At the Mind's Limits*, 34). Perhaps it is best to speak of an ongoing process of healing that takes place over time—a process which may, in fact, never truly, or only with great difficulty, reach an end.

23. Pinochet's London detention confirmed that the General still had the support of a significant sector of Chileans. Most estimates confirm the number to be somewhere around one third of the population, although that number is now steadily declining.

24. The *Revista de crítica cultural*'s articles have reflected (primarily from the local Chilean viewpoint, but frequently from an international perspective) on issues as diverse as gender, modernity, the free market, the city, the status of cultural studies, the function of politics, structures of power, the logic of consensus, and the manipulation of memory. Numerous dossiers have been dedicated to debates on memory (see especially numbers 5, 17, 18 and 22), making the topic a cornerstone of the journal's composition and intellectual mission.

25. "A Klee painting named 'Angelus Novus' shows an angel looking as though he is about to move away from something he is fixedly contemplating. His eyes are staring, his mouth is open, his wings are spread. This is how one pictures the angel of history. His face is turned toward the past. Where we perceive a chain of events, he sees one single catastrophe which keeps piling wreckage upon wreckage and hurls it in front of

his feet. The angel would like to stay, awaken the dead, and make whole what has been smashed. But a storm is blowing from Paradise; it has got caught in his wings with such violence that the angel can no longer close them. The storm irresistibly propels him into the future to which his back is turned, while the pile of debris before him grows skyward. This storm is what we call progress" (Benjamin, *Illuminations*, 257–258).

26. Ricardo Piglia's novel, *Respiración artificial* [Artificial Respiration], opens with an ambiguous question: "¿Hay una historia?" [Is there a story?] (13). With this sentence, Piglia capitalizes on the double meaning of the word *historia* in Spanish (history/story), thus calling into question both the possibility of writing a univocal "history" and of writing a "story" of the disaster.

Chapter 1. The Poetics of Impossibility (Diamela Eltit's *El padre mío*)

1. The Commission was created by "Supreme Decree #355" on 25 April 1990.

2. *El padre mío* was republished in a second edition for the thirtieth anniversary of the coup (Santiago: LOM, 2003).

3. The film reels were shown publicly only once in 1996 at Santiago's Instituto Cultural Francés [French Cultural Institute]. I would like to thank Lotty Rosenfeld for sharing the film reels with me, as they have given me a better sense of the genesis of the Padre Mío project.

4. Readers of Latin American literature may perceive a similarity between Eltit's *loco* and a figure like Moncada in Arguedas's *El zorro de arriba y el zorro de abajo* [The Fox from up Above and the Fox from Down Below], a character who "speaks the truth that madmen speak." Ricardo Piglia's "La loca y el relato del crimen" [The Madwoman and the Story of the Crime] is also an important text that raises questions about the relationships among testimony, madness, and truth.

5. The fragment was a common aesthetic element used by many Chilean artists under dictatorship, particularly artists of the *Avanzada*. For a discussion of the *Avanzada*, see Richard's *La insubordinación de los signos* [The Insubordination of Signs]. Regarding her use of the fragment, Eltit has said the following: "Frente a lo monolítico, frente a lo hegemónico, me parece que tengo una política de fragmentos. Me interesa lo heterogéneo y lo heterodoxo; me interesa como proyecto de escritura. Y me interesa precisamente porque me parece que el sujeto escritural no es homogéneo sino un conjunto de antagonismos y diferencias. Pero estamos obligados por los aparatos sociales a unir esas partes (hasta donde se pueda, por supuesto). Pero no creo que haya un sujeto único, sino que dentro de uno coexisten muchos sujetos, muchas pulsiones, muchas interferencias, muchas crisis, muchas fracturas. Entonces, a mí me parece adecuado, en ese sentido, elegir el fragmento como una opción de escritura" [Therefore, pitted against the monolithic and the hegemonic, I feel I practice a politics of the fragment. I like the heterogeneous and the heterodox; I am interested in these things as a writing project. I am interested in them precisely because I feel that the writing subject is not homogeneous, but rather a collection of antagonisms and differences. We are obliged by society to unify these differences (to the extent possible, of course). But I don't believe that there is such a thing as a unified subject. Rather, within a person there

are many subjects, many impulses, many interferences, many crises, many fractures. Because of this, it seems fitting to me to elect the fragment as an option for writing]" (Lazzara, *Los años de silencio*, 125).

6. The Pinochet regime's official story is well known and documented in books like *El día decisivo* [The Decisive Day] (1980) and *Camino recorrido: memorias de un soldado* [My Path: Memoirs of a Soldier] (1990–1994), both ghost-written works attributed to Pinochet. See also Raquel Correa and Elizabeth Subercaseaux's book-length interview with Pinochet, *Ego Sum Pinochet* [I Am Pinochet] (1989).

7. Baltra Montaner (1988) has done the most complete study to date on the way in which the Pinochet regime curtailed freedom of expression. Her book catalogues the military's official censorship decrees and the names of many writers and journalists who were persecuted by the regime. Decree Law #5 (1973), established in the Code of Military Justice, gives a sense of the severity of censorship under Pinochet: "Toda persona que sea sorprendida durante el Estado de Sitio imprimiendo o difundiendo por cualquier medio propaganda subversiva y atentatoria contra el Supremo Gobierno, será juzgada seriamente por los Tribunales Militares de Tiempo de Guerra y se les aplicarán drásticamente las penas correspondientes" [During the State of Siege, anyone who by any means is caught printing or distributing subversive propaganda against the Supreme Government will be judged harshly by the military's Wartime Tribunals and punishments will be applied drastically]" (12). Military Band #11 (1973) established an office of censorship: "Se ha designado una Oficina de Censura de Prensa, que funcionará en la Academia Politécnica Militar del Ejército (San Ignacio #242), que tendrá bajo su control las publicaciones escritas autorizadas; el sistema a emplear será el de CENSURA a la edición impresa" [An Office of Censorship of the Press has been established. It will function in the Army's Polytechnic Institute (San Ignacio #242), and will have control over all authorized publications. The system to be implemented will be the CENSORSHIP of published materials] (10). Many such offices were established throughout Chile and functioned until official censorship was lifted in 1983.

8. Eltit also works with the figure of the *loco* in another project entitled *El infarto del alma* (1994). This project, done in conjunction with Chilean photographic artist Paz Errázuriz, juxtaposes texts and photographs of mental patients interned in the famous psychiatric hospital in Putaendo, Chile. The project differs from *El padre mío*, however, in an important way. Whereas in *El infarto del alma* Eltit fictionally constructs the words of the mental patients, in *El padre mío* she simply transcribes the vagabond's own words. Both projects, however, share in a common a desire to give voice to the voiceless and express an overarching concern with marginality and exclusion in their relation to power.

9. Nelly Richard echoes this point elegantly in *Residuos y metáforas* [Cultural Residues]: "En el caso de *El padre mío*, la única 'verdad' insocializable que exhibe el relato evocando el Chile enfermo de la dictadura, es su desfile hiperbólico de identificaciones falsas, de referencias inconexas, de frases desintegradas, de sentencias erráticas, de locas interpretaciones" [In the case of *El padre mío*, the only nonsocializable "truth" exhibited by the story evoking the sick Chilean world of the dictatorship is its hyperbolic

parade of false identifications, disconnected references, disintegrating phrases, erratic pronouncements, and crazy interpellations] (84, 53 in trans.).

10. Marguerite Feitlowitz's impressive analysis of the Argentine junta's discourse is enlightening for understanding how military regimes, despite their guise of absolute candor, dismantle the relationship between *language* and *truth*. Feitlowitz notes that as the discourse of the military regime began to penetrate ever more deeply into the collective psyche, people became disoriented when they found that language, though "comprehensible" (and seemingly transparent), was "incongruous" with reality. She quotes one Mother of the Plaza de Mayo as having noted that the military's rhetoric "made you *psychotic*. . . . We could barely 'read,' let alone 'translate' the world around us. And that was exactly what they wanted" (*A Lexicon*, 20).

11. Doris Sommer's work on Rigoberta Menchú (1991), for example, shows that "secrets" or intentional silences can also be a strategy used by the testimonial subject when engaged in dialogue with an interviewer.

12. I will address the topic of shame at greater length in Chapter 2.

13. The question of how to say the "unsayable" is a source of reflection not only for Eltit but also for other authors who have written about dictatorships. The Argentine novelist, Ricardo Piglia, for example, reflects on this question in his novel *Respiración artificial* [Artificial Respiration]. Toward the end of the novel, one of Piglia's characters thinks about the way in which Kafka used literature as a space in which to probe the limits of the sayable: "¿Cómo hablar de lo indecible? Ésa es la pregunta que la obra de Kafka trata una y otra vez de contestar. O mejor, dijo, su obra es la única que de un modo refinado y sutil se atreve a hablar de lo indecible, de eso que no se puede nombrar. ¿Qué diríamos hoy que es lo indecible? El mundo de Auschwitz. Ese mundo está más allá del lenguaje, es la frontera donde están las alambradas del lenguaje. Alambre de púas: el equilibrista camina, descalzo, solo allá arriba y trata de ver si es posible decir algo sobre lo que está del otro lado" [How to speak of the unspeakable? That is the question that Kafka's work tries constantly to answer. Or better yet, he said, Kafka's is the only body of work that, in a subtle and refined way, dares to speak of the unspeakable, of that which cannot be named. What might the unspeakable be today? The world of Auschwitz. That world is beyond language. It is the limit where we find the barbed wire of language. Barbed wire: the tightrope-walker walks, barefoot and alone, and tries to see if it is possible to say anything about what's on the other side] (Piglia, *Respiración artificial*, 209–210).

14. Diamela Eltit made the following remarks about her search for a subject: ". . . desde 1980, más o menos, estaba estableciendo yo un recorrido subjetivo por la ciudad. Quería yo . . . no sé lo que quería. No sé lo que quería. Quería no más. Quería. Tenía un deseo de ciudad, pero no sabía cuál era exactamente el objeto de mi deseo hasta que encontré al Padre Mío. Y en ese camino deseante me había encontrado con muchos sujetos marginales, todos ellos, por supuesto, relevantes. Sin embargo, cuando encontré al Padre Mío, me di cuenta que efectivamente mi deseo se encarnaba. Ese *quería*, *quería*, *quería*, *quería* encontró un cuerpo con el cual establecer una estética" [. . . since 1980, more or less, I had been taking a subjective journey through the city. I wanted . . . I

don't know what I wanted. I don't know what I wanted. I just wanted. I had a desire for the city, but I didn't know exactly what the object of my desire was until I met El Padre Mío. On that path of desire I had met many marginal subjects—all of them, of course, relevant. Nevertheless, when I met El Padre Mío, I understood that my desire had become flesh. That *wanting, wanting, wanting, wanting* found a body through and upon which to establish an aesthetic] (Lazzara, *Los años de silencio*, 129).

15. By 1983 the military government's policies had driven Chile into a severe economic crisis, which in turn prompted rowdy protests by labor unions. These protests set the stage for more massive demonstrations all over Santiago in which the opposition called for an end to dictatorship. The regime would not fall, however, until after the mobilization of the NO campaign and the Concertación's victory in the October 1988 plebiscite.

16. In his essay "La insurrección de las sobras" [The Insurrection of Remains], Federico Galende notes that the "residual" and the "fragmentary" are what historical narratives tend to leave aside. He claims that these fragments of voices and experiences ". . . habrán de comunicarse con 'lengua secreta' sus derechos a la contemporaneidad. Esto es lo que los desperdicios le deben a la historia, pues sin ellos no tendríamos críticas ni revoluciones, sino apenas el juego de un 'tiempo liso' que buscaría cerrarse sobre sí mismo" [. . . will have to make known, through a "secret language," their right to contemporaneity. This is what "remains" owe to history, for without them we would not have critiques or revolutions, but rather a "smoothed-over conception of time" that would seek to devour itself] (24).

Chapter 2. The Poetics of Reconciliation (Luz Arce's *El infierno*)

1. Although I will only consider Luz Arce in this chapter so as to do justice to the complexities of her individual case, I intend for the framework I establish for analyzing *El infierno* to serve as a starting point for reading similar narratives like Merino's *Mi verdad*.

2. A number of survivors of the Chilean concentration camps have questioned whether the facts of Arce's testimony are accurate or sufficient. Lautaro Videla, for example, whose sister Lumi was killed by DINA in November 1974 and whose story Arce recounts in her book, published an accusatory article in the magazine *Apsi* (March 1991) bearing the title "Lo que no vio Luz Arce" [What Luz Arce Did Not See]. His goal is to complete and correct Arce's account of his sister's detention and murder.

3. The following paragraph is taken from Arce's declaration before the Truth and Reconciliation Commission (9 October 1990). The complete transcript is housed in the archive of the Vicaría de la Solidaridad, Santiago de Chile: "Deseo hacer presente que declaro ante esta Comisión por un deber de conciencia, porque creo que tengo una deuda, y me parece necesario hacerlo, si esto contribuye de algún modo a reparar mis acciones, derivadas de mi colaboración con la DINA y el hecho de haber sido funcionaria de ese organismo. Me importa también contribuir al esclarecimiento de la verdad, y a la realización de la justicia, en un contexto de reconciliación. Desde hace varios años, he experimentado un proceso de encuentro con el Señor, y he vivido profundamente

mi compromiso con la Fe cristiana, y por eso, dentro de mis posibilidades, quiero ser fiel con los dictados de mi conciencia" [I want to add that I am testifying before this commission as a matter of conscience, because I believe that I owe a debt, and it seems necessary to do so, if it contributes in some way to making amends for my collaboration with DINA and for having been a functionary in that organization. It is also important to me to contribute to the construction of the truth and to the realization of justice in a context of reconciliation. For a number of years I have been going through a process of coming to know the Lord, and I have lived in accordance with my deep commitment to the Christian faith. For this reason, insofar as I am able, I want to remain faithful to the dictates of my conscience.]

4. Perhaps the long, rocky history of the Chilean transition belies the very possibility of reconciliation, particularly in the short term. In his inaugural speech delivered at the National Stadium on 12 March 1990, Patricio Aylwin founded the transition based on a demand for truth, a desire for justice "en la medida de lo possible " [insofar as it was possible] and a wish for national reconciliation. But reconciliation, specifically in the political arena, implied a future-oriented politics of forgetting. The following words, spoken by Aylwin at his inauguration, capture the tenor of the Concertación's project in the early 1990s and exemplify the type of wishful political discourse to which I am referring: "Considero mi deber evitar que el tiempo se nos vaya de entre las manos mirando hacia el pasado. La salud espiritual de Chile nos exige encontrar fórmulas para cumplir estas tareas de saneamiento moral, de modo que más temprano que tarde llegue el momento en que, reconciliados, todos miremos con confianza hacia el futuro y aunemos esfuerzos en la tarea que la patria nos demanda" [I consider it my duty to make sure that time does not slip away from us as we focus on the past. Chile's spiritual health demands that we find formulas for achieving moral healing such that, sooner rather than later, the moment arrives in which, reconciled, we can all look confidently toward the future and turn our attention to the tasks that the fatherland demands] (Aylwin, *La transición*, 21).

5. Susan Brison reminds us that although the reasons narrative plays such an important role in the aftermath of trauma remain something of a mystery, trauma survivors have repeatedly stressed the importance of "living to tell" and "telling to live," that is, the importance of narration as a necessary means for surviving and coping with trauma. She writes: "The act of bearing witness to the trauma facilitates this shift [from being the subject of another's speech to being the subject of one's own speech], not only by transforming traumatic memory into a narrative that can be worked into a survivor's sense of self and view of the world, but also by reintegrating the survivor into a community, reestablishing connections essential to selfhood" (Brison, *Aftermath*, 68).

6. Jean Améry makes the important point that recurring images of trauma often make it impossible for the victim to forget. Even many years beyond the camp, the torture he suffered remains an inescapable reality: "It was over for awhile. It still is not over. Twenty-two years later I am still dangling over the ground by dislocated arms, panting and accusing myself. In such an instance there is no 'repression.' Does one repress an unsightly birthmark? One can have it removed by a plastic surgeon, but the

skin that is transplanted in its place is not the skin with which one feels naturally at ease" (*At the Mind's Limits*, 36).

7. Agamben reads this last type of shame (often referred to as *survivor guilt*) in the writings of Primo Levi, Bruno Bettelheim, and Elie Wiesel: "I live, therefore I am guilty" (*Remnants*, 87–95). This is the shame that arises when a survivor realizes that he or she has lived in the place of another.

8. Arce's decision to speak as a victim—to say in no uncertain terms that she is *not* a perpetrator—amounts to what Sartre once called the "radicalization of evil." When evil is radicalized, judgment of one's actions is accepted, but reversed, so that the brunt of the shame falls not on oneself but on the ultimate perpetrators of the crime. For more complete commentary on the "radicalization of evil" see Heller, *The Power*, 23.

9. The "cog in the wheel" argument brings to mind the Argentine concept of "Due Obedience" [Obediencia Debida], often invoked by the military during the public trials of the Junta (1985). The argument that one was "just following orders" is well exemplified, too, in Horacio Verbitsky's book *El vuelo* [The Flight], another confessionary text in which a retired Argentine military officer, Francisco Scilingo, publicly exposes the military's crimes and his own role with respect to the torture center known as ESMA [Escuela de Mecánica de la Armada/ Navy School of Mechanics]. See especially Chapter 10, "El juicio de los hombres" [The Judgment of Mankind].

10. Agamben wonders what borders separate ethics from legality and posits Adolf Eichmann as a quintessential case in which a perpetrator felt himself "guilty before God, not the law." Eichmann's case (and perhaps Arce's too) begs certain questions: Is claiming responsibility for one's actions valuable only if one is willing to do so *both* morally and legally? If ethics is anterior to the law, how then is it possible to admit moral guilt, while refusing to be held legally accountable for one's actions? (Agamben, *Remnants*, 21–24)

11. The 1978 Amnesty Law made it all but impossible to prosecute perpetrators during the transition's early years and has been one of the greatest impediments to justice in Chile. José Zalaquett, one of Aylwin's close political advisors and a member of the Truth and Reconciliation Commission, conscious of the difficulties of obtaining justice, offers the idea that in democratic transitions acceptance of moral responsibility may be even more important than judicial action, since justice can only be meted out symbolically and imperfectly: "In the moral reconstruction we are discussing, punishment is of lesser importance. It's important, but acknowledgement is more important. . . . [P]unishment is an instrument . . . [b]ut the bigger objective was this more comprehensive theory of moral reconstruction. It includes elements of shaming, truth telling, institution building, punishment, but also of forgiveness, to the extent that forgiveness is legitimate" (qtd. in Roht-Arriaza, "The Need," 206). In another moment, Zalaquett comments that unfortunately "the military wanted it both ways: no punishment and no shame" (Roht-Arriaza, "The Need," 203).

12. In an argument that to some extent seems to counter Levi's, Hannah Arendt holds that although "the system cannot be left out of account altogether," we must be

wary of shifting responsibility from the individual onto the system. Individuals are ultimately responsible for their own actions. Regarding the Eichmann trial, where the defense attorneys tried to portray the collaborator as a simple cog in the machinery of the totalitarian state, Arendt writes: "In a courtroom there is no system on trial, no History or historical trend, no ism, anti-Semitism for instance, but a person, and if the defendant happens to be a functionary, he stands accused precisely because even a functionary is still a human being, and it is in this capacity that he stands trial" (*Responsibility*, 30, 32).

13. Both Eltit (*Emergencias*) and Richard (*Residuos*) have taken a particularly critical stance toward Arce and have condemned her for her moral shortcomings. Perhaps only Hernán Vidal (*Política cultural*) has offered a more favorable reading of Arce's testimony.

14. In a revealing passage, Arce writes a page-long "catalog" of her false identities: "El oficial me entregó un archivador con toda la documentación que comprueba mi calidad de funcionaria de la DINA y la CNI. Contenía las hojas de vida, el original de mi renuncia a la CNI, presentada en octubre de 1979 . . . todas las tarjetas de identificación que tuve tanto en DINA como en CNI . . . la chapa completa incluyendo cédula y pasaporte a nombre de Mariana del Carmen Burgos Jiménez, identidad con la que viajé y viví en la República Oriental de Uruguay. Cédulas de identidad falsas a nombre de Ana María Vergara Rojas . . . otra a nombre de Patricia Pizarro" [The official handed me a file containing all the documentation that proved my role as a functionary of DINA and CNI . . . my complete false identity including an ID and a passport in the name of Mariana del Carmen Burgos Jiménez—the identity with which I traveled and lived in the Oriental Republic of Uruguay—[f]alse ID cards in the name of Ana María Vergara Rojas . . . and another in the name of Patricia Pizarro] (Arce, *El infierno*, 314–315).

15. Foucault delivered his lecture "Christianity and Confession" in English at Dartmouth College on 24 November 1980.

16. See particularly Tertullian's "On Repentance."

17. Dori Laub emphasizes the importance of an "empathic listener" as a necessary precondition for verbalizing one's story: "The absence of an empathic listener, or more radically, the absence of an *addressable other*, an other who can hear the anguish of one's memories and thus affirm and recognize their realness, annihilates the story" (Felman and Laub, 68).

18. For more complete information on Romo, see Nancy Guzmán's extensive interview: *Romo: confesiones de un torturador*. Romo, currently in prison, holds firm to his position that he carried out a patriotic duty by torturing left-wing militants. He states that his conscience is clean and that he would act in the same way if given a second opportunity. At one point in his interview with Guzmán, he mentions in his typically brash manner that the vast majority of torture victims "talked": "En la tortura todos hablan. . . . Los cabros del MIR eran valientes, pero igual . . . todos tarde o temprano cantan como pajaritos" [Under torture, everyone talks. . . . The kids from MIR were

brave, but they talked just the same . . . [E]veryone, sooner or later, sings like a bird] (Guzmán, *Romo*, 100). Later, Romo refers specifically to the cases of La Flaca Alejandra and Luz Arce: "La Luz fue re harto torturá, a ella hasta le dispararon en un pie y casi se fue cortá, pero la Flaca no. Después ella se acostó con todo el mundo igual que la Luz, así compraron su vida, ellas eligieron eso. Claro, ahora se quejan y cuentan y hablan pero cuando andaban como perros falderos y no les importaban los que habían sido sus compañeros, eso no lo cuentan na" [Luz was tortured a lot. They even shot her in the foot, almost cut her in half. But not la Flaca. Later she slept with everybody, just like Luz. That was how they bought their lives. They chose it. Sure, now they complain and speak out, but they don't say anything about when they were like lapdogs who didn't care at all about those who had been their *compañeros*] (*Romo*, 100).

19. Regarding this encounter with Romo in 1992, Arce added some relevant details in our personal interviews that point to further acts of compassion toward her former torturer: "Me pidió papel higiénico y papel para escribir cartas a su mujer. Le dije que sí, que le enviaría. Me pidió dinero porque dijo no tener desodorante, jabón y esas cosas esenciales. Como a mí me llevarían en vehículo a casa, le pasé todo lo que tenía en la cartera y con posterioridad le envié con gente de la Policía lo que me pidió: papel higiénico, un block de papel para cartas aéreas y unos sobres para cartas. Me nació hacerlo. A ninguna persona, ni al peor criminal, le negaría esas cosas. Yo sé lo que es carecer de ellas, sobre todo, si uno está en prisión" [He asked me for toilet paper and paper to write letters to his wife. I told him yes, that I'd send it to him. He asked me for money because he said he didn't have deodorant, soap or other essential items. Since they were going to take me home in a car, I gave him everything I had in my purse and later sent him the other things he asked for via the police: toilet paper, a block of paper for air mail letters and some envelopes. I did it out of the goodness of my heart. I wouldn't deny those things to anyone, not even to the worst criminal. I know what it's like to be without, especially when you're in prison].

20. Aylwin's use of the word "excesses" is a curious reiteration of the military regime's own vocabulary.

21. Loveman and Lira write: "La consigna de 'reconciliación' respondía al anhelo de paz de las mayorías; también al deseo de terminar con el estado casi permanente de amenaza y de miedo experimentado por muchos chilenos entre 1973 y 1990. En el debate cotidiano, sin embargo, se perdían las implicaciones y los significados de la 'reconciliación' y de las diferencias entre los requisitos propios de reconciliaciones personales, sociales o políticas. Existía una confusión permanente entre los duelos y dolores personales, las condiciones morales y religiosas para 'perdonar' y 'reconciliarse' y los requisitos jurídicos y políticos para la justicia y la convivencia" [The term "reconciliation" responded to the majority's desire for peace and to a desire to end the nearly permanent state of threats and fear felt by many Chileans between 1973 and 1990. Nevertheless, in quotidian debates, the implications and meanings of "reconciliation" were lost, as were the differences among the specific requirements for personal, social, and political reconciliation. There was permanent confusion regarding personal pain, the moral and religious conditions for "pardoning" and "reconciling" and the judicial

and political requirements for justice and communal living] (Loveman and Lira, *Las ardientes cenizas*, 14–15).

22. Derrida holds that it is not the right of heads-of-state to forgive in the place of victims. He distinguishes between "pure forgiveness" (which is something that can occur only between victims and victimizers) and political processes of reconciliation (which involve third-party arbiters): "Of course, no one would decently dare to object to the imperative of reconciliation. It would be better to put an end to crimes and discords. Once again, however, I believe it necessary to distinguish between forgiveness and this process of reconciliation, this reconstitution of a health or a 'normality,' as necessary and desirable as it would appear through amnesties, the 'work of mourning,' etc. A 'finalized' forgiveness is not forgiveness; it is only a political strategy or a psycho-therapeutic economy" (Derrida, *On Cosmopolitanism*, 50).

23. As I conclude the writing of this book, there have been certain recent developments that might be taken as positive signs that the military is beginning to heed society's demands for atonement. Two events, in particular, stand out. First, on 22 November 2003 a group of former detainees from the concentration camp at Isla Dawson were guided by 20 representatives of the Chilean Navy to the remote island in the Strait of Magellan where they had been imprisoned in 1973. The visit, inspired by the thirtieth anniversary of the coup, was agreed to by the navy at the behest of Defense Minister Michelle Bachelet, whose father had been a victim of the Pinochet regime. The Chilean media portrayed the return to Isla Dawson as a moving experience for all involved, and focused on images of reconciliation: most notably the image of former prisoners and naval officers singing together an impromptu version of the Chilean national anthem. *El Mercurio* described the event as a "ritual of spiritual purification." Second, on 2 December 2003, the Chilean Air Force arranged a ceremony in Quintero (Region V) in which it welcomed back into the "military family" 130 ex-members of the Air Force who had been dishonorably discharged and judged as war criminals in 1973. In the ceremony, the former airmen's military ID cards were returned to them and their benefits reinstated (a symbolic restitution of identity). This event was portrayed by the media as an emblem of reconciliation *within* the military's ranks.

24. Derrida's definition of "pure forgiveness" reads like a secular version of Christian rhetoric. Derrida, in fact, is interested, precisely, in how the "Abrahamic language" of forgiveness and reconciliation saturates political discourses in post-authoritarian, post-conflict societies.

25. The following elements might be considered some of the pre-conditions for reconciliation: (1) truth-telling; (2) acknowledgment of wrongdoing by perpetrators; (3) public recognition of victims' suffering in the form of monuments, apologies, ceremonies, commemorative dates, reparations, and so on; (4) justice; (5) forgiveness or empathy; and (6) solidifying broken bonds of trust. However, these pre-conditions, taken individually or collectively, may not be necessary or sufficient.

26. The ability to punish may not, however, be required for forgiveness. The question remains open for debate: Can there be forgiveness without justice?

Chapter 3. Presence and Absence (On Art and Disappearance)

1. In reference to Argentina's disappeared, Marguerite Feitlowitz notes, "In Argentina the infernal mist of *Nacht und Nebel* [Night and Fog] was ushered in by the unprecedented, obscurant rage of a single word: *desaparecido*. It was coined by the Argentine military as a way of denying the kidnap, torture, and murder of thousands of citizens. Then-commander of the army Roberto Viola put it this way: A *desaparecido* was someone who was 'absent forever,' whose 'destiny' it was to 'vanish.' Officially, a *desaparecido* was neither living nor dead, neither here nor there. The explanation was at once totally vague and resoundingly final. Night and fog drawn like a curtain in the collective mind" (*A Lexicon*, 49).

2. Notwithstanding the parallels I draw, I by no means wish to imply that *Muselmänner* and *desaparecidos* should be understood as equivalent terms. Each term undoubtedly points to a particular historical context that cannot and should not be reduced to the other. Nevertheless, I think certain aspects of Agamben's reflections can be extrapolated to the *desaparecidos* of Latin America, and it is on these points of intersection that I will focus here.

3. Antonia García ("Por un análisis") points out, quite insightfully, that one of the mechanisms of disappearance under Pinochet was "indiscretion." Although the regime made every effort to cover up its crimes, every so often a dead body would intentionally appear before the public eye as a scare tactic, as a way of saying "this could happen to you." Such was the case with Lumi Videla. In 1974 Lumi Videla's body was thrown over the wall of Santiago's Italian Embassy as a way of threatening militants who had sought refuge within and of cowing the public in general.

4. One of the most striking images of the Chilean post-dictatorship is that of family members holding shovels, digging in remote mountainous or desert areas to find bodies of their disappeared loved ones. As has happened repeatedly throughout Chile's recent history, when the government fails family members, they have not been afraid to take matters into their own hands. The "digging" photos testify to the families' obstinate will and to the overwhelming importance of unearthing material traces for burial.

5. Although during the Mesa de Diálogo the military recognized that some bodies of the disappeared had been thrown into the sea, no individual military official ever spoke publicly about how such missions were carried out. This changed on 7 July 2003 when a retired officer, Subofficial Juan Carlos Molina H., testified on TVN's nightly news program *24 Horas* that he had participated in two missions in 1979 to dispose of the bodies of nine *desaparecidos*. In his interview with reporter Claudio Fariña, Molina admitted having witnessed the dumping of bodies from Puma helicopters into waters off the coast of Quintero. This type of dumping, which according to Molina continued to occur until at least 1981, was a reaction by the military to the 1978 discovery (and subsequent publicity) of a common grave located at Lonquén, outside Santiago. The military's fear of future discoveries caused them to dig up victims' remains and dispose of them in undisclosed locations. Molina, a mechanic asked to provide technical support for the helicopters, told Fariña that the bodies were placed in sacks and bound to railroad ties so that they would sink in the ocean. Though for years he could not admit

what he witnessed, the death of his child in 2003 prompted him to come forward and voice his shame publicly. TVN's report was an important public revelation of the official silences that had surrounded such missions for thirty years. A similar Argentine testimony can be found in Horacio Verbitsky's interviews with Francisco Scilingo (*El vuelo*).

6. To date, Caiozzi's documentary has not been shown in its entirety on Chilean network television. It has aired only in severely fragmented form late at night (as part of an interview with Caiozzi) on TVN. The cable channel SKY has shown the documentary in full, but every other network (either on cable or in syndication) has shied away.

7. The film has also had a transformative effect on individual viewers. A screening at the 1998 Valdivia Film Festival left many audience members in tears. According to Caiozzi, one unsuspecting *pinochetista* in the crowd approached him after the film and told him that although she had always staunchly supported the ex-dictator, *Fernando ha vuelto* made her realize, many years later, that "Pinochet went too far." (This anecdote, presented by Kristen Sorensen at SUNY Albany's conference on "Democratization in Latin America: 30 Years after Chile's 9/11," 10–12 October 2003, strikes me as a moving reminder of art's ability to effect change in the real world).

8. The most complete study of the Agrupación's strategies of resistance is Vidal's *Dar la vida por la vida*.

9. Sandra Lorenzano calls attention to the importance of the *siluetazo* in Argentina: "El 'siluetazo,' el *Nunca Más*, fueron modos de recuperar a nuestros desaparecidos. También lo fueron, desde la cultura, algunas voces marginadas: unas pocas revistas, ciertos grupos de rock, novelas publicadas dentro y fuera del país. La parte más consciente y combativa de nuestra cultura jugó así el papel de Antígona. Como ella, desafió la ley del Estado enterrando simbólicamente a quienes permanecían insepultos 'fuera de los muros de la ciudad'" [The "siluetazo" and *Never Again* were ways of reviving our disappeared. In the realm of culture, so too were certain marginalized voices: a few journals, certain rock groups, novels published within and outside the country. The most conscious and combative part of our culture thus played the role of Antigone. Like her, they challenged the law of the State, burying symbolically those who remained unburied "beyond the walls of the city"] (Lorenzano, *Escrituras*, 53). On the *siluetazo*, see also Taylor, *Disappearing Acts*.

10. Another important photographic installation was put together for the thirtieth anniversary of the military coup (11 September 2003). Four walls of photographs of the disappeared were displayed at Santiago's Salvador Allende Museum as part of an exhibit entitled "Memory and Hope: 30 Years after the Coup."

11. The ceramic tiles were made by artisan Sergio Porflidt and plastic artist Luis Acosta.

12. For a complete history of Juan Alsina's murder by military officials on 19 September 1973, see Jordá Sureda, *Martirologio*.

13. I bring Caruth into my discussion for her emphasis on trauma's recurrence as well as for her compelling insights regarding the voice that emanates from the wound.

I would like to note, though, that I see certain shortcomings in her theory, especially regarding the notion of trauma as "missed experience." Contrary to Caruth, I am convinced that many survivors do, in fact, remember certain aspects of the traumatic moment, either cognitively or somatically, and that these memories subsequently influence the narratives survivors produce. The availability of narrative frameworks for speaking trauma strikes me as a separate (though related) issue from whether memory traces are registered. I say this because the absence of *modes of narrating* does not necessarily imply that the experience was "missed" entirely. Memory traces may exist even if no framework for organizing them does. The problem of relaying trauma is therefore fundamentally a narrative problem. I am left questioning the implications of Caruth's choice of terms: Is it really true that in the case of *all* survivors traumatic experience is "missed"? I find it difficult to generalize on this point and choose to leave the question open for debate.

Chapter 4. Lenses of Memory (On Narrating Villa Grimaldi)

1. For a detailed history of some of Chile's sites of memory, see Tamayo and Lagos, "Casas de tortura."

2. Between 1974 and 1990, the house at 1367 José Domingo Cañas served two primary functions. For a number of years it was used to house unmarried agents of DINA and CNI, and later, it became an orphanage operated by SENAME [Servicio Nacional de Menores/ National Service for Minors]. When the dictatorship ended, the house was abandoned until legislation passed in 1996 stating that all properties expropriated by the dictatorship should be returned to their original owners. Ownership thus passed back into the hands of a Brazilian university professor who was living in São Paolo at the time. When the professor decided to sell the property, human rights activists immediately began lobbying the Chilean government to purchase it and establish a cultural center for human rights. The proposal, however, became mired in red tape and never came to fruition. Meanwhile, a neighbor who operated a toy factory located at José Domingo Cañas 1395, Pablo Rochet Araujo, purchased the property and destroyed the house in order to expand his workshop.

In the case of Londres 38, soon after it ceased to function as a detention center, the house was given by the dictatorship to the Instituto O'Higginiano (named, ironically, for Chile's "liberator," Bernardo O'Higgins). The Institute's leadership, comprising mostly retired military officers, quickly changed the number on the building from 38 to 40 so that people looking for the site would not be able to find it.

3. An article entitled "La prueba de la blancura" [The Test of Whiteness], published in the online version of the Chilean magazine *Qué pasa* (26 February 2001), describes the polemic surrounding Lagos's renovation of La Moneda: "Mientras sacaban el familiar estuco grisáceo que cubre el edificio, se encontraron balas que quedaron incrustadas el 11 de septiembre de 1973. El descubrimiento de los proyectiles, que serán llevados a un museo, no ha podido silenciar la polémica en la que se ha visto involucrada la casa de gobierno ante su próxima coloración. La casa presidencial, a partir del 11 de marzo, lucirá una remozada fachada blanca por petición del presidente electo Ricardo Lagos,

como parte de un plan mayor para renovar el barrio cívico con motivo del Bicentenario de la Independencia. . . . No se discute el valor de la modernización, la novena que ha sufrido La Moneda en su historia. El debate versa más bien sobre la pertinencia del tinte albo en la edificación creada por Toesca e inaugurada en 1807" [While they removed the familiar gray stucco covering the building, they found bullets encrusted there on 11 September 1973. The discovery of the projectiles, which will be taken to a museum, has not been able to silence the polemic surrounding the painting of La Moneda. The presidential palace, starting on 11 March will, at the request of President-elect Ricardo Lagos, sport a renovated white façade, as part of a larger plan to renovate the civic center of the capital for the Bicentennial of Chilean Independence. . . . The value of this modernization—the ninth that La Moneda has undergone in its history—is not being discussed. Rather, the debate revolves around the appropriateness of the white color for the building which Toesca created and which was inaugurated in 1807].

4. Such practices are not unique to Chile but can be seen time and again in other parts of Latin America and the world. In Argentina, we might note the relatively recent unearthing of The "Club Atlético" [Athletic Club], whose ruins are currently under excavation by archaeologists from the University of Buenos Aires. In Uruguay, one notorious example of a forgotten site is the Punta Carretas shopping mall (Montevideo), where a torture center once stood.

5. Jay Winter and Emmanuel Sivan note the following: "Salient events are more vividly remembered and recalled, especially when they are associated with a specific time and place. This is what is meant by the term 'context dependency.' *Context dependency* may be *extrinsic* or *intrinsic*. On the one hand, memory traces may be associated with certain external or 'extrinsic' features originating outside the individual: smell, color, sounds. Such memories, on the other hand, may be linked powerfully with 'intrinsic' aspects of our mood or personal situation at the time the memory trace was encoded" (*War and Remembrance*, 14).

6. Maurice Halbwachs's work has been particularly important for establishing a connection between physical sites and the construction of memory narratives. Halbwachs wrote about the ways both individuals and groups use physical sites as markers in which to ground their memories—to give them "stability"—and argued that memory unfolds within a spatial framework. Nevertheless, his discussion does beg certain questions in light of the twentieth century's tragic realities. What happens, for example, if the physical surroundings that Halbwachs sees as a vehicle for memory's "stability" change or disappear completely? What if the structure of the physical world is somehow altered so that the "illusion of not having changed over time" that allows people to identify with a particular physical space loses its viability (Halbwachs, *The Collective Memory*, 140)? That is, what if memory has to be reconstructed on shaky, ruinous ground? This has certainly been the case in the history of the Americas since the Conquest, where the "conquered" have long faced the difficulty of reconstructing the past on the ruins left behind by their conquerors. Though Halbwachs doesn't provide sufficient answers to these particular questions, he does make room for the possibility that "space" does not have to refer "solely to physical space" (*The Collective Memory*, 140). Space, to the

contrary, can be understood as a mental construct, as an "image of space" in the mind that exists even beyond the physical eradication of a given site in the world. Perhaps on these grounds it is possible to speak of a mental space (a "space of memory") that is opened up based on the ruins of a physical site.

7. Salvatore Settis observes that "ruins potently epitomize the perennial tension between what is preserved and what is lost, what seems immediately understandable (or usable) and what needs interpretation (or reconstruction). . . . Ruins operate as powerful metaphors for absence or rejection, and hence, as incentives for restoration" (Roth et al., *Irresistible Decay*, vii).

8. Svetlana Boym notes that the "value" of ruins has changed throughout history: "In the baroque age, the ruins of antiquity were often used didactically, conveying to the beholder 'the contrast between ancient greatness and present degradation.' Romantic ruins radiated melancholy, mirroring the shattered soul of the poet and longing for harmonic wholeness. As for the modern ruins, they are reminders of the war and the cities' recent violent past, pointing at coexistence of different dimensions and historical times in the city. The ruin is not merely something that reminds us of the past; it is also a reminder of the future, when our present becomes history" (Boym, *The Future*, 79).

9. Nelly Richard reminds us that we must critically assess narrative and artistic strategies of representation. The questions *What should we remember?* and *How should we remember?* are vitally important: "La formulación del recuerdo pasa por una incesante disputa entre diferentes conceptualizaciones del *qué* y *cómo* recordar. La voluntad de inscribir el recuerdo del pasado en un circuito de referencialidad pública supone, entonces, debatir críticamente sobre los nudos entre *acontecimiento* y *representación* que la memoria es llamada a deshacer y rehacer cada vez que se propone llevar el pasado de la simple revelación de los hechos a un complejo proceso de entendimiento crítico. Este debate concierne las relaciones entre arte público, memoria social y contexto urbano, y atañe también al problema de las *estrategias de la conmemoración*, de las retóricas expresivas y de los montajes simbólicos con los que una determinada narrativa de la memoria elige darle *figuración* al recuerdo [The formulation of memory passes through an incessant dispute among different conceptualizations of *what* and *how* to remember. The will to inscribe memory in a circuit of public referentiality supposes, then, a critical debate about the connections among *experience* and *representation* that memory is called to unmake and remake every time the past becomes more than a simple revelation of facts, but rather a complex process of critical understanding. This debate concerns the relationships among public art, social memory, and the urban context, and also accounts for the problem of *strategies of commemoration*, of rhetorical expression and of the symbolic montages through which a given memory narrative chooses to give *form* to memory]" (Richard, "Sitios de la memoria," 11).

10. Among the sites acknowledged to date are the Estadio Chile—whose name was changed in 2003 to Víctor Jara Stadium in memory of the famous Chilean folk singer assassinated there in 1973—and the Hornos de Lonquén [Lonquén Ovens], a place situated on the outskirts of Santiago where some small plaques and crosses have been

placed by human rights activists to commemorate the 1978 murder of fifteen farmers. A visitor to Lonquén can still see the rubble left after the military destroyed the site.

11. One of the most noteworthy commemorative acts took place on 21 March 2001, when Ernesto Cardenal, Gonzalo Rojas, Juan Gelman, Adrienne Rich, Amanda Berenguer, and other prominent Latin American poets gathered at the park to read their poetry. The poets were in Santiago to commemorate the thirtieth anniversary of Pablo Neruda's Nobel Prize (Bacic, "Amidst Poetry").

12. I have been unable to locate Luis Santibáñez to formally request his permission to reprint fragments of our interview. The interview was carried out, however, with the mutual understanding that I would use its contents in this book.

13. Shortly before this book went to press, I was shocked to see a thirty-second spot about the Park for Peace on Chile's National Television Network (TVN). In between its regular programming, TVN occasionally features a brief segment called "Parks and Plazas of Santiago." Since the thirtieth anniversary of the coup, I have noticed that the segment on Villa Grimaldi has aired sporadically. What I find interesting is that the segment offers a reading of the park as "space of encounter" that leads visitors toward the renewing waters of a fountain located at the park's center. Yet the segment says nothing about the horrors committed at Villa Grimaldi. It focuses exclusively on the park as a space of healing and reconciliation. Although I find the publicity encouraging, I am also quite concerned about what TVN is silencing through its whitewashed presentation.

14. In a personal interview conducted in January 2002, Mr. Pedro Matta, one of the principal activists who fought for the creation of the Park for Peace, alluded to the political conflicts that the park elicited, even among representatives of the political left. Matta said: "I remember particularly a meeting with a Socialist deputy who was very active in human rights matters. Unexpectedly, and much to our surprise, he told us that he would not support the construction of a Park for Peace because he believed that Chile's fledgling democracy and its recently established institutions could not handle it. He thought there might be a reaction by the army that could endanger the status quo or undermine the agreements and understandings that had been reached to establish 'governability' in the country. Because of this, he was willing to support the construction of a human rights park anywhere but at Villa Grimaldi."

15. A complete record of the speeches delivered at the inauguration is housed in Santiago in the archives of the Vicaría de la Solidaridad.

16. Funding has been a constant impediment to the construction of a Human Rights Museum at Villa Grimaldi. However, new progress is being made toward that goal. On 11–12 August 2005, a symposium entitled "A Museum at Villa Grimaldi: A Space for Memory and Human Rights Education" was held in Santiago. Organized by the Park for Peace Corporation and the Municipality of Peñalolén, the event brought together representatives from the Ann Frank Foundation (Holland), Open Memory (Argentina), The University of Notre Dame's Center for Human Rights (USA), and other entities. The museum plans to incorporate photographic material, audiovisual

testimonies, and historical artifacts from the era of repression (for example, railroad ties found in the ocean by Judge Juan Guzmán that were used to make "disappeared" bodies sink).

17. A documentary like Gloria Camiruaga's *La venda* [The Blindfold] (2000) helps us understand that torture generates a multiplicity of experiences. Camiruaga's documentary focuses on the testimonies of female prisoners at Villa Grimaldi, with an eye toward understanding the particularities of gender differences in the context of repression.

18. A good example of Matta's memory narrative can be found in Elizabeth Farnsworth's report "Confronting the Past," created for the "News Hour with Jim Lehrer" (13 March 2000). Matta also appears prominently in Tony Comiti and Manolo D'Arthuy's documentary *Chili: des bourreaux en liberté* [Chile: Torturers at Large](France 1999). He has worked closely with the University of Wisconsin at Madison's "Legacies of Authoritarianism" project, and in 2003 was named resident director of Trinity College's study abroad program in Santiago. Information on the program and a link to Matta's personal human rights library can be found at <www.humanrights.cl>.

19. I want to clarify that by using the term "performance" I do not wish to imply that Matta's tours are in any way fictional, false, or contrived. Instead, I employ the term in some of the senses that Diana Taylor ascribes to it in *The Archive and the Repertoire: Performing Cultural Memory in the Americas.* "Performances," Taylor writes, "function as vital acts of transfer, transmitting social knowledge, memory, and a sense of identity through reiterated, or what Richard Schechner has called 'twice-behaved behavior.' . . . On another level, performance also constitutes the methodological lens that enables scholars to analyze events *as* performance. Civic obedience, resistance, citizenship, gender, ethnicity and sexual identity, for example, are rehearsed and performed daily in the public sphere" (2–3).

20. The seeds for Marín's novel first appeared as a poem published in exile in 1978 (Marín, "El Palacio," 1978).

21. The narrative situation Marín creates calls to mind a text like Jorge Semprún's *Literature or Life* (1994). In his final chapter, Semprún tells of his return to Buchenwald years after he had been a prisoner: "The watchtower over the entrance gate was still there, just as I'd remembered it. As well as the crematory, the washhouse, and the store for the prisoners' belongings. Everything else had been leveled, but as an archaeological excavation site, the positions and foundations of each wooden or concrete hut were indicated by rectangles of fine gray gravel, edged with stone, with a marker at one corner bearing the number that had once identified the vanished building. The effect was unbelievably powerful. The empty space thus created, surrounded by barbed wire, dominated by the crematory chimney, swept by the wind off the Ettersberg, was a place of overwhelming remembrance" (295–296). As in the case of Villa Grimaldi, the grounds at Buchenwald have changed with the passage of time. Yet certain aspects of the landscape allow Semprún an entryway to his past. The empty space bears important traces of the disaster (the barbed wire, the crematory chimney, the foundations of the wooden huts) which act as memory triggers that lead Semprún to reconnect to his for-

mer self, to finish the story he repressed for so many years. Yet Marín's narrator differs from Semprún in an important way: he is not a torture survivor but rather a returned exile trying to piece together a past that is at once personal and *remote*.

22. For more on Luz Arce and Marcia Alejandra Merino, see Chapter 2, "The Poetics of Reconciliation."

23. The figure of María del Carmen Posada seems to be based on the real life collaborators Luz Arce and Marcia Alejandra Merino. Marín's character, like Arce and Merino, seeks pardon for her transgressions. She wants to assuage her shame and, to that end, confides in the narrator as an empathic Other. In addition, the figure of Mónica also appears to be based loosely on Arce and Merino. Toward the end of the novel, we discover that one of Mónica's jobs as a functionary of DINA was to archive newspaper articles published in other countries about the dictatorship (Marín, *El Palacio*, 189). This, of course, was one of Arce's assignments as well.

24. Insofar as the exile is constantly struggling to understand his past, establishing a connection to physical spaces in the world can help him feel "rooted." Of his frequent visits to Straus Park in New York City, André Aciman, himself an exile, writes: "My repeated returns to Straus Park make of New York not only the shadow city of so many other cities I've known but a shadow city of itself, reminding me of an earlier New York in my own life, and before that of a New York that existed before I was born and which has nothing to do with me but which I need to see—in old photographs, for example—because, as an exile without a past, I like to peek at others' foundations to imagine what mine might look like had I been born here" (Aciman, *False Papers*, 48).

Bibliography

Aciman, André. *False Papers: Essays on Exile and Memory*. New York: Farrar, Straus and Giroux, 2000.

Adorno, Theodor W. "Commitment." *Notes to Literature*. Ed. Rolf Tiedemann. Trans. Sherry Weber Nicholsen. Vol. 2. New York: Columbia University Press, 1992.

———. "What Does Coming to Terms with the Past Mean?" *Bitburg in Moral and Political Perspective*. Ed. Geoffrey H. Hartman. Trans. Timothy Bahti and Geoffrey H. Hartman. Bloomington: Indiana University Press, 1986.

Agamben, Giorgio. *Remnants of Auschwitz: The Witness and the Archive*. Trans. Daniel Heller-Rozen. New York: Zone Books, 1999.

Agosín, Marjorie. *Las zonas del dolor/ Zones of Pain*. Trans. Cola Franzen. New York: White Pine Press, 1988.

Améry, Jean. *At the Mind's Limits: Contemplations by a Survivor of Auschwitz and Its Realities*. Trans. Sidney Rosenfeld and Stella P. Rosenfeld. New York: Schocken, 1990.

Anderson, Benedict. *Imagined Communities: Reflections on the Origin and Spread of Nationalism*. New York: Verso, 1996.

Appelfeld, Aharon. "After the Holocaust." *Writing and the Holocaust*. Ed. Berel Lang. New York: Holmes and Meier, 1988.

Arce Sandoval, Luz. "Declaration before the Rettig Commission for Truth and Reconciliation." Santiago: Archive of the Vicaría de la Solidaridad. 9 October 1990.

———. *El infierno*. Santiago: Planeta, 1993.

———. Personal interviews. June 2002–September 2005.

Arendt, Hannah. *Eichmann in Jerusalem: A Report on the Banality of Evil*. New York: Penguin, 1994.

———. *The Human Condition*. Chicago: University of Chicago Press, 1958.

———. *Responsibility and Judgment*. Edited with an introduction by Jerome Kohn. New York: Schocken, 2003.

Arguedas, José María. *El zorro de arriba y el zorro de abajo*. Buenos Aires: Editorial Losada, 1971.

Arteagabeitía, Rodrigo de. *Corporación Parque por la Paz Villa Grimaldi: una deuda con nosotros mismos*. Santiago: Ministerio de Vivienda, 1997.

Augustine. *Confessions*. Trans. F. J. Sheed. Introduction by Peter Brown. Indianapolis: Hackett, 1993.

Avelar, Idelber. "Five Theses on Torture." *Journal of Latin American Cultural Studies* 10, no. 3 (2001): 253–271.

———. *The Untimely Present: Postdictatorial Latin American Fiction and the Task of Mourning*. Durham, N.C.: Duke University Press, 1999.

Aylwin Azócar, Patricio. *El reencuentro de los demócratas: del golpe al triunfo del No.* Santiago: Ediciones Grupo Zeta, 1998.

———. *La transición chilena: discursos escogidos, marzo 1990–1992.* Eds. Secretaría de Comunicación y Cultura and Ministerio Secretaría General de Gobierno. Santiago: Editorial Andrés Bello, 1992.

Bacic, Roberta. "Amidst Poetry, Pain, Memories, Magic and Rage: A Re-encounter with Villa Grimaldi." *Strange Ways* 5, no. 2 (2001): 9–10.

Baer, Ulrich. *Spectral Evidence: The Photography of Trauma.* Cambridge: MIT Press, 2002.

Baltra Montaner, Lidia. *Atentados a la libertad de información y a los medios de comunicación en Chile: 1973–1987.* Santiago: CENECA, 1988.

Bakhtin, Mikhail. "The Problem of Speech Genres." *Speech Genres and Other Late Essays.* Eds. Caryl Emerson and Michael Holquist. Trans. Vern W. McGee. Austin: University of Texas Press, 1986.

Barahona de Brito, Alexandra. *Human Rights and Democratization in Latin America: Uruguay and Chile.* New York: Oxford University Press, 1999.

Barthes, Roland. *Camera Lucida: Reflections on Photography.* Trans. Richard Howard. New York: Hill and Wang, 1981.

Beckett, Samuel. *Not I.* London: Faber, 1973.

Belpoliti, Marco, et al. *The Voice of Memory: Primo Levi, Interviews, 1961–1987.* Trans. Robert Gordon. New York: The New Press, 2001.

Benjamin, Walter. *Illuminations.* Ed. Hannah Arendt. Trans. Harry Zohn. New York: Schocken, 1969.

———. *Walter Benjamin: Selected Writings, 1927–1934.* Ed. Michael William Jennings, et al. Cambridge: Harvard University Press, 1999.

Beverley, John, et al. *The Postmodernism Debate in Latin America.* Durham, N.C.: Duke University Press, 1999.

Blanchot, Maurice. *The Writing of the Disaster.* Trans. Ann Smock. Lincoln: University of Nebraska Press, 1995.

Boym, Svetlana. *The Future of Nostalgia.* New York: Basic Books, 2001.

Brison, Susan J. *Aftermath: Violence and the Remaking of a Self.* Princeton, N.J.: Princeton University Press, 2002.

Brito, Eugenia. *Campos minados (literatura post-golpe en Chile).* Santiago: Cuarto Propio, 1990.

Campusano, Mauricio. "Ricardo Lagos llamó a los chilenos a mirar hacia el futuro." *El Mercurio Online* 11 September 2002. <www.emol.com/noticias/detalle/prt_nd.asp?idnoticia=94359>, accessed 11 September 2002.

Camus, María Eugenia. "30 años después: ¿se puede cerrar esta herida?" *Rocinante* 6, no. 57 (July 2003): 7–9.

Caruth, Cathy. *Unclaimed Experience: Trauma, Narrative and History.* Baltimore: Johns Hopkins University Press, 1996.

Caruth, Cathy, ed. *Trauma: Explorations in Memory.* Baltimore: Johns Hopkins University Press, 1995.

El caso Pinochet. Dir. Patricio Guzmán. Nueva Imagen/First Run/Icarus Films, 2001.

Cavallo, Ascanio. *La historia oculta de la Transición: memoria de una época, 1990–1998*. Santiago: Grijalbo, 1998.

Cerda, Carlos. *Una casa vacía*. Santiago: Alfaguara, 1996.

Chabín, Paula. "La conversión de Luz Arce." *Apsi* 381 (25 March–7 April 1991): 12–15.

Cheyre, Juan Emilio. Address. "Declaraciones del Comandante en Jefe en el Regimiento Reforzado no. 1 'Topater,' Calama." 13 June 2003. <www.ejercito.cl>, accessed 8 February 2006.

———. "Ejército de Chile: el fin de una visión." *La Tercera* online. 4 November 2004.

Chile: la memoria obstinada. Dir. Patricio Guzmán. Nueva Imagen/First Run/Icarus Films, 1997.

Chili: des bourreaux en liberté. Dirs. Tony Comiti and Manolo D'Arthuy. Videocassette. France, 1999.

Constable, Pamela, and Arturo Valenzuela. *A Nation of Enemies: Chile under Pinochet*. New York: Norton, 1991.

Correa, Raquel, and Elizabeth Subercasseaux. *Ego Sum Pinochet*. Santiago: Zig-Zag, 1989.

Delbo, Charlotte. *Auschwitz and After*. Trans. Rosette C. Lamont. New Haven: Yale University Press, 1995.

Déotte, Jean-Louis. *Catástrofe y olvido: las ruinas, Europa y el museo*. Santiago: Cuarto Propio, 1998.

———. "El arte en la época de la desaparición." *Revista de crítica cultural* 19 (1999): 12–14.

Déotte, Martine. "Desaparición y ausencia de duelo." *Políticas y estéticas de la memoria*. Ed. Nelly Richard. Santiago: Cuarto Propio, 2000.

Derrida, Jacques. *On Cosmopolitanism and Forgiveness*. Trans. Mark Dooley and Michael Hughes. New York: Routledge, 2002.

Digeser, P. E. *Political Forgiveness*. Ithaca, N.Y.: Cornell University Press, 2001.

"La DINA hoy." Special edition of *El Siglo*. No. 7797. 9–15 February 1992.

Dinges, John. *The Condor Years: How Pinochet and His Allies Brought Terror to Three Continents*. New York: The New Press, 2004.

Dorfman, Ariel. *Exorcising Terror: The Incredible Unending Trial of General Augusto Pinochet*. New York: Seven Stories Press, 2002.

———. *Viudas*. Mexico City: Siglo XXI Editores, 1981.

Drake, Paul W., and Iván Jaksic, eds. *The Struggle for Democracy in Chile*. Lincoln: University of Nebraska Press, 1991.

Droguett, Carlos. "Literatura del exilio." *Texto crítico* 22–23 (1981): 209–237.

Eltit, Diamela. *Emergencias: escritos sobre literatura, arte y política*. Santiago: Planeta, 2000.

———. *Lumpérica*. Santiago: Ediciones del Ornitorrinco, 1983.

———. *El padre mío*. Santiago: Francisco Zegers, 1989.

———. *Por la patria*. Santiago: Ediciones del Ornitorrinco, 1986.

———. *Los vigilantes*. Santiago: Sudamericana, 1994.

Eltit, Diamela, and Paz Errázuriz. *El infarto del alma*. Santiago: Francisco Zegers, 1994.

Ercilla, Alonso de. *The Araucanid: A Version in English Poetry of Alonso de Ercilla y Zúñiga's "La Araucana."* Trans. Charles Maxwell Lancaster and Paul Thomas Manchester. Nashville: Vanderbilt University Press, 1945.

Feher, Michel. "Terms of Reconciliation." *Human Rights in Political Transitions: Gettysburg to Bosnia*. Eds. Carla Hesse and Robert Post. New York: Zone Books, 1999.

Feitlowitz, Marguerite. *A Lexicon of Terror: Argentina and the Legacies of Torture*. New York: Oxford University Press, 1998.

Feld, Claudia. *Del estrado a la pantalla: las imágenes del juicio a los ex-comandantes en Argentina*. Buenos Aires/ Madrid: Siglo XXI Editores, 2002.

Felman, Shoshana. *The Juridical Unconscious: Trials and Traumas in the Twentieth Century*. Cambridge: Harvard University Press, 2002.

Felman, Shoshana, and Dori Laub. *Testimony: Crises of Witnessing in Literature, Psychoanalysis and History*. New York: Routledge, 1992.

Fernando ha vuelto. Dir. Silvio Caiozzi. Videocassette. Chile: Caiozzi y García Ltda., 1998.

La Flaca Alejandra: vidas y muertes de una mujer chilena. Dirs. Carmen Castillo, Erica Chanfreau, and Guy Girard. Videocassette. France: INA, 1994.

Foucault, Michel. "Christianity and Confession." *The Politics of Truth*. Eds. Sylvére Lotringer and Lysa Hochroth. Boston: Semiotext(e)/MIT Press, 1997.

———. *Discipline and Punish: The Birth of the Prison*. Trans. Alan Sheridan. New York: Vintage Books, 1995.

———. *Madness and Civilization: A History of Insanity in the Age of Reason*. Trans. Richard Howard. New York: Vintage Books, 1988.

———. "Truth and Juridical Forms." *Power: The Essential Works of Foucault, 1954–1984*. Ed. James D. Faubion. Trans. Robert Hurley. New York: The New Press, 2000.

Freud, Sigmund. "Mourning and Melancholia." *Freud: General Psychological Theory*. Ed. Philip Rieff. New York: Collier, 1963.

Galende, Federico. "El desaparecido, la desdicha del testigo." *Revista de crítica cultural* 22 (2001): 32–34.

———. "La insurrección de las sobras." *Revista de crítica cultural* 10 (1995): 24.

———. "La izquierda entre el duelo, la melancolía y el trauma." *Revista de crítica cultural* 17 (1998): 42–47.

García, Antonia. "Por un análisis político de la desaparición forzada." *Políticas y estéticas de la memoria*. Ed. Nelly Richard. Santiago: Cuarto Propio, 2000.

Gide, André. *La secuestrada de Poitiers*. Trans. Michèle Pousa. Barcelona: TusQuets, 1969.

Grunebaum, Heidi. "Talking to Ourselves 'among the Innocent Dead': On Reconciliation, Forgiveness and Mourning." *PMLA* 117, no. 2 (2002): 306–309.

Gubar, Susan. *Poetry after Auschwitz*. Bloomington: Indiana University Press, 2003.

Gugelberger, Georg M., ed. *The Real Thing: Testimonial Discourse and Latin America.* Durham, N.C.: Duke University Press, 1996.

Guzmán, Nancy. *Romo: confesiones de un torturador.* Santiago: Planeta, 2000.

Halbwachs, Maurice. *The Collective Memory.* New York: Harper, 1980.

Heller, Agnes. *The Power of Shame: A Rational Perspective.* Boston: Routledge and Kegan Paul, 1985.

Huyssen, Andreas. "Present Pasts: Media, Politics, Amnesia." *Public Culture* 12, no. 1 (2000): 21–38.

I Love Pinochet. Dir. Marcela Said. Videocassette. Chile, 2001.

Irigaray, Luce. *To Speak Is Never Neutral.* Trans. Gail Schwab. New York: Routledge, 2002.

Jelin, Elizabeth. *Los trabajos de la memoria.* Madrid/Buenos Aires: Siglo XXI Editores, 2002.

Jelin, Elizabeth, ed. *Las conmemoraciones: las disputas en las fechas "in-felices."* Madrid/Buenos Aires: Siglo XXI Editores, 2002.

Jocelyn-Holt Letelier, Alfredo. *El Chile perplejo: del avanzar sin transar al transar sin parar.* Santiago: Planeta, 1998.

———. *Espejo retrovisor: ensayos histórico-políticos, 1992–2000.* Santiago: Planeta, 2000.

Joignant, Alfredo, and Amparo Menéndez-Carrión, eds. *La caja de Pandora: el retorno de la transición chilena.* Santiago: Planeta, 1999.

Jordá Sureda, Miguel. *Martirologio de la iglesia chilena: Juan Alsina y víctimas del terrorismo del estado.* Santiago: LOM, 2001.

Kofman, Sarah. *Smothered Words.* Trans. Madeline Dobie. Evanston, Ill.: Northwestern University Press, 1998.

Kohut, Karl, and José Morales Saravia, eds. *Literatura chilena hoy: la difícil transición.* Frankfurt: Vervuert, 2002.

Kornbluh, Peter. *The Pinochet File: A Declassified Dossier on Atrocity and Accountability.* New York: New Press, 2003.

LaCapra, Dominick. *Writing History, Writing Trauma.* Baltimore: Johns Hopkins University Press, 2001.

Lacoue-Labarthe, Philippe. *Poetry as Experience.* Trans. Andrea Tarnowski. Stanford: Stanford University Press, 1999.

Lagos, María Ines, ed. *Creación y resistencia: la narrativa de Diamela Eltit, 1983–1998.* Santiago: CEGECAL/Cuarto Propio, 2000.

Lagos, Ricardo. Address. "No hay mañana sin ayer." 12 August 2003. <www.gobiernodechile.cl/discursos/discurso_presidented.asp>, accessed 4 October 2005.

Lazzara, Michael J. *Los años de silencio: conversaciones con narradores chilenos que escribieron bajo dictadura.* Santiago: Cuarto Propio, 2002.

———. "Tres recorridos de Villa Grimaldi." *Monumentos, memoriales y marcas territoriales.* Edited by Elizabeth Jelin and Victoria Langland. Madrid/Buenos Aires: Siglo XXI Editores, 2003.

Lemebel, Pedro. *De perlas y cicatrices: crónicas radiales.* Santiago: LOM, 1998.

León-Portilla, Miguel. *Visión de los vencidos: crónicas indígenas.* Madrid: Historia 16, 1985.

Lértora, Juan Carlos, ed. *Una poética de literatura menor: la narrativa de Diamela Eltit.* Santiago: Cuarto Propio, 1983.

Levi, Primo. *The Drowned and the Saved.* Trans. Raymond Rosenthal. New York: Vintage International, 1988.

———. "On Obscure Writing." *Other People's Trades.* Trans. Michael Joseph Rosenthal. New York: Summit Books, 1989.

———. *The Reawakening.* Trans. Stuart Woolf. New York: Touchstone, 1996.

———. *Survival in Auschwitz.* Trans. Stuart Woolf. New York: Touchstone, 1996.

Levinas, Emmanuel. *De L'évasion.* Montpellier: Fata Morgana, 1982.

Lira, Elizabeth. "Mesa de diálogo de derechos humanos en Chile: 21 de agosto 1999–13 de junio de 2000." *Chile 1999–2000, Nuevo gobierno: desafíos de la reconciliación.* Santiago: FLACSO, 2000.

Lira, Sonia. "Luz Arce presentó libro con su historia." *La Época* 18 November 1993: 22.

Lombardo, Francesca. "Cuerpo, violencia y traición." *Revista de crítica cultural* 11 (1995): 35–39.

Lorenzano, Sandra. *Escrituras de sobrevivencia: narrativa argentina y dictadura.* Mexico City: UNAM, 2001.

Loureiro, Ángel G. *The Ethics of Autobiography: Replacing the Subject in Modern Spain.* Nashville: Vanderbilt University Press, 2000.

Loveman, Brian. "La reconciliación nacional en América Latina: utopía y 'pomada' de los noventa." *Chile 1999–2000, Nuevo gobierno: desafíos de la reconciliación.* Santiago: FLACSO, 2000.

Loveman, Brian, and Elizabeth Lira. *Las ardientes cenizas del olvido: vía chilena de reconciliación política, 1932–1994.* Santiago: LOM/DIBAM, 2000.

———. *El espejismo de la reconciliación política: Chile, 1990–2002.* Santiago: LOM, 2002.

"Luz Arce lloró al presentar 'El infierno.'" *La Tercera* 18 November 1993: 6.

Margalit, Avishai. *The Ethics of Memory.* Cambridge: Harvard University Press, 2002.

Marín, Germán. "Mudo." *Conversaciones para solitarios.* Santiago: Sudamericana, 1999.

———. *El Palacio de la Risa.* Santiago: Planeta, 1995.

———. "El Palacio de la Risa: antecedentes para una investigación." *Araucaria de Chile* 3 (1978): 179–181.

Masiello, Francine. *The Art of Transition: Latin American Culture and Neoliberal Crisis.* Durham, N.C.: Duke University Press, 2001.

Matta Lemoine, Pedro Alejandro. Personal interview. 23 January 2002.

———. *Villa Grimaldi, Santiago de Chile: A Visitor's Guide.* Santiago: Gráfica Andros Ltda., 2000.

Mercado, Tununa. *En estado de memoria.* Mexico City: UNAM, 1992.

Merino Vega, Marcia Alejandra. *Mi verdad: más allá del horror, yo acuso*. Santiago: A.T.G., 1993.

Mifsud, Tony, S. J. "La reconciliación: un camino ético en la verdad y en la justicia." *Historia, política y ética de la verdad en Chile, 1891–2001: reflexiones sobre la paz social y la impunidad*. Edited by Elizabeth Lira, Brian Loveman, Tony Mifsud S.J., and Pablo Salvat. Santiago: LOM, 2001.

Minow, Martha. *Between Vengeance and Forgiveness: Facing History after Genocide and Mass Violence*. Cambridge: Harvard University Press, 2002.

Minow, Martha, ed. *Breaking the Cycles of Hatred: Memory, Law and Reapir*. Introduced and with commentaries edited by Nancy L. Rosenblum. Princeton, N.J.: Princeton University Press, 2002.

Mistral, Gabriela. *Desolación-Ternura-Tala-Lagar*. Mexico City: Porrúa, 1999.

Molloy, Sylvia. *At Face Value: Autobiographical Writing in Spanish America*. New York: Cambridge University Press, 2001.

Morales T., Leonidas. *Conversaciones con Diamela Eltit*. Santiago: Cuarto Propio, 1998.

Moulián, Tomás. *Chile actual: anatomía de un mito*. Santiago: LOM/ARCIS, 1997.

———. "La liturgia de la reconciliación." *Políticas y estéticas de la memoria*. Ed. Nelly Richard. Santiago: Cuarto Propio, 2000.

Muller, John P., and William J. Richardson, eds. *The Purloined Poe: Lacan, Derrida and Psychoanalytic Reading*. Baltimore: Johns Hopkins University Press, 1988.

Munizaga, Giselle. *El discurso público de Pinochet: un análisis semiológico*. Santiago: CESOC/CENECA, 1988.

Murphy, Jeffrie G. *Getting Even: Forgiveness and Its Limits*. London: Oxford University Press, 2003.

Neustadt, Robert. *CADA DÍA: la creación de un arte social*. Santiago: Cuarto Propio, 2001.

Nietzsche, Friederich. *The Use and Abuse of History*. Trans. Adrian Collins. Indianapolis: Liberal Arts Press and Bobbs-Merril, 1957.

Nora, Pierre. "Between Memory and History: Les Lieux de Mémoire." *Representations* 0, no. 26 (1989): 7–24.

Norat, Gisela. *Diamela Eltit and the Subversion of Mainstream Literature in Chile*. Newark: University of Delaware Press, 2002.

Olea, Raquel, and Olga Grau, eds. *Volver a la memoria*. Santiago: LOM, 2001.

Otano, Rafael. *Crónica de la Transición*. Santiago: Planeta, 1995.

El padre mío. Dir. Lotty Rosenfeld. Videocassette. Chile: CADA, 1986.

Paz, Octavio. *Libertad bajo palabra*. Mexico: Texontle, 1949.

Pérez, Claudio, and Rodrigo Gómez. *Muro de la memoria*. 2002. Monument located at Puente Bulnes, Santiago de Chile.

Pey, Coral, and Dante Donoso. *Villa Grimaldi, un parque por la paz*. Santiago: Taller Piret/Revista Con Tacto, 1996.

Piglia, Ricardo. *Formas breves*. Barcelona: Anagrama, 2000.

———. *Nombre falso*. Buenos Aires: Seix Barral, 1994.

———. *Respiración artificial*. Buenos Aires: Seix Barral, 1994.

Pinochet Ugarte, Augusto. *Camino recorrido: biografía de un soldado*. 4 vols. Santiago: Instituto Geográfico Militar de Chile, 1990–1994.

———. *Carta a los chilenos*. Santiago: Ismael Espinosa S.A., 1998.

———. *El día decisivo: 11 de septiembre de 1973*. Santiago: Editorial Andrés Bello, 1980.

Polomer, Azún Candina. "El día interminable: memoria e instalación del 11 de septiembre de 1973 en Chile (1974–1999)." *Las conmemoraciones: las disputas en las fechas "in-felices."* Edited by Elizabeth Jelin. Madrid/Buenos Aires: Siglo XXI Editores, 2002.

Preminger, Alex, T.V.F. Brogan, et al. *The New Princeton Encyclopedia of Poetry and Poetics*. Princeton, N.J.: Princeton University Press, 1993.

"La prueba de la blancura," *Qué pasa* online. 26 February 2001. <www.quepasa.cl/revista/1507.6.html>, accessed 15 March 2001.

Renan, Ernest. "What Is a Nation?" *Becoming National: A Reader*. Eds. Geoff Eley and Ronald Grigor Suny. New York: Oxford University Press, 1996.

Rettig, Raúl, et al. *Summary of the Truth and Reconciliation Commission Report*. Santiago: Chilean Human Rights Commission/Centro IDEAS/Ministry of Foreign Affairs of Chile, 1991.

Richard, Nelly. *Arte en Chile desde 1973: Escena de Avanzada y sociedad*. Santiago: FLACSO 46, 1987.

———. "Las confesiones de un torturador y su (abusivo) montaje periodístico." *Revista de crítica cultural* 22 (2001): 14–19.

———. *Cultural Residues: Chile in Transition*. Trans. Alan West-Durán and Theodore Quester. Foreword by Jean Franco. Minneapolis: University of Minnesota Press, 2004.

———. *La insubordinación de los signos (cambio político, transformaciones culturales y poéticas de la crisis)*. Santiago: Cuarto Propio, 1994.

———. "Lo impúdico y lo público." *Revista de crítica cultural* 11 (1995): 29–34.

———. "Historia, memoria y actualidad: reescrituras, sobreimpresiones." *Nuevas perspectivas desde/ sobre América Latina: el desafío de los estudios culturales*. Ed. Mabel Moraña. Santiago: Cuarto Propio/Instituto Internacional Iberoamericana, 2000.

———. *Margins and Institutions: Art in Chile since 1973*. Melbourne, Australia: Art & Text, 1986.

———. *Residuos y metáforas (Ensayos de crítica cultural sobre el Chile de la Transición)*. Santiago: Cuarto Propio, 1998.

———. "Sitios de la memoria, vaciamiento del recuerdo." *Revista de crítica cultural* 23 (2001): 11-13.

Richard, Nelly, ed. *Utopía(s) 1973–2003: revisar el pasado, criticar el presente, imaginar el futuro*. Santiago: ARCIS, 2004.

Richard, Nelly, and Alberto Moreiras, eds. *Pensar en/ la postdictadura*. Santiago: Cuarto Propio, 2001.

Roht-Arriaza, Naomi. "The Need for Moral Reconstruction in the Wake of Past Human Rights Violations: An Interview with José Zalaquett." *Human Rights in Political Transitions: Gettysburg to Bosnia*. Edited by Carla Hesse and Robert Post. New York: Zone Books, 1999.

Roth, Michael, et al. *Irresistible Decay: Ruins Reclaimed*. Los Angeles: Getty Research Institute for the History of Art and the Humanities, 1997.

Saer, Juan José. *El entenado*. Buenos Aires: Seix Barral, 2000.

Said, Edward. *Reflections on Exile and Other Essays*. Cambridge: Harvard University Press, 2002.

Santa Cruz, Guadalupe. "Capitales del olvido." *Políticas y estéticas de la memoria*. Ed. Nelly Richard. Santiago: Cuarto Propio, 2000.

———. "Santiago fugaz: memoria y territorio." *Revista de crítica cultural* 19 (1999): 44–46.

Santibáñez, Luis. Personal interview. 11 February 2002.

Sarlo, Beatriz. "La historia contra el olvido." *Punto de vista* 36 (1989): 11–13.

Scarry, Elaine. *The Body in Pain: The Making and Unmaking of the World*. New York: Oxford University Press, 1985.

Semprún, Jorge. *Literature or Life*. Trans. Linda Coverdale. New York: Viking, 1997.

Sigmund, Paul E., ed. *Chile 1973–1998: The Coup and its Consequences*. Princeton University: Program in Latin American Studies, PLAS Cuadernos 3, 1999.

Sommer, Doris. "Rigoberta's Secrets." *Latin American Perspectives* 70.18, no. 3 (1991): 32–50.

Sontag, Susan. *Regarding the Pain of Others*. New York: Farrar, Straus and Giroux, 2003.

Stern, Steve J. "De la memoria suelta a la memoria emblemática: hacia el recordar y olvidar como proceso histórico (Chile, 1973–1998)." *Memoria para un nuevo siglo: Chile, miradas a la segunda mitad del siglo XX*. Eds. M. Garcés et al. Santiago: LOM, 2000.

———. *Remembering Pinochet's Chile: On the Eve of London 1998*. Durham, N.C.: Duke University Press, 2004.

Sturken, Marita. *Tangled Memories: The Vietnam War, the AIDS Epidemic and the Politics of Remembering*. Berkeley: University of California Press, 1997.

Tamayo, Tania, and Claudia Lagos. "Casas de tortura y centros de detención: arquitectura de espanto." *Rocinante* 6, no. 57 (July 2003): 10–13.

Taylor, Diana. *The Archive and the Repertoire: Performing Cultural Memory in the Americas*. Durham: Duke University Press, 2003.

———. *Disappearing Acts: Spectacles of Gender and Nationalism in Argentina's Dirty War*. Durham, N.C.: Duke University Press, 1997.

"Texto íntegro de la declaración pública de los tenientes generales." *La Tercera* online. 7 July 2003.

Tierney-Tello, Mary Beth. "Testimony, Ethics and the Aesthetic in Diamela Eltit." *PMLA* 114, no. 1 (1999): 78–96.

Tertullian. "On Repentance." Trans. Reverend S. Thelwall. <www.ccel.org/fathers2/ANF-03/anf03-47.htm#P11261_3190842>, accessed 20 September 2005.

Todorov, Tzvetan. *Facing the Extreme: Moral Life in the Concentration Camps*. Trans. Arthur Denner and Abigail Pollack. New York: Phoenix, 1996.

Trujillo Correa, Iván. "La construcción sacrificial de la memoria." *Cyber Humanitatis* 19 (2001): 28 pars. 20 September 2005 <www.uchile.cl/facultades/filosofia/publicaciones/cyber/cyber19/itrujillo.html>.

Tutu, Desmond. *No Future without Forgiveness*. New York: Doubleday, 1999.

Uribe, Armando. *El fantasma de la sinrazón y El secreto de la poesía*. Santiago: Editores Be-uve-dráis, 2001.

Valdés, Hernán. *Tejas Verdes: diario de un campo de concentracion en Chile*. Barcelona: Editorial Ariel, 1974.

La venda. Dir. Gloria Camiruaga. Videocassette. Chile, 1996.

Verbitsky, Horacio. *El vuelo*. Buenos Aires: Planeta, 1995.

Victoriano, Felipe. "Lo desaparecido, su espera." *Revista de crítica cultural* 17 (1998): 38–41.

Vidal, Hernán. *Dar la vida por la vida: Agrupación Chilena de Familiares de Detenidos Desaparecidos*. Santiago: Mosquito Editores, 1996.

———. *Política cultural de la memoria histórica*. Santiago: Mosquito Editores, 1997.

Videla, Lautaro. "Lo que no vio Luz Arce." *Apsi* 381 (25 March– 7 April 1991): 21–27.

Weeks, Gregory. *The Military and Politics in Postauthoritarian Chile*. Tuscaloosa: University of Alabama Press, 2003.

White, Hayden. *Tropics of Discourse: Essays in Cultural Criticism*. Baltimore: Johns Hopkins University Press, 1978.

Wilde, Alexander. "Irruptions of Memory: Expressive Politics in Chile's Transition to Democracy." *Journal of Latin American Studies* 31 (1999): 473–500.

Winter, Jay, and Emmanuel Sivan, eds. *War and Remembrance in the Twentieth Century*. New York: Cambridge University Press, 1999.

Young, James E. *At Memory's Edge: After-Images of the Holocaust in Contemporary Art and Architecture*. New Haven: Yale University Press, 2000.

———. *The Texture of Memory: Holocaust Memorials and Meaning*. New Haven: Yale University Press, 1993.

———. *Writing and Rewriting the Holocaust: Narrative and the Consequences of Interpretation*. Bloomington: Indiana University Press, 1988.

Zurita, Raúl. *Literatura, lenguaje y sociedad (1973–1983)*. Santiago: CENECA, 1983.

Index

www.ingramcontent.com/pod-product-compliance
Lightning Source LLC
LaVergne TN
LVHW090936080826
845145LV00003B/768

* 9 7 8 0 8 1 3 0 3 5 6 8 0 *